Elizabethan Society

Derek Wilson

ROBINSON

Constable & Robinson Ltd.
55–56 Russell Square
London WC1B 4HP
www.constablerobinson.com

First published in the UK by Robinson,
an imprint of Constable & Robinson Ltd., 2014

ISBN: 978-1-4721-0233-1 (paperback)
ISBN: 978-1-4721-0234-8 (ebook)

Typeset by TW Typesetting, Plymouth, Devon

Printed and bound in the UK

1 3 5 7 9 10 8 6 4 2

CONTENTS

INTRODUCTION

Another book about what everyday life was like in late-sixteenth-century England? Not really. We have studies in plenty about what the Elizabethans wore, what they ate, what houses they lived in, and so on. The following pages, *per contra*, are about *society*. Society is not things; it is people. So what we will be exploring is how the subjects of Queen Elizabeth I coped with the world in which they had been placed. What did they believe? What did they think? What did they feel? How did they react towards one another? What, indeed, did they understand by the word 'society'? What did they expect from it? What were they prepared to contribute towards it? Some were intent on preserving it as it was. Others were eager to change it.

For the majority such profound reflections were outside their remit. They were involved in a struggle for survival that occupied all their waking hours. Life was a contest with poverty, hunger, disease and injustice. Even those who lived above the subsistence level did not enjoy the freedoms to which we are accustomed. English society was fiercely hierarchic. Patronage was the glue that held it together. Men and women paid allegiance to their social superiors – landlords, guild masters, stewards, magistrates, members of the royal court and officials appointed by the nobility and gentry who ruled the shires. They had no legitimate means of voicing complaints or demanding redress. Parliament only represented the interests of the landed class and the urban rich. This was why what government feared most was popular rebellion. Without a constitutional escape valve the pressure of discontent always had the potential to reach danger point. Laws were, therefore, harsh. People had to be deterred from getting together to discuss their grievances.

They even had to be deterred from moving about the country. For Elizabeth and her ministers a safe society was a static society, in which, as far as possible, the queen's subjects remained in the towns and villages where they were born. 'Vagabondage' was something the government was constantly trying to control. Just as important as physically staying put was spiritually staying put. Between 1530 and 1558 England had passed through the biggest upheaval since the Norman Conquest. The struggle between Catholicism and Protestantism had divided the nation. The new reign brought a new religious settlement. It was intended to do just what the name implies – to 'settle' all points of religious difference. English men and women were to attend their parish churches and show themselves as obedient to Elizabeth's bishops and clergy as they did to the queen's secular officers.

But not all the first Elizabethans were disposed to subservience. Necessity and ambition alike drove men from their homes to seek jobs elsewhere and to make a living – either inside or outside the confines of the law. The establishment of an official church did not stop people asking questions – and arguing over the answers. And if religion did not provide enough matter for speculation and debate, what Elizabethans called 'science' added to the subjects thinking men and women wrestled with. As the Renaissance entered the bloodstream of common life more and more, books on more and more subjects poured from the printing presses. And more and more people were able to read them. Education came within the scope of thousands, widening their mental horizons. At the same time mariners were widening their geographical horizons, bringing back tales of strange lands and a world that was bigger by far than previous generations could possibly have imagined.

If we are to get to grips with this strange world which was, at the same time, drab and colourful, static and expansive, traditionalist and 'modern', we do it best by exploring the lives of individuals. So, in this book we will meet scores of men and women from all levels of sixteenth-century life and, hopefully, we will gain a 'feel' (and it can be nothing more substantial than that) for what 'Elizabethan society' really was.

I

THE STATESMAN

O! when degree is shak'd,
Which is the ladder of all high designs,
The enterprise is sick. How could communities,
Degrees in schools, and brotherhoods in cities,
Peaceful commerce from dividable shores,
The primogenitive and due of birth,
Prerogative of age, crowns, sceptres, laurels,
But by degree, stand in authentic place?
Take but degree away, untune that string,
And, hark! What discord follows . . .

Troilus and Cressida, I. iii. 101–10

When, in the early days of Queen Elizabeth I's reign, Nicholas Bacon took his place upon the woolsack in the House of Lords, as Lord Keeper of the Great Seal, the action was doubly significant. Not only was the forty-eight-year-old lawyer a highly distinguished member of his profession, he was also a Suffolk man. Suffolk meant wool, and wool had been the backbone of England's prosperity ever since the woolsack had been given its honoured position in the parliament chamber more than two centuries before.

Bacon came of a family long established at Drinkstone, between Bury St Edmunds and Stowmarket. It was not a remarkable village by local standards. Nearby Rattlesden and Woolpit could boast splendid 'wool' churches, while, to the south, Lavenham's fine half-timbered merchants' houses testified to its status as one of the wealthiest towns in the realm, and impressive country mansions, such as those at Hengrave and Long Melford, were the focal points of county high society. But humble Drinkstone shared in the wealth arising from the manufacture and sale of woollen cloth, which was still England's staple export and highly prized in all the leading European markets. Even families of modest yeoman stock shared in the general wellbeing.

Robert Bacon, Nicholas's father, farmed a scattering of fields in Drinkstone and the neighbourhood and also worked as sheep-reeve for Bury St Edmunds Abbey, supervising the care of the monastery's extensive flocks. In this capacity he had to be able to write reports and keep accounts, so we know that he had what was, by the standards of the day, a more than basic education. This was something he clearly prized, for he ensured that his sons received the best academic grounding he could afford, in order to help them reach higher rungs than his own on the social ladder. Nicholas was his second son and, as soon as possible, Robert used his influence to place the boy in the abbey school at Bury St Edmunds. From there he progressed, at the age of about thirteen, to Benet College, Cambridge (later renamed Corpus Christi). The dictum, 'It's not what you know but who you know that counts' was as true in the sixteenth century as it is now. Just as Eton is the nursery of those who aspire to prominence in today's Conservative party, so Cambridge was the breeding ground of Tudor progressive politicians. At the university Bacon became part of a circle of upwardly mobile men who influenced his future career. John Cheke was the greatest humanist scholar of the day and became Professor of Greek. Matthew Parker would be Elizabeth's first Archbishop of Canterbury. Younger men drawn, a few years later, into the same circle were Roger Ascham, future tutor of Princess Elizabeth, and William Cecil, her principal minister for most of the reign. Having graduated in 1527, Bacon probably gravitated to London, where his two brothers were already established in the commercial life of the capital. However, it was the law that attracted Nicholas and he was admitted to Gray's Inn in 1532. A few years later, he was joined at this elite social club by William Cecil. By the end of the decade both men were moving in royal court circles.

This is not the place to rehearse the tumultuous politico-religious upheavals of the mid-century years or discuss how Bacon and his friends survived them. By a mixture of opportunism and prudence Cecil emerged, in November 1558, as the right-hand man of the twenty-five-year-old new queen. Elizabeth appointed him as her first minister and Cecil selected Nicholas Bacon's name from a short list of equally talented contenders as the new Lord Keeper. At the same time Bacon received the honour of a knighthood. It is not without significance that, by this time, the two friends were related by marriage. Nicholas's second wife, Anne, was the younger daughter of yet another prominent humanist scholar, Anthony Cooke, and her sister, Mildred, was Cecil's wife. This brief summary of Bacon's early life merely serves as an introduction to the way his own career influenced (but not necessarily determined) his policies once he reached his exalted office.

Contemporary portraits depict Bacon as somewhat corpulent, with heavy jowls, thick lips and a gaze at once searching and sardonic. The position he now enjoyed was essentially that of Lord Chancellor but the queen declined to bestow that title upon an arriviste of humble origin. His varied responsibilities tested to the full his legal expertise and his intellectual stamina. He was a member of the Privy Council, head of the Court of Chancery, the queen's representative in Parliament, chairman of various judicial committees and generally the leading expert on the law. Together with his fellow councillors – and, particularly, Secretary Cecil – he had to guide a young woman who was as inexperienced as she was strong-minded.

Two facts were perfectly clear to all observers: England's security depended on the health and safety of this one woman, and, after decades of bewildering change and chronic unrest, the nation was in desperate need of firm government. The Treasury was strapped for cash. War and domestic upheaval had played havoc with trade and industry. Religious division made a nonsense of any immediate prospect of national unity. Poverty and vagabondage were at an all-time high. In 1558 no one was in any doubt that the young queen would select a husband from among Europe's royal houses, thus providing that constitutional respectability and stability the realm needed and also, God willing, an heir to the throne. But as the years passed and it became increasingly clear that Elizabeth would not marry, a novel pattern of government emerged which placed Bacon and his colleagues in a unique position of authority. Professor Collinson dubbed it a 'monarchical republic'. Queen, Privy Council and Parliament were partners in an uneasy alliance, which controlled and executed policy, often lurching from crisis to crisis.

Right at the beginning of the reign, Bacon chaired a committee which drew up a proposed legislative schedule setting out what Elizabeth and her advisers saw as the most urgent measures necessary to bring England out of its current malaise and set it on a course of peace and prosperity. This is where our story really begins because the list of 'Considerations' Bacon prepared for Parliament provides us with a summary of the 'state of the nation' – at least as it was viewed from the top.

It was a reactionary and repressive document. The solution to the disordered state of the realm was to be sought, not in reform or careful consideration of what might or might not be justified grievances, but in reinforcing the divinely ordained hierarchy and giving the courts sharper teeth in dealing with anyone who sought to disturb it. Social mobility was expressly rejected. One wonders how Bacon, the yeoman's son, who had pursued his own ambition by every means that fell to hand and who was now well placed on the upper rungs of the social and political ladder, could, with a clear conscience, close the door of opportunity to other men of humble origin. For example, the Considerations decreed, 'That none study the laws, temporal or civil, except he be immediately descended from a nobleman or gentleman, for they are the entries to rule and government, and generation is the chiefest foundation of inclination'.[1]

From the premise that all Englishmen are born either to rule or be ruled followed a schedule of regulations governing many aspects of national life. An anti-vagrancy act of 1547 which had subsequently been repealed was to be reinstated. It made provision for vagabonds (i.e. men and women with no settled abode or employment) to be forcibly enslaved. The movements of labourers and servants were to be rigidly regulated. In future no one would be permitted to go in search of employment without a written testimonial from his previous employer, endorsed by parish officials, so that, 'servants may be reduced to obedience' and, thus, become more loyal 'to the Prince and God'.[2] The system of apprenticeship was to be tightened up. Theoretically, it was governed by regulations set by craft guilds, but the flooding of the labour market had encouraged many young men to bind themselves to merchants and professionals. The masters, in their turn, had happily flouted the rules in order to obtain the services of such would-be trainees 'on the cheap'. Now only the

sons of gentlemen and noblemen were to enjoy this freedom. Lesser mortals would have to produce a substantial
financial bond before they could be engaged as apprentices.
Restraints were to be placed on wealthy tradesmen who
aspired to buy their way into high society. Merchants were
forbidden to purchase land above a prescribed value. Other
items on the list included fixing wages in various occupations, restricting the activities of foreign merchants and
obliging noblemen to have their sons educated at the universities. Long though the list of proposed reforms was, it
was considerably lengthened when presented to Parliament
and eventually emerged as the Statute of Artificers (1563),
which ran to forty clauses (see below, p. 167).

As the new government set out on its perilous course,
Bacon and all men involved in the preservation of law and
order at national or local level were concerned above everything else with preventing insurrection. One did not
have to be very old to have heard about or witnessed at
first hand the Pilgrimage of Grace (1536–7), which had
convulsed much of midland and northern England, the
disturbances of 1549 in East Anglia and the south-west
and Wyatt's Rebellion, which had reached the gates
of London and threatened Mary Tudor's reign in 1554.
Contemporary unrest in France and the Netherlands was
brought home to Englishmen by Protestants fleeing from
persecution and Elizabeth's reign would not be very old
before full-scale wars of religion were raging on the other
side of the Channel. All hierarchic societies are acutely
wary of social unrest and that was the underlying reason
for the detailed (and largely unworkable) restrictions contemplated by Bacon and his colleagues. They were aimed
at 'freezing' the social structure and, in particular, at
stopping unemployed or unemployable people from wandering the realm as free agents and potential criminals or
troublemakers. They proclaimed an end of the changes
that had riven society ever since Elizabeth's father had

outlawed the pope and they proclaimed zero tolerance of all unsettling influences.

Religion was the most worrying of these influences. Henry VIII had severed the English Church from continental Catholicism and pronounced himself the head of that Church. Those who governed the country during the minority of Edward VI had pushed the Reformation much further, moving the nation quite decisively into the Protestant camp. Mary Tudor had reversed all this, reconciled the English Church with Rome and launched a vigorous campaign against 'heretics'. Several of the most dedicated Protestants had sought sanctuary in Reformation hotspots such as Geneva, Zurich and Strasbourg. They lost little time in returning after Mary's death and were intent on picking up the momentum of religious change. The Church's hierarchy, meanwhile, had been filled with Mary's nominees. Any attempt at settling the religious issue once and for all thus had to steer a course between the Scylla and Charybdis of Catholic and Protestant extremism.

There was no doubt on which side of the divide Bacon and his close colleagues were placed. They were still the men who had learned their religion at Cambridge, the Inns of Court and other centres of progressive faith. They were, however, more cautious than most of the returning exiles. Having kept their heads down during Mary's reign, they were now poised to clear away the superstructure of the Marian Church and build afresh on the foundations laid by the queen's father and brother. This would mean forcing Catholic bishops and clergy to conform or be sacked. It would also mean holding in check their more hot-headed co-religionists, who desired a 'thorough' Reformation polity along the lines of those established in Geneva or Zurich. But the councillors' biggest problem was not with extremist partisans of either side, but with the queen herself. Though firmly Protestant in her beliefs, she was decidedly more 'middle-of-the-road' than Bacon and co. would have liked. Moreover, she was convinced that her royal prerogative covered all aspects of religion. The stage was set for a struggle in which queen, Council, Parliament and church leaders would be involved throughout the reign.

The first decision to be made was that of choosing a new Archbishop of Canterbury, the previous incumbent of that office having conveniently died on the same day as his royal mistress. Bacon knew just the man for the job – his old friend Matthew Parker. Parker was, understandably, far from enthusiastic about assuming the hot seat. It took Bacon nine months of persuasion and cajolery to bring him to accept the preferment. Meanwhile the Lord Keeper had to induce Parliament to endorse the religious settlement proposed by the government. Opening the first session, he reminded members that they were gathered primarily to make laws, 'for the according and uniting of the people of this realm into an uniform order of religion, to the honour and glory of God, the establishment of his Church and tranquillity of the realm'. In their deliberations they were to avoid sophistical, captious and frivolous arguments and refrain from hurling at one another such terms of abuse as 'heretic' and 'papist'.[3]

He can hardly have hoped that his irenic appeal would elicit the desired response, nor did it. Ill-tempered debate raged back and forth from January 1559 to Easter, without any agreement on the necessary legislation. The bishops who had served under Mary were supported in the upper house by several of the peers, while the radicals had a sizeable presence in the Commons. Determined to end the gridlock, the government announced a theological debate to take place during the recess under the 'impartial' chairmanship of the Lord Keeper. Bacon was determined not to preside over another slanging match that would have no positive outcome. The rules of the debate were rigged against the Catholics and the chairman tried to bully them into submission. When they protested, their two leading spokesmen were conveyed to the Tower. Even then the opponents of the government's policy were not completely cowed. Hard-edged debate continued and, though the act re-establishing the royal supremacy passed with relative ease, that imposing a new English Prayer Book had the distinction of being the first piece of religious legislation to be brought into being without the support of the bishops.

When Bacon closed the session in May he declared that the government would be vigilant in enforcing unity, being equally severe with those 'that go before the law or beyond the law as those that will not follow'.[4] In other words, he was declaring war on both Catholics and the Protestant zealots who were now being dubbed 'Puritans'.* However, in practice, he was very far from being even-handed. He served on the commissions for the dioceses of Norwich and Ely, where radical religious elements were very active. However, the reports of his commissions contained no whisper of Puritan discontent with the Elizabethan settlement and Sir Nicholas used his prominent position in East Anglia to further the moderate radical cause.

He was, by now, the most powerful man in the region, second only to the Duke of Norfolk. Indeed, the reception he customarily received on arrival was almost ducal; all the local gentry turned out to greet him as he crossed the Suffolk border. He had added substantially to his land-holdings over the years and had built himself an impressive country mansion at Redgrave, some fifteen miles north of his natal village. This, however, proved to be inconveniently placed for a man of his increasing importance. He needed a rural retreat within easy reach of London. In the 1570s Bacon built a grander house at Gorhambury, near St Albans. It was scarcely a coincidence that Cecil's architects

---

* This term of ridicule was very imprecise. G.R. Elton suggested, with some justification, that 'the puritans were all those people that the queen disliked'. (*The Parliament of England*, 1559–1581, 1986, 199.)

were busy constructing Theobalds, a spectacular country seat not sixteen miles away at Cheshunt. The 1570s were boom years for English domestic architecture when courtiers and country squires were falling over themselves to make status statements. Sir Nicholas Bacon was among the trendsetters.

His influence, locally and nationally, was now immense. Patronage was the cement that held Tudor society together. Ambitious men commended themselves to their betters in the hope of gaining preferment. A scholar seeking financial help to get through university, a priest looking for a lucrative benefice, a country gentleman hoping to find a place for his daughter in the queen's entourage, a political zealot wanting to be elected to the House of Commons – these and other hopefuls approached influential members of the establishment begging them, as the term went, to be 'good lord' to the supplicant. The system worked in both directions. When a petitioner was successful, he was helped up the social ladder, but his patron also gained the loyalty of someone who could be useful to him. Bacon, like his conciliar colleagues, built up a following of men he could rely on to support his policies. Throughout East Anglia he appointed several JPs and parish priests. He supported candidates for Parliament and for government offices. Some of those advanced in this way were his own relatives, for nepotism was ingrained in the system. For example, his four sons, Nicholas, Nathaniel, Francis and Edward, all held parliamentary seats as well as being active in provincial politics. A letter he wrote to Nicholas junior in 1569 indicates the kind of problems to which family loyalties could give rise. The Lord Keeper's son had written in support of a candidate for the office of under-sheriff of Suffolk. His father protested, 'you tell me not his name and expect me to write in favour of a man I know not, which I am not accustomed to doing.'[5]

The Bacon network connected East Anglian life to the

government, but, while it was generally very effective in ensuring the implementation of official policy, the Lord Keeper could not always maintain complete control of his clientage. This was particularly true in religious affairs. In 1571 he fell out with his old friend, Matthew Parker. The Archbishop dragged several extreme Puritans before the Privy Council for promoting beliefs and practices against the authority of himself and his bishops. Bacon's problem with this was that some of the alleged offenders were his own protégés. Percival Wiburn, one of his chaplains, had written and preached against the 'half-reformed' Church of England and travelled to Geneva and Zurich to enlist the support of leading Protestant theologians. He frequently enlisted his patron's aid in having radical friends appointed to parishes. The embarrassed Bacon was obliged to support the ecclesiastical establishment and unrepentant radicals were forbidden to preach. However, when the dust had settled, the offenders were soon back in the pulpits. In the overheated religious climate of the 1570s personal convictions often came into conflict with professional responsibilities. These were tense days, and public opinion was increasingly polarized between Catholic and Puritan extremes.

In 1577, Bacon's friend and colleague, Sir Francis Walsingham, wrote to a friend in Strasbourg, 'the times in which we live are abounding in dangers, and the dispositions of the men with whom we have to contend, are not without their infinite recesses and deep concealments'.[6] As Elizabeth's reign progressed so did the possibility of foreign conflict, and her councillors were acutely aware of the potential dangers her realm faced. Religion-inspired terror stalked the streets of neighbouring states. In 1570 Elizabeth's envoy to the Scottish court was gunned down in Edinburgh. Within weeks Pope Pius V issued a bull, *Regnans in Excelsis*, excommunicating Elizabeth, declaring her deposed and absolving her subjects of all allegiance to her. France was in a state of political and religious chaos. Elizabeth's reign coincided with that of five French kings and the instability this caused contributed to utterly horrendous events. In 1572 the notorious St Bartholomew's Day Massacre occurred, when at least 13,000 French Protestants (Huguenots) were slaughtered with the approval of the government. The same year brought to a head the long-running bloody conflict in the Netherlands between the Spanish rulers and those of their subjects who had embraced Calvinism. The territory was plunged into bloody civil war. The impact of these conflicts on England was twofold: trade across the Narrow Seas was severely disrupted and large numbers of refugees arrived, fleeing from religious persecution.

The government also had its own internal problems. In 1569–70 the Catholic earls of Northumberland and Westmorland raised the standard of revolt in the North. The rising was swiftly dealt with and scores of participants were executed for treason but, in the process of examining suspects, a network of Spanish agents was uncovered. They had connections with Mary, the Queen of Scotland, who claimed the English crown and was currently held captive by Elizabeth, having fled her own country. Bacon and his colleagues were frustrated because Elizabeth refused to read the signs of the times. She believed that England could remain aloof from the conflicts convulsing the continent and, particularly, declined to do anything that would upset the rulers of Spain and France. She refused to tighten restrictions against English Catholics, send military aid to Protestants in the Netherlands or apply the 'final solution' to Mary. Even the disgrace and execution of the Duke of Norfolk failed to alert her to her danger. Thomas Howard, England's premier Catholic peer and a member of the Privy Council, was implicated in the plotting that centred on Mary Queen of Scots and was sent to the block in 1572.

The removal of this Catholic champion from government made life easier for the Protestant majority. It also greatly enhanced Bacon's standing in East Anglia. The Howard family was finished as the main force in local politics for a generation. In the parliamentary election of 1572, all the successful candidates for Suffolk and Norfolk shire seats were Bacon's protégés and one was the younger Nicholas Bacon. Another son, Edward Bacon, took his seat as MP for Great Yarmouth and, thanks to his father's influence, yet another, Nathaniel, became member for Tavistock. The entire clan was now at the heart of English politics.

Yet the greatest accolade they received came in July of this eventful year. The queen came to stay. Every spring and summer Elizabeth took her entire court touring parts of southern and midland England, lodging along the way in the towns and country houses of her more prosperous subjects. These were PR exercises, designed to show herself to and receive the adulation of her people. For those selected to act as hosts having the queen under their roof was a great mark of favour – if an expensive one. Lords, courtiers and country gentlemen vied with each other to provide the very best entertainment for their royal guest. There were banquets, hunting parties, dances and plays. Sometimes locals put on amateur theatricals for Elizabeth's delectation. The antics of Bottom, Quince and co. in *A Midsummer Night's Dream* will have readily been recognized by the sophisticates of the court. When Puck demanded, 'What hempen homespuns have we swaggering here, so near the cradle of the fairy queen'(*A Midsummer Night's Dream*, III. i. 68–9), images of provincial entertainments will have sprung readily to mind for Elizabeth and her attendants. We do not know how Sir Nicholas diverted the queen during that first visit to Gorhambury from 25 to 28 July 1572 but we do know that the responsibility filled him with anxiety. He turned to his brother-in-law (now Lord Burghley) for guidance:

Understanding . . . that the Queen's Majesty means to come to my house . . . I have thought good to pray you that this bearer might understand what you know therein . . . and that I might understand your advice what you think to be the best way for me to deal in this matter . . . no man is more raw in such a matter than myself and I would gladly take that course that might best please her Majesty, which I know not how better to understand than by your help.[7]

Elizabeth visited Gorhambury three times in the next five years, so Bacon must have got something right.

By no means was a royal visit always a matter for rejoicing. After Elizabeth had been entertained by Edward Rookwood at Euston, near Thetford, in 1578, her host was berated as a stubborn Catholic. He and twenty-two other leaders of recusant households (places where Catholic rites were sometimes performed) were examined by the Council at Norwich a few weeks later and suffered various penalties. By contrast, Nicholas Bacon junior was among a group of safely Protestant gentlemen to receive knighthoods. The Bacon caucus was dominant in the region, according to at least one commentator who described 'the gentlemen of these parts' as 'being great and hot Protestants'.[8] The temperature of religious conflict was now rising rapidly and increasingly affected the workings of local government and the relationships between the county leaders and the crown. There was, for example, a long-running feud between Edmund Freke, who was Bishop of Norwich between 1575 and 1584, and several of Bacon's friends and appointees in the magistracy. Freke, not unreasonably, believed that it was his responsibility to ensure the proper teaching of official Anglican doctrine and attempted to discipline Puritan preachers. Several Suffolk and Norfolk gentry countered by accusing the bishop of being soft on recusants.

As a leader of society in the eastern counties, Bacon was acutely conscious of the menacing situation on the other side of the North Sea. He carefully monitored contacts between English Catholics and their friends abroad. In August 1576, Nathaniel passed on to his father information about raids being carried out against Dutch Protestant shipping by pirates based in East Anglian ports. The leading figures in this activity were Thomas Hubbart and Christopher Heydon, both Norfolk recusants. Hubbart was already under suspicion as a result of loose talk about sending troops to Spain to take part in the 'Enterprise of England', the invasion plan that King Philip II was already ruminating upon. The Lord Keeper saw in this a chance to make political capital. He and his colleagues had long been urging on the queen a pro-Dutch policy but she continued to prefer amity with the leading Catholic powers. By skilful manoeuvring he had the accused brought before the Council, examined, condemned and sent to prison. Elizabeth could not stop this judicial process and, though she subsequently pardoned the offenders, Bacon and his associates had made their point, in both court and county.

Their relationship with the queen was always frustrating. Elizabeth and her Council were alike concerned for the security of the realm but they understood that security differently. They all knew that the various elements in society were finely balanced and that the job of government was to maintain that balance. That meant, for example, reinforcing the authority of local magistrates, strengthening the laws against the criminally inclined, the itinerant unemployed and those who preferred begging to working for a living. On such things they could agree. But Elizabethan society was built on regional hierarchies of power and networks of patronage. Maintaining that status quo was an issue over which the queen and her advisers not infrequently fell out. Bacon was among those for whom the signs of the times were very clear. England was a Protestant nation fighting for its identity in a largely Catholic Europe.

It should be in firm alliance with leaders like the Prince of Orange, champion of the Dutch rebels, it should be vigilant in dealing with Catholic fifth columnists and it should remove their potential figurehead, Mary Queen of Scots. It was also necessary for Elizabeth to marry in order to ensure the Protestant succession and to end speculation about the future. The queen, by contrast, wanted to keep her foreign policy options open, declined to upset her Catholic subjects by stringent application of the recusancy laws, regarded radical preachers with grave suspicion and had no inclination to weaken her own authority by taking a husband. Bacon was not averse to straight talking with Her Majesty:

> Most gracious Sovereign, by my former letters [there were] three things that . . . I with all humbleness did advise Your Majesty to do as the best [for] your surety . . . The first was to assist the Prince of Orange; the second to [make sure] of Scotland; the third to make all safe and ready at home. Now, seeing it has not pleased God to move Your Majesty's heart to give that assistance to the Prince in time, as was wished and desired, which I cannot remember but greatly to my grief, the best counsel I can give is that care be taken for the other two . . .[9]

Yet, Bacon was at all times the queen's man. Particularly, he was her mouthpiece when addressing Parliament. During the course of the reign the House of Commons became increasingly difficult to handle. It contained a sizeable and vocal number of Puritans and used its power of granting taxation to discuss subjects that the queen regarded as belonging to her prerogative – particularly her marriage (see below, pp. 44–6). Elizabeth became extremely adroit in using flattery and delaying tactics to keep Parliament sweet. It was often Bacon who was put in the difficult position of delivering these orations. Much as he shared the Commons' concerns, he had to mouth gracious words which promised much and delivered nothing.

> . . . it doth not only content you to have her Majesty to reign and govern over you, but also you do desire that some [issue] proceeding of her Majesty's body, might by perpetual succession reign over your posterity also; a matter greatly to move her Highness, she saith, to incline to this your suit . . . for your sakes and for the benefit of the realm she is content to be disposed that way provided conditions are favourable . . .[10]

This speech was made at the closing of the 1576 session of Parliament. It was to be Bacon's last address to the assembly. By the time it was convened again, five years later, he was dead.

Elizabeth never married. With her the Tudor dynasty came to an end. By contrast, Sir Nicholas Bacon had five sons and three daughters by his two wives. All the boys became Members of Parliament and were prominent in national as well as regional politics. The girls were all married into major gentry families. The descendants of a Drinkstone sheep reeve exercised considerable and widespread influence for many years to come.

2

KING LAND

This blessed plot, this earth, this realm, this England,
This nurse, this teeming womb of royal kings,
Fear'd by their breed and famous by their birth,
Renowned for their deeds as far from home –
For Christian service and true chivalry –
As is the sepulchre in stubborn Jewry
Of the world's ransom, blessed Mary's Son:
This land of such dear souls, this dear, dear land.

King Richard II, I. 52–9

'Land' meant different things to different people in Elizabeth's England. For councillors, trying to persuade the queen to take up the sword against the tyrannical rulers of Catholic Europe, it was the home of Protestant truth, destined to lead the fight against the Counter-Reformation. Patrons of the Globe would have had their hearts stirred by John of Gaunt's famous speech, which wrapped nationalist sentiment in religion's glittering robe. For the vagabond and the destitute, 'land' meant a friendless country of rutted roads, linking sparse settlements, winding through forests, 'by nature made for murders and for rapes'.[1] For the athletic courtier it was private ground owned by the queen or her wealthy nobles where he could enjoy the sport of hunting the deer. For the great territorial magnates it was power and a degree of local independence from central authority. For the farmer it was a hard taskmaster, who demanded long hours of wearying toil in return for modest crop yield. For the gentleman and yeoman it was, simply, security, a title to a few acres to be jealously guarded and passed on to the next generation. But for all English men, women and children land was king. It ruled their lives, provided their income and demanded their loyalty. Preachers might insist that heaven is our home and we are but strangers and pilgrims here but those of the queen's subjects who could do so acquired areas of the ground beneath their feet which provided them with the illusion of permanence.

Few were more acquisitive than Elizabeth Talbot, widely known as Bess of Hardwick. She was born into the middle-income Derbyshire family of John Hardwick but never knew her father, who died within a year of her birth. Since her only brother, the heir to the family's estate, was a minor, the management of his affairs now became the responsibility of the Crown – more specifically the master of the King's Wards (replaced in 1540 by the Court of Wards and Liveries). This meant that all income became part of royal revenue, except for an allowance (usually a third) allotted to the widow. In practice what happened was that the wardship was sold to the highest bidder, usually a neighbouring landowner eager to incorporate the heir's property with his own. Not infrequently this was a prelude to marriage. The wardship holder, if a bachelor or widower, might wed the heir's mother or arrange a union between the heir and his own daughter, thus permanently amalgamating their estates. This was a common way of creating large landholdings. This money-earner for the Crown notionally prevented the death of a major landowner leading to a free-for-all of ambitious rivals but was much resented as interference by central government in the affairs of shire families. In the case of Elizabeth, it led to her mother becoming the wife of Ralph Leche of Chatsworth, some twelve miles distant.

The arrangement was not a happy one. Despite being the lord of extensive lands, Leche appears to have been incapable of adequately supporting his enlarged family and spent several years in a debtors' prison. Early hardship must have strengthened Bess's resolve to better herself and put straitened circumstances behind her. As a teenager she was briefly the wife of a neighbour's son (he died within a year of the wedding). However, by 1558, she had come to London and was moving in very different circles. She had managed to gain access to the royal court, probably by securing a position as lady-in-waiting to Frances Grey, Marchioness of Dorset, first cousin to the queen. Here she met a man who was her match in ambition and energy. Sir William Cavendish, some twenty years Bess's senior, was a gifted administrator who was steadily working his way up the social ladder. He had held a succession of financial offices at court and used them to good personal advantage. Though he came under suspicion for sharp practice on more than one occasion, he survived, probably because he had made himself indispensable to the right people. It was during her ten years of marriage to Sir William (1547–57) that Bess began to build the extensive Midlands holdings that became the basis of her wealth and power.

Cavendish had accumulated various estates in the Home Counties. These he now sold in order to acquire land in his wife's native county of Derbyshire. He bought Chatsworth from her relatives, the Leches. Over the next few years he added several other parcels of land to his holding and made the mansion, which he rebuilt, the centre of an extensive empire. He and Bess lived and entertained in style, their expenditure frequently outpacing their income. Bess, it seems, was determined to impress upon Midlands society that the daughter of a notorious debtor and wastrel had 'made it'. She had also learned the lesson of the wardship trap. Like a modern wheeler-dealer stashing his assets in offshore accounts to avoid tax, Bess ensured that the Crown could not gain access to her landed investments. Cavendish was well versed in every financial dodge going. He ensured that all the Cavendish properties were held jointly by himself and his wife. This meant that, if Sir William died before his heir had come of age (as seemed likely), the Crown could not step in to take charge of his property. Thus, after the death of her second husband, Bess continued to be 'queen' of Chatsworth. But earlier profligacy brought its consequences. She found herself heavily in debt. Time for another advantageous marriage.

Sir William St Loe had two advantages: he was immensely wealthy and, as Captain of the Guard, he was one of the men closest to the new queen. Marriage to him solved Bess's financial problems and placed her at the centre of court life. She now became a gentlewoman of the privy chamber. The relationship of the two Elizabeths was sometimes stormy. The possessive queen always resented the wives of her favourite courtiers and this partly explained Bess's long absences from court. However, Lady St Loe was well occupied building up her Midlands estates. Another fly in the ointment was Sir William's brother, Edward, who was convinced, probably not without reason, that Bess was after her husband's fortune. Edward was a passionate and unstable character who was suspected of having murdered his first wife. On a visit to William and Bess, after 'much unnaturalness and unseemly speeches' he tried – or so it was believed – to poison them. If he thought by such behaviour to secure William's property for himself, he certainly miscalculated. St Loe made Bess the sole beneficiary to his estate and, though the will was contested,

nothing prevented Bess adding substantially to her growing fortune.

Two years after Sir William's death (c.1567) the forty-
year-old widow made her fourth and final marriage. This
time she reached the top of the social tree. Her husband,
George Talbot, was Earl of Shrewsbury, a man of long
and distinguished aristocratic lineage. His possessions in
the North were extensive. As well as a large acreage, he
owned castles and substantial houses at Rufford, Tutbury,
Sheffield, Pontefract, Handsworth and Worksop. By now,
Bess was a property tycoon with a wide knowledge of the
law. This she used to make a cast-iron marriage settlement
that would perpetuate her dynasty. Two of her daughters
were pledged in wedlock to two of Shrewsbury's sons.
The relationship began amicably enough but the management of their joint empire almost inevitably placed
strains upon it. Husband and wife disagreed over prior-
ities and Shrewsbury particularly resented the money Bess
spent on extending her Derbyshire holdings. Then, when
Queen Elizabeth placed the earl in charge of the captive
Mary Queen of Scots (1569–84) a poisonous ménage à trois
developed. Bess was becoming a jealous termagant and
convinced herself that George Talbot was having an affair
with his royal guest. In any case her property portfolio
now occupied most of her time and energy. In 1584 the
couple formally separated – an unusual process in those
days. In the legal battle that followed Bess made good her
claim to Chatsworth and a substantial financial settlement.

For the remaining twenty years of her life the Countess
of Shrewsbury was able to concentrate on her building projects, in what was almost a frenzy of creative activity and
self-glorification. She bought the family home of Hardwick
from her brother and set in hand a major rebuilding programme. Not satisfied with that, when she inherited more
wealth on the death of her estranged husband, she called
upon the architect, Robert Smythson, and builders to

construct for her a new Hardwick Hall, which was to be
the archetypal grand house. Her creation stands today as
the finest example of Elizabethan domestic building, a
symmetrical, multi-windowed mansion crowned with the
repeated 'ES' motif in stone. It is a tour de force and was
even more so in the days of its first owner, who filled it
with the most exquisite furniture, hangings and paintings.
Bess was an early advocate of the Mel Brooks adage, 'when
you got it, flaunt it'.

This was an age of ostentatious display and the lady of
Hardwick was far from being alone in building to impress.

> The Queen's Majesty, contrary to the appetite of all that be
> about the Court, will needs make her progress to Collywes-
> ton and being here I think her Majesty will visit my cottage
> and my Lord Admiral's house, who is at home preparing great
> things for the same, and poor I am constrained to remain here
> and yet shall not thereby spare my purse.[2]

So wrote William Cecil in 1566. The 'cottage' he referred
to was Burghley House, near Stamford, one of the two
country residences on which he lavished a not inconsid-
erable fortune. These courtly owners of stately homes
maintained the conceit that they built their stunning rural
palaces for the sole purpose of entertaining their sovereign.
This was part of the ritual royal worship. Sir Christopher
Hatton, one of Elizabeth's closest friends, spent lavishly on
Holdenby Hall in Northamptonshire, calling it a 'shrine' to
England's 'holy saint'. He was to be disappointed, though
– his angelic queen never visited his mansion. The lengths
to which sycophancy could go is illustrated by Thomas
Gresham's response to a queenly comment made when
Elizabeth visited his Middlesex home at Osterley. She
remarked that his expansive courtyard might look better
if divided by a wall running down the middle. When she
emerged from the house the following morning, the wall

was dutifully in place. Gresham had brought in builders to effect the desired change by working through the night. Such flamboyant gestures signalled not only the devotion of Elizabeth's leading subjects but also their magnificence.

If there existed, as presumably there did, some unofficial competition to see who could entertain the queen most sumptuously, that contest must have been won, hands down, by the Earl of Leicester in July 1575, when he welcomed the royal court to Kenilworth castle. At the outer gate the queen and her attendants were welcomed by a fanfare sounded by 'giant' trumpeters on the ramparts.

> Thenceforth, for the next eighteen days, the worlds of actuality and myth completely overlapped. When Elizabeth went hunting, a savage man and satyrs appeared to recite flattering verses. Returning on another day to the castle, she was surprised by Triton who emerged from the lake dripping weeds and water, to make another oration. Even at her departing she found Sylvanus running at her stirrup and urging her to stay for ever. There were masques and pageants in plenty, banqueting and bear-baiting. There was a rustic wedding and games arranged for the townsfolk in the tilt-yard. There were mummers and a troupe of actors from Coventry who came to present traditional plays. There were tumblers and jugglers and firework displays. There were picnics and minstrelsy on the lake. And everywhere 'magic' surprises – bushes that burst into song, pillars that grew fruit and gushed wine, trees decked with costly gifts.[3]

The lavish expenditure on pleasure palaces by the leaders of society trickled down to lesser mortals who emulated their betters as far as their resources would allow. The Dissolution of the Monasteries had provided the impetus for a revolution in domestic building, but the first Tudor mansions were either conventual buildings adapted for family use or others following traditional patterns. Elizabethan owners and architects introduced Renaissance style. Earlier grand houses had been inward-looking, arranged round enclosed courtyards. The grand houses of the new era, like Hardwick Hall, Longleat, Montacute and others, gazed proudly out on their surrounding parkland through glittering facades of large windows. Features from Italy and the Netherlands were incorporated and, indeed, often created by craftsmen brought over from the continent. A new breed of designer-masons was much in demand as owners rivalled each other to create residences which reflected the latest fashion.

Robert Smythson, who was employed at Hardwick, already had a long and impressive career behind him. His memorial tablet in Wollaton church, Nottinghamshire (1614), describes him as 'architector and surveyor unto the most worthy house of Wollaton, and divers others of great account'. This much-in-demand craftsman had indeed worked on many impressive mansions, including Longleat (where he collaborated with the French master mason, Alan Maynard), Wollaton Hall, Welbeck Abbey and Worksop Manor). Among his early patrons was no less a person that Sir Francis Knollys, Elizabeth's Vice Chancellor. By 1568 Smythson was in a position to dictate terms. An intermediary, recommending him to Sir John Thynne of Longleat, stipulated that he should be paid,

16d. a day whole that is to say 8s. a week and a nag kept at your worship's charges and the rest of his men 12d. a day. Secondly his men to have day wages for their travel, that is to say 12d. a day whiles they are coming and the carriage of their tools paid for . . .[4]

It is interesting that Smythson was described on his memorial as an 'architector', for the word 'architect' was new to the English language. The theory of building design was first explained by John Shute, a member of the Painter Stainers' Company, who, after several years' study in Italy, published, in 1563, *The first and chief groundes of architecture used in all the auncient and famous monymentes* . . . He brought to the attention of builders and ambitious landowners, who desired to be regarded as cultured and avant-garde, the mathematical principles upon which classical craftsmen had founded their art. This obsession with form, order and harmony extended into the immediate surroundings of the country house and led to the development of the pleasure garden. Taking their inspiration from Italian villas and their grounds, architects 'tamed' nature to provide for wealthy families and their guests areas where they might take their ease when the weather permitted sedate outdoor exercise. Gravel paths bordered flower beds constrained within box hedges arranged in geometrical patterns. Hitherto, gardens had been kept for utilitarian purposes – providing vegetables, fruit and herbs for the kitchen and simples for medicines. Of course, they remained so for the majority of people, but for the privileged few they connected earth with the harmonious beauties of Elysium, as defined by classical poets. In the arbours and shaded walks they might fancy themselves catching a glimpse of Oberon, Titania, Ariel or any of the other magical creatures of whom Shakespeare wrote and who were portrayed in court masques.

If the rich man's garden was an art form, gardeners were becoming artists or, at least, superior craftsmen influenced by foreign trends and the developments made possible by the introduction of plants and seeds brought back from lands now being reached by English mariners.

> Our orchards . . . were never furnished with so good fruit nor with such variety as at this present. For, beside that we have most delicate apples, plums, pears, walnuts, filberts, etc., and those of sundry sorts, planted within forty years past, in comparison of which most of the old trees are nothing worth, so have we no less store of strange fruit, as apricots, almonds,

peaches, figs, corn-trees [of the species *cornus* or dogberry] in noblemen's orchards. I have seen capers, oranges and lemons, and heard of wild olives growing here, beside other strange trees, brought from far, whose names I know not.[5]

So the controversial historian and topographer, William Harrison, explained in 1577. This Puritan clergyman wrote extensively about terrestrial chronology, seeking to describe in detail how the human story revealed the workings of divine providence. He attracted criticism from the opponents of religious extremism but also from Puritans of a more radical stamp, who insisted that a man of the cloth had no business writing secular history. However, Raphael Holinshed regarded Harrison's descriptions of the contemporary scene worthy of incorporation into his *Chronicle*. Harrison was eager to demonstrate the superiority of England to Catholic countries and we need to take his patriotic zeal into account when reading his glowing descriptions of English husbandry.

> We have ... such workmen as are not only excellent in grafting the natural fruits, but their artificial mixtures, whereby one tree bringeth forth sundry fruits, and one and the same fruit of divers colours and tastes, dallying, as it were, with nature and her course ... Divers also have written at large of these several practices, and some of them ... of small fruit to make far greater, and to remove or add superfluous or necessary moisture to the trees, with other things belonging to their preservation, and with no less diligence than our physicians do commonly show upon our own diseased bodies ... And even so do our gardeners with their herbs, whereby they are strengthened against noisome blasts, and preserved from putrefaction and hindrance: whereby some such as were annual are now made perpetual.[6]

The new architecture was the inspiration of the classically educated landlord class. It was the estate owners who had the vision. Masons, gardeners and 'architectors' were simply craftsmen who carried out their patrons' detailed instructions. Since many of these patrons were members of the government and attendees at the royal court, the over-sight of building works usually fell to the estate steward. Sir John Thynne was often absent from Somerset but, as a quaint observation, supposedly made by his great house, states, he was always 'thinking of me, framing and erecting me, raising many a time with great care and now and then pulling down this or that part of me to enlarge sometimes a foot or some few inches, upon a conceit, or this or that man's speech'.[7] Much of this activity fell to Thynne's agent, John Dodd, to carry out and working for such a perfec-tionist was far from easy. Thynne gave precise instructions on every aspect of the work and warned, 'If I shall find any fault with the workmanship . . . they shall make it again'. As the intermediary, Dodd often had to stomach his mas-ter's wrath. 'I do not a little marvel that since my departure you have not obeyed my instructions to the letter,' Thynne complained on one occasion, and, on another, 'you have used yourself very lewdly'.[8]

Sir John and his breed were building for posterity; establishing very tangible monuments in the landscape to proclaim the power and permanence of themselves and their descendants. But these great estates had a practical, economic raison d'être. They were, as far as possible, self-sustaining. Rented farmland provided the owners' basic income. Timber for building came from the woodland and, in some cases, stone was quarried on site. Meat and fish were reared in the fields and lakes. Heating and cooking consumed a vast amount of wood. Grain was brought in for the kitchen and the brewhouse. Bess Hardwick informed her steward at Chatsworth, 'If I lack either good beer or good charcoal or wood I will blame nobody so much as I will do you.'[9]

Substantial landlords were frequently on the lookout

to maximize income from their estates. George Talbot, Earl of Shrewsbury, was the most active noble entrepreneur of his generation. Despite his considerable landed wealth he frequently pleaded that he was in dire financial straits. He certainly had plenty to complain about. In 1569, Elizabeth assigned to him the care of Mary Queen of Scots, a responsibility he was forced to shoulder for fifteen years. Shrewsbury accommodated the prisoner and her entourage in various of his northern houses and received grossly inadequate financial recompense from his parsimonious sovereign. He often asked to be relieved of the burden. Not only, he claimed, as it was impoverishing him, but it was also keeping him away from the royal court and, thus, depriving him of preferment. If we took his complaints at face value we would have to conclude that the demands of the two Elizabeths – his wife and his queen – were driving him to the brink of ruin. In fact, he was able to add to his considerable fortune by dabbling in numerous financial ventures. He was a shipowner. He mined coal, iron and lead on various of his estates. He had a steel mill. And he owned a glass-making factory. It is reasonable to call George Talbot one of England's first industrialists. Perhaps we should also regard him as prone to paranoia.

Few entrepreneurs may have followed the earl's lead by diversifying into mining and manufacture but there were many who were determined to enhance their income by agricultural innovation. Changing land use usually meant converting arable to pasture, enclosing common land and employing fewer labourers. 'There have grown many more depopulations by turning tillage into pasture than at any time for the like number of years heretofore.'[10] So ran the preamble to the Act for the Maintenance of Husbandry and Tillage (1597–8). For decades enclosure had been a common cause of grievance. For the most part this meant the conversion of ploughland to grazing for

sheep to feed the flourishing wool industry but enterprising landlords were students of the market and responded
to its fluctuations. In parts of the Midlands more profit
was to be obtained from dairy farming and cattle breeding (for beef and hides) than from sheep. Population
increase created a growing demand for basic foodstuffs
so that there were even examples of pasture being recon-
verted to wheat cultivation. Another way of increasing
agricultural productivity was by reclamation. Towards
the end of the century serious efforts were being made to
bring wasteland under cultivation (notably around The
Wash, where Dutch engineers were brought in to design
and construct drainage ditches). Woodland clearance had
a double value. It produced saleable timber for which the
price was high thanks to the demands of the building and
shipbuilding industries. It also made land available for
other kinds of husbandry.

The agricultural scene was complicated – perhaps more
complicated than even contemporaries appreciated. The
problems of unemployment and vagabondage were so
acute that it was tempting to assume simple reasons for
them. In the popular imagination the person responsible
for most of society's ills was the ubiquitous, 'cormorant'
landowner. Unscrupulous squirearchs certainly existed,
who thought little about encroaching on the common
ground, enclosing tillage and sacking those who had
earned their living by the plough, or even levelling villages. It was easy for a nobleman living at a distance from
an area designated for 'development' to issue instructions to his steward to make the necessary changes and
either to remain indifferent to the social consequences
or to observe that efficient land use was good for the
country, even if it involved a certain amount of collat-
eral damage. But it was just as easy for legislators in the
capital to assume that such landlords were solely to blame
and to ignore underlying economic factors. The 1597 Act

was an attempt to put the clock back by reversing recent enclosure activity. It ordered that any land that, since the beginning of the reign, had been converted from agrarian to pastoral use must, by 1 May 1599, be

> Restored to tillage or laid for tillage in such sort as the whole ground according to the nature of that soil and course of husbandry used in that part of the country be within three years at the least turned to tillage by the occupiers and possessors thereof, and so shall be continued for ever.[11]

It was one thing to enact a statute but quite another to enforce it, as Anthony Cope pointed out. Cope was a veteran MP who had sat for Banbury, Oxfordshire, in almost every parliament of the reign. As a substantial landowner and one who was upwardly mobile, he knew what he was talking about. He inherited the family estate at Hanwell and steadily added to it over the years. He accumulated further lands in Northamptonshire, Surrey and Lincolnshire, was able to entertain the Earl of Leicester in 1585 and later married one of his daughters to a son of the Marquis of Exeter. Cope was a dyed-in-the-wool Puritan, a friend and supporter of Peter Wentworth (see pp. 43–4) who used his influence in the shires to support radical preachers and who was sometimes in trouble for the religious views he expressed in the Commons. But he certainly did not have a one-track mind and his concern for the wellbeing of the commonwealth extended beyond simply supporting his own class. This he showed when he wrote to Burghley, pointing out the weaknesses in the new legislation. It would be naive, he said, to expect the leaders of rural society to enforce the Act impartially. It would have to be given sharper teeth. Assize judges ought to be invested with power to inquire into every complaint and the results of such inquiries should be recorded:

The Clerk of the Peace or some other public officer to keep a
book of the defaults and restitutions, and to notify the same
twice in the year, upon oath, into the Chancery, that the Lord
Keeper may take true knowledge and certify her Majesty and
your Lordships of the Council what is done therein.[12]

Cope's argument found little favour with landlords who
insisted that they were the best judges of what constituted
good husbandry. Francis Bacon spoke for them when he
suggested that, 'high corn prices invited and enticed men
to break up . . . ground and convert it to tillage more than
all the penal laws could ever by compulsion'. The argument
continued.

Reading the volumes of paperwork engendered by these
disputes tends to obscure the fact that there were contrary
trends in operation. Clearance of woodland or reclamation
provided space for new houses to be built. Specialist occupations such as mining and iron-working brought together
small communities. Such activities led to the development
of settlements and villages beyond the existing bounds of
human habitation. Though it is indisputable that depopula-
tion and vagrancy were major problems, land ownership,
use and occupation were becoming more complicated.
People are always aware of (and usually deplore) change
but the disappearance of traditional homesteads and rural
occupations are only part of the story.

The social structure of rural England was no less complex. The commonly used terms – 'labourer', 'peasant',
'husbandman', 'yeoman' and 'gentleman'– tend to conceal
an economy that was more fluid than such fixed categories suggest. At the bottom of the heap was the scantily
employed labourer. He worked for his neighbours at harvest time or when hedges or ditches had to be repaired but,
if he was at all enterprising, he might also discover a skill he
could exploit, such as that of carpenter, thatcher or brewer.
His wife might earn money as spinner, basket-weaver

or midwife. If he could raise the finance to buy a horse and wagon he might become the village carter, carrying goods and people to and from the nearest market. Harrison had little sympathy for those who had 'neither voice nor authority in the commonwealth'. These were the people, he observed, who tended to make trouble or fall into criminal activity. Yet, he pointed out that it was often from their ranks that minor village officers were drawn – sidesmen, churchwardens, aleconners (men who tested the quality of ale – doubtless an agreeable chore) and even constables. The husbandman was a landless farmer, working fields rented from the lord of the manor or a local yeoman or gentleman but he, or other members of his family, might provide services and help to fulfil some of the varied needs of the community. The yeoman farmed a more extensive acreage, at least some of which he owned. He employed others to till his ground and tend his stock but was essentially a 'hands-on' landowner, unlike the gentleman, whose estates might be scattered and who was free from the drudgery of day-to-day farming. He could afford the time to acquire an education, serve as a JP, play a role in shire politics and plan to increase his inheritance through marriage and purchase. But the gentleman was not necessarily wealthier than the yeoman or the yeoman than the landless farmer. Rising prices and fixed rents tended to close the gap between those who owned land and those who leased it. And, as we have seen, anyone with intelligence, skill, a willingness to work hard and a modicum of luck could earn enough to better himself. The ranks of Elizabethan society were not so rigidly exclusive as to discourage enterprise. By the same token, younger sons of the gentry who had no chance of inheriting property had to rely on their education, their wits or their contacts if they wished to maintain their social status. Meanwhile, their fathers had the worry of keeping their family holdings intact. One creature they always had to watch out for was the gold-digger.

FENTON: I see I cannot get thy father's love . . .
He doth object I am too great of birth;
And that, my state being gall'd with my expenses,
I seek to heal it only by his wealth.
Besides these, other bars he lays before me,
My riots past, my wild societies;
And tells me 'tis a thing impossible
I should love thee but as a property.

ANNE: Maybe he tells you true.

FENTON: No, heaven so speed me in my time to come!
Albeit I will confess thy father's wealth
Was the first motive that I woo'd thee, Anne;
Yet, wooing thee, I found thee of more value
Than stamps in gold, or sums in sealed bags.

Merry Wives of Windsor, III. iv. 1–16

Anne's father, Master Page, has no intention of seeing the family fortune falling into the hands of a ne'er-do-well son-in-law. Fortunes, carefully garnered, could be easily lost and such was the tyranny of King Land that men of property were obsessed with preserving it for their posterity. A gentleman wished, above all things, to be blessed with sons. Daughters existed for the purpose of sealing favourable alliances but sex might at any time intrude, enabling a dashing lad of yeoman stock to force his way up the social ladder.

The life of the Elizabethan village was a human jigsaw. Ploughmen, labourers, carters, blacksmiths, bakers, brewers, other artisans, small landowners, the priest, the steward and servants from the 'big house' fitted together in a community that was largely self-contained. They lived a humdrum existence dominated by the need to keep themselves and their families above subsistence. Much of the excitement that entered these people's lives came from their visits to the nearest market town.

Here we see the hub of regional life – the economic,

social and administrative centre of the wider community. It was, first and foremost, a place of commercial exchange. To the weekly open-air market villagers took their crop surplus to sell. Here they bought necessities unavailable in the village. But here they also gossiped with folk from nearby communities. Here they rubbed shoulders with townsmen, merchants and travellers whose fine clothes and well-caparisoned horses displayed their wealth and importance. Here they discovered what was going on in the wider world and, when a preacher stood up by the market cross, they gathered to enjoy a display of religious oratory. And, of course, there was always the alehouse. Harrison was scathing about the drinking habits of the lower orders. He probably did not exaggerate when he complained of the numbers of men who could be seen on any market day rendered witless by strong drink, which rejoiced under a number of nicknames – 'huffcap, mad dog, father Whoreson, angel's food, dragon's milk, stride wide, go-by-the-wall and lift-leg'. But there were worse evils to which he drew attention – various kinds of sharp practice. He went into detail about engrossers, who cornered the market in corn or other commodities, in order to force up the price. He waxed eloquent about false measures. Every market was officially under the eye of the enforcers of the assize of ale and bread, a statutory order governing the price and quality of those commodities. However,

As these have been in times past erected for the benefit of the realm, so are they in many places too too [sic] much abused: for the relief and ease of the buyer is not so much intended, as the benefit of the seller. Neither are the magistrates for the most part (as men loth to displease their neighbours . . .) so careful in their offices as in right and duty they should be. For in most of these markets neither the assizes of bread, nor order for the goodness and sweetness of grain, and other commod-

ities that are brought thither to be sold, are any whit looked
upon; but each one suffered to sell or set up what and how
himself listeth . . .[13]

It is difficult to know to what extent, if at all, Harrison
was exaggerating, but it is not difficult to see how town-
based merchants might cultivate the JPs to their own
advantage and how the system could work to the disadvantage of the poor countryman who lacked the influence to
challenge it. In King Land's domain good men often strug-
gled for a living.

3

THE PARLIAMENTARIAN

IST CITIZEN: *They ne'er cared for us yet: suffer us to famish,*
and their storehouses cramm'd with grain; make edicts for
usury, to support usurers; repeal daily any wholesome act
established against the rich, and provide more piercing
statutes daily to chain up and restrain the poor. If the wars
eat us not up, they will; and there's the love they bear us.
                                        Coriolanus, I. i. 76–84

Politicians have never been popular. There has always
been a gap between those who make the laws and those
who have to obey the laws. In the centuries before 1558
scarcely a generation had passed without a popular revolt
of greater or lesser seriousness. Subjects rebelled over harsh
taxes, religious change, issues of land usage or other matters which touched their everyday lives. It is significant,
therefore, that throughout the forty-four years and four
months of Queen Elizabeth's reign there was no concerted
uprising of the common people, demanding political and
social reform.

There are many reasons for this internal peace but one was the emergence of the House of Commons as a self-conscious political entity acting as a partner in government. The lower house of parliament was as unpopular with the queen as it had been with her predecessors. There was a fundamental difference of viewpoint between the monarch and those who sat in the 'High Court of Parliament', where laws were made. The substantial men of the realm conceived of themselves as having the right to be consulted on important matters. Elizabeth's concept, by contrast, was well enunciated in the words of Sir Nicholas Bacon, spoken at the opening of the queen's first parliament:

> Although divers things that are to be done here in Parliament might by means be reformed without Parliament, yet the Queen's majesty, seeking in her consultations of importance contentation [satisfaction] by assent and surety by advice, and therewith reposing herself not a little in your fidelities, wisdoms and discretions, meaneth not at this time to make any resolution in any matter of weight before it shall be by you sufficiently and fully debated, examined and considered.[1]

In other words, Parliament was an advisory body, summoned by the queen's gracious favour, and one whose advice she was free to accept or reject. The story of the ten parliaments of her reign is, in large measure, the account of how these differing viewpoints clashed or were accommodated.

Elizabeth summoned the assembly of the people as rarely as possible, but recurring crises obliged her to instigate sixteen separate sessions, some of which turned into political sparring matches. However, it would be wrong to think of Crown and Parliament being constantly in conflict. They shared a common concern for the security and wellbeing of the nation and, in any case, the two houses spent much of their time in the humdrum task of drafting legislation. If constitutional crisis was avoided, that was in large measure

due to the consummate skill with which the queen handled
Parliament. She did not harangue and bully; she wooed and
cajoled. For their part, the members were, by and large,
charmed by their sovereign. The initiative lay firmly with
the monarch, who summoned parliaments as infrequently
as possible and only when she needed something – usually
money. The principle had been long established that new
taxes could only be 'granted' to the government and not
exacted by a rapacious ruler.

Throughout the reign ten parliaments were summoned,
but that does not mean that they met almost continuously
as long as Elizabeth was on the throne. On the contrary,
all the sessions, taken together, amounted to no more than
five per cent of the period 1558–1603. This was because
sittings rarely lasted more than a few weeks. The reason
was not just that the queen prorogued or dissolved parliament at the earliest opportunity, once she had got what she
wanted from it. The members themselves were anxious to
get home and resume their interrupted lives. Attendance
was an expensive business and electors who paid their
members' expenses did not want them extending their stay
in the capital.

Parliament was not representative of the nation, just the
political classes. Originally, this meant the nobility and
the 'spirituality' (bishops and, until 1539, abbots) – these
were the major stakeholders in 'England PLC'. No designated space existed for such an ad hoc assembly. The Lords
were allotted an old, lofty hall at the south end of the
Westminster complex, known as the Queen's Chamber.
However, with the steady shift of economic power to
embrace non-aristocratic country landowners and wealthy
urban merchants, it had become necessary to admit other
influential subjects to the deliberative assembly. For more
than two centuries the House of Commons had been in
existence, comprising knights of the shire, representing
the English counties, and burgesses selected to speak for

the major towns and cities. However, it was not until the 1530s that the status of the lower house was acknowledged. Henry VIII assigned to the Commons St Stephen's Chapel, part of the property he had confiscated from the Church. Having their own 'home' certainly gave members a sense of permanence and they began to consider the implications of their partnership with Crown, Privy Council and Lords in the political life of the nation.

But even the men chosen to attend could not all be said to be representatives of their constituencies in any real sense. This was because patronage played a vital part in parliamentary elections, just as it did in other areas of Elizabethan life. The system worked like this: a writ of summons went out to every sheriff who, in turn, ordered the electors to select their members. In the shires, those eligible to vote were freeholders having property with a rentable value of forty shillings or more. Converting sixteenth-century values into modern equivalents is notoriously difficult, but when we realize that a minimum living wage was between forty and sixty shillings per annum we can see that a voter was a financially substantial man. Since inflation was increasing the value of land, while the property qualification remained fixed, a growing minority of landowners became eligible to vote.

Borough franchise was more complicated and varied from town to town, but effectively belonged to the civic leaders; that is, the wealthier members of the mercantile community. To take one urban constituency at random, Worcester had a governing body comprising two bailiffs, a recorder, a town clerk, a city council of twenty-four and a council of forty-eight freeholders. The city council members would choose their candidate, after which the freeholders or 'as many as would come' were invited to have a say. Then 'the bailiffs and the whole council together went up to the council chamber and . . . proceeded to their election'. If there was disagreement a poll was taken of all present from the two councils.[2] Originally, candidates had been chosen from their own community, but patronage had made deep inroads into this tradition. When the electors of Denbigh made a hurried choice of the man they wanted to represent them, they received the following letter from the Earl of Leicester, who happened to be the biggest land-owner in the region:

> ... if you do not ... choose such a one as I shall nominate ... be ye well assured never to look for any friendship or favour at my hand in any of your affairs hereafter ... It will haply be alleged that your choice was made before the receipt of my let-ters ... I would little have thought that you would have been so forgetful or rather careless of me as, before your decision, not to make me privy thereto, or at least to have some desire of my advice therein.[3]

Many Commons seats were in the gift of the men who wielded real power in the regions. If they were intent on bolstering their own influence in Parliament or if, as in Leicester's case, they wanted to fill as many seats as pos-sible with men loyal to the government, they put forward their own candidates. Election then became a formality and many electors did not even trouble to vote. For some ambi-tious young men gaining a place in Parliament was one way of advancing their career, of raising their profile in the cor-ridors of power. In 1597, William Slingsby, an adventurer who had decided to put his military life behind him and, 'come and do my duty in Yorkshire', wrote to his brother: 'We have news here of a Parliament to begin 12 October next; if it be so, good brother, put my father in mind to make me a burgess of the Parliament, for it is a thing I do exceedingly desire.'[4] He was duly elected as a member for Knaresborough, which his father and brother before him had represented.

In very few cases were elections contested. However,

some municipal corporations were not composed of spine-less forelock-tuggers. Having had a courtier foisted on them in 1581, Canterbury's council decreed that in future only residents were to be elected. In November 1562, Exeter rejected the stranger being presented to them by the Earl of Bedford and returned the sitting member, Thomas Williams, a local man and an experienced parliamentarian who ended his career in the Commons as Speaker. Bedford seems to have been losing the influence he had once held in the West Country and the city burgesses wanted someone at Westminster who would look after *their* interests. They paid their MP's wages and also offered rewards to those who represented them well.

Sometimes elections could become lively affairs. In 1588, John Edwards was proposed as a candidate in Denbighshire against the sitting member, William Almer. Almer enjoyed majority support but he had enemies and, in a long and tenacious campaign, Edwards made a point of securing their support. He used his standing among Catholic gentry in the shire as another bulwark and he even imposed electoral loyalty on anyone seeking to lease land. Finally, he persuaded the sheriff to announce the result in his favour. Such corruption, more commonly associated with eighteenth- and nineteenth-century elec-toral shenanigans, created quite a stir at the time and became the subject of a lawsuit brought in the court of Star Chamber.

When the new member arrived, he was directed to St Stephen's Chapel, the internal layout of which would play a large part in the development of English political life over the following centuries. St Stephen's had been a collegiate chapel in which the pews were arranged facing each other on either side of the chancel. These were now occupied by the MPs, not with any confrontational intent, but simply because that was the existing seating plan. At the east end, where the altar had once stood, was the chair occupied by the president, who had recently become known as the 'Speaker'. This was because he was the officer who had to speak for the house in any communication with the sovereign. He was not elected by the house; he was appointed by the sovereign to control the behaviour of members and to relay royal messages to them. The seats closest to the Speaker's chair were occupied by privy councillors who made sure that the government's agenda was followed. They could always rely on their own clients.

The initiative, thus, remained with the supporters of royal policy. Councillors proposed most of the business. They presented the government's case, controlled the membership of committees and could usually rely on the support of the upper house. Even if Parliament passed legislation that was not to the queen's liking, she had the power of veto and she did not flinch from using it. But the mood of the Commons was changing. Town members now accounted for almost three-quarters of the 460 or so complement of the house and they were less likely than the shire gentry to be restricted by traditional attitudes. They represented the merchant class, men with foreign contacts, open to new ideas, especially about religion. They also had an agenda and they took every opportunity to propose it. Thus, there was a real potential for discord and this is displayed very clearly in the career of Peter Wentworth.

Wentworth came from an established and well-connected Oxfordshire family. His first wife was a cousin of Queen Catherine Parr and his second was the sister of Francis Walsingham, Elizabeth's secretary. His religious affiliations placed him firmly within the advanced Protestant camp and he probably owed his first election to Parliament to the Earl of Bedford, a leading patron of Puritans. He was presented to the burgesses of Barnstaple in 1571 and to those of Tregony the following year. Thereafter, perhaps because of Bedford's declining West Country influence, he

sought the support of the ruling clique in Northampton, a
Puritan 'hot spot', where local clergy and gentry attended
one of the radical 'exercises' the queen so fervently detested
(see p. 62). Wentworth was in no hurry to enter Parliament;
he was already forty-three when he took his seat for the
first time. His younger brother, Paul, had been an MP
since the beginning of the reign but, for some reason, he
was unable to stand in 1571. Peter's decision to take Paul's
place was made because, as he later explained, he felt called
by God and was pressed by 'sundry grave and wise men'.
Once he had committed himself to a political career, he
remained an MP for the rest of his life.

The major issues which concerned parliamentarians
and to which they returned over and again during these
years were security and succession. The two were closely
related. English Catholic groups were in league (or, at least,
in contact) with foreign courts and agents who hoped to
see an end to Protestantism and the placing of Mary Queen
of Scots on the throne. It was important to discover and
thwart any Catholic plots that were hatched, but the long-
term safeguard for the Protestant realm was for the queen
to marry and provide England with an heir. Elizabeth persistently resisted calls for draconian action against Catholic
activists and refused to be dragooned into marriage. This
created tensions between Queen and Parliament, which
were not eased with the passing of time. Indeed, matters could only get worse. Elizabeth's Protestant subjects
looked to the past and remembered the fires of Smithfield
and were keenly aware of the sacrifices that had been made
in establishing a nation independent of Rome. They were
aware in the present of the atrocities being carried out in
France and the Netherlands. They looked to the future
with mounting anxiety about what would happen to their
children and grandchildren should England be brought
back to Roman allegiance, either by invasion or by the
accession of a Catholic monarch. Their position in society

would certainly be under threat in any regime that tried to turn back the clock. To many of her subjects it seemed that Elizabeth was guilty of grave dereliction of duty by refusing to deal with their concerns.

As long as she could, the queen stalled. She ended the first session of the 1563 parliament in April and did not summon it again until September 1566. In the interim the 'big issue' had not gone away. Sermons were preached, pamphlets were distributed and wherever people met – in markets, in alehouses and around private dinner tables – the succession to the throne was on their lips. The reconvened Commons intimated politely but firmly that the granting of taxation was inextricably bound up with the settlement of their grievances. Elizabeth was furious. She denounced MPs as 'rebels'. For almost two months arguments raged back and forth between court and Parliament. Anxious ministers tried to find some compromise statement that would paper over the constitutional crack that was now widening, but there was no escaping the incompatibility of the rival principles; the succession issue was either a matter of royal prerogative or one in which the representatives of the people had lawful interest.

It was Paul Wentworth who clearly identified the crux of the matter. After the queen had roundly ordered Parliament not to meddle in succession issues he rose in his place in the Commons chamber. He asked the house, 'Whether her Highness' commandment, forbidding the Lower House to speak or treat any more of the succession and of any their excuses [reasons] in that behalf, be a breach of the liberty of their free speech of the House or not?'[5] His question sparked an earnest debate, which occupied members 'from nine of the clock till two after noon'.[6] Everyone knew that Wentworth's question was demanding a definition of what had always remained undefined: the right to free speech within Parliament. The principle had been acknowledged but never spelled out. For example, did it imply that

Parliament could initiate debate on any subject its members wished or did their freedom only extend to offering opinions on matters referred to them by the Crown? No answer was forthcoming during the remainder of the session. Elizabeth found a gracious form of words that put the lid back on the snake basket for the time being, by which time most parliamentarians were relieved at the easing of tension. On the following 2 January the queen dissolved her troublesome parliament. It would be more than five years before she summoned another. By that time Paul Wentworth's more outspoken elder brother was ready to enter the fray.

Elizabeth did not want to call a new parliament and put off doing so for as long as possible. It was only a series of grave crises that made it necessary to send out writs for a reconvened assembly. When it did meet she made sure that it did not last long enough for the Commons to settle down and organize opposition to royal policy. The 1571 parliament opened on 2 April and closed on 29 May.

In 1569, the northern earls had risen in revolt (see above, p. 12). Their rebellion had been easily suppressed but it had still cost money, which meant that a reluctant queen had to go cap in hand to the political classes asking for more cash. Elizabeth also had an unwanted guest on her hands. Mary Queen of Scots had taken refuge in her cousin's realm and was already proving a focus of pro-Catholic hopes. As if that were not bad enough, other events had forced religion to the top of the agenda. Sectarian war had broken out in France and the Netherlands, inevitably prompting Englishmen to express their own sympathies. The pope had issued a bull dethroning Elizabeth and absolving her subjects of their loyalty. Relations with Catholic Spain were steadily deteriorating. So, the queen hoped that Parliament might express and help to consolidate national unity. The major fly in the ointment was religion. Contemporary conflicts in Europe had the effect of raising the profile of doctrinal and liturgical issues and polarizing opinion. Elizabeth considered that the position of the English Church had been settled but radical Protestants (well represented in Parliament) still looked for further reform. Preaching at the opening service, the Bishop of London (doubtless well primed) warned that debate about religious beliefs 'must needs be dangerous to the Commonwealth ... One God, one king, one faith, one profession, is fit for one Monarchy and Commonwealth. Division weakeneth: concord strengtheneth ... Let conformity and unity in religion be provided for; and it shall be as a wall of defence unto this realm ...'[7]

One listener who turned a deaf ear to this entreaty was the new man, Peter Wentworth. It may be that he had sought election because his brother was, for some reason, unable to stand, but he wasted little time in making his mark. Only a few days later, he showed clearly his position on church authority. He was part of a Commons delegation sent to discuss with the bishops a bill relating to the Church's doctrinal articles. When the archbishop intimated that laymen should leave such theological matters to the bishops, Wentworth responded, 'No, by the faith I bear to God! We will pass nothing before we understand what it is, for that were to make you popes. Make you popes who list, for we will make you none.'[8] That indignant retort reveals the real man. A contemporary described him as 'of a whet [sharp] and vehement spirit'. As a person of conviction, he saw issues in black and white. As a person with an acute conscience, he had no time for compromise. As a Bible-based Christian he could accept no other authority in matters of faith and church organization. As a Protestant Englishman he insisted on Parliament's right to legislate on religious matters.

Wentworth was very far from being a lone voice. The recent election had returned a larger number of religious extremists, many of whom were eager to air their opinions. This was doubly irritating to the government. Not only were the Commons' members dabbling in matters that were none of their business, they were using up time that should have been employed in dealing with the business drafted by the queen's ministers. Discussion became heated and came to a head over the Strickland affair. William Strickland, a Yorkshire member, put forward a bill aimed at removing from church life all those ceremonies and customs to which Puritans objected. He was summoned before the Privy Council and ordered not to attend Parliament. This produced a furore in the lower house. After the Easter recess, Strickland was quietly allowed to return. Elizabeth hoped that gestures such as this would make her point without the need to recourse to more confrontational tactics. Wentworth and Strickland either were or became close friends and, within a few years, Wentworth's daughter, Frances, was married to Strickland's son and heir, Walter.

When Elizabeth dissolved this brief parliament she hoped and assumed that it would be a long time before she needed another, but the reign was now entering a time of deep crisis and within a year writs were sent out for the convening of a new assembly. A wide-ranging conspiracy (the Ridolfi Plot) had been uncovered, aimed at replacing Elizabeth with Mary Queen of Scots (to be married to the Catholic Duke of Norfolk) with the aid of foreign troops and money. The entire political nation looked to the queen for decisive action – not least the execution of Mary and Norfolk. During the seven-week session, covering most of May and June 1572, speech after speech urged the queen to deal firmly with her enemies. The emergency also raised again the question of the succession. Elizabeth's people urgently needed to know what would happen in the event of a successful attempt on her life. No one was more frustrated than Wentworth. On at least four occasions he rose in his place to demand that Norfolk and Mary ('the most notorious whore in all the world') should be immediately despatched (Norfolk was executed on 2 June).

Wentworth had plenty of time to ruminate on the place of Parliament within the framework of government, for it did not assemble again until 8 February 1576. Now that he had seen for himself how the system worked, he discussed his misgivings with friends and colleagues back in rural Oxfordshire and the neighbouring shires. He was more than ready to be their indignant mouthpiece when the house reconvened. Immediately he gave the Commons the benefit of a long, prepared and rehearsed speech, which has gone down as one of the most famous in parliamentary history:

> Mr Speaker, I find written in a little volume these words, 'Sweet indeed is the name of liberty and the thing itself a value beyond all inestimable treasure' . . . in this House which is termed a place of free speech there is nothing so necessary for the preservation of the prince and state as free speech, and without it is a scorn and mockery to call it a Parliament house, for in truth it is none, but a very school of flattery and dissimulation and so a fit place to serve the Devil and his angels in and not to glorify God and benefit the Commonwealth . . .

The members listened aghast as this Midlands squire threw etiquette to the winds and went on to criticise the queen:

> Her Majesty hath committed great faults, yea dangerous faults to herself and the state . . . It is a dangerous thing in a prince unkindly to entreat and abuse his or her nobility and people as her Majesty did the last Parliament . . .

Wentworth complained that Elizabeth had summoned Parliament to advise on the perilous political situation and had then declined to follow their advice.

> Is this a just recompense in our Christian Queen for our faithful dealings? The heathen do require good for good; then how much more is it dutiful in a Christian prince?

Now the fervent orator came close to threats.

> ... will not this her Majesty's handling, think you, Mr Speaker,
> make cold dealing in many of her Majesty's subjects toward
> her? . . . I fear it will. And hath it not caused many already
> . . . to seek a salve for the head that they have broken (i.e. find
> some non-constitutional means to deal with the Catholic
> threat)? I fear it hath. And many more will do the like if it be
> not prevented in time.[9]

Wentworth attacked specifically the means most
commonly used by the court in 'handling' Parliament
– forbidding discussion of certain subjects and sending
messages indicating the queen's displeasure at Parliament's
proceedings. 'We are incorporated into this place to serve
God and all England,' he insisted, 'and not to be timeserv-
ers and humour feeders.'

Serving 'God and all England' rather than serving the
queen came perilously close to a definition of treason
and it is hardly surprising that Elizabeth took umbrage
at the speech. She had Wentworth whisked away to the
Tower, where he was obliged to cool his heels for a month.
Meanwhile his words reverberated around England and
were reported abroad. It may be that Wentworth himself
supplied the printers with a copy. Like anti-government
protesters before and since, he insisted that his criticisms
were motivated by loyalty towards the very institutions he
attacked.

The experience of temporary incarceration did nothing
to weaken Wentworth's terrier-like resolve. If anything,
he may have regarded persecution as evidence of the
righteousness of his cause. In subsequent parliaments he
continued to campaign over issues closest to his heart.
This earned him another sojourn in the Tower in March
1587. By this time freedom of speech had become a campaign. The nation was faced with monumental issues and

Wentworth was one of the few men prepared to forfeit his freedom in the hope of forcing the queen to acknowledge them. After the execution of Mary Queen of Scots (February 1587) the immediate threat of a Catholic seizing the throne had passed, but the big question still remained: who would Elizabeth choose as her successor? She either could not or would not decide. Wentworth wrote a tract entitled, *A Pithie Exhortation to her Majestie for establishing her successor to the crowne*. Its language was frank to the point of being abusive. But it was no more than many Englishmen – including members of the Privy Council – were thinking: what would happen when the queen died? Even to mention the death of the sovereign was treason. Had the pamphlet been published it might well have earned its author something worse than a spell in prison. When a few copies leaked out the Council had Wentworth confined again, probably for his own safety and to prevent him becoming a figurehead for political demonstration.

The degree of support he enjoyed is suggested by the fact that the electors of Northampton continued to select him as their MP. Before the parliament of 1593 met, Wentworth tried to assemble a group of radical younger members to launch a well-orchestrated attack on royal policy. But by now he was a watched man. Within days he found himself back in the Tower and this time he was not released. He could easily have regained his freedom by promising to abandon his crusade but this he declined to do. His prison conditions were not harsh. The last glimpse we have of this self-appointed campaigner is that of an old man, shuffled aside, rather than punished:

[He] is much impaired in health, by reason of his close imprisonment and especially owing to the great heat of the present season. The Council allow him the liberty of the Tower in company with some trusty servant and also to see his sons, friends and physicians for his better comfort and recovery of health; but he shall not be permitted to have any conference with them except in the presence of the Governor or his servants.[10]

There he lived until his death in 1599.

Wentworth was a loose cannon, an advocate of parliamentary freedom who was an embarrassment to most parliamentarians and may, indeed, have actually hindered the reforms he so vociferously advocated. Like all zealots he took a principle and drove it to its logical conclusion. England's political hierarchy was not ready for that conclusion. Councillors and parliamentarians handled the queen with kid gloves. It would be forty years after Elizabeth's death before the gloves came off. Wentworth identified what was fundamentally at stake in the relations between the monarch and the legislature. His contemporaries, though shunning him and his methods, did learn something from him. For example, in 1589, a standing committee of the house was established to examine and rule on all matters of Commons privilege.

In his last lonely days in the Tower this unruly man penned an autobiographical poem. It closed with the lines,

Syth I have said, and done my best
Meekly with prayer, God grant me rest.

4

THREE MEN OF RELIGION

... Who would fardels bear,
To grunt and sweat under a weary life,
But that the dread of something after death –
The undiscovered country from whose bourn
No traveller returns – puzzles the will ...

Hamlet, III. i. 76–80

Hamlet, philosophizing about life after death, refers to it as a mystery, a sleep which might be oblivion or one which might be haunted by unwelcome dreams. Earlier in the play the troubled prince has had an encounter with the ghost of his murdered father, who gives the merest hint of the soul's existence in purgatory:

But that I am forbid
To tell the secrets of my prison-house,
I could a tale unfold whose lightest word
Would harrow up thy soul, freeze thy young blood,
Make thy two eyes, like stars, start from their spheres,

Thy knotted and combined locks to part,
And each particular hair to stand on end,
Like quills upon the fretful porpentine:
But this eternal blazon must not be
To ears of flesh and blood.

Hamlet, I. v. 13–22

And Macbeth concludes that life has no eternal significance; it is but a 'walking shadow', 'a tale told by an idiot . . . signifying nothing'.[1] Such lines have fuelled scholarly debate about the playwright's religious allegiance. One could argue, by selective quotation, that Shakespeare was an agnostic, an atheist or that he assented to Catholic or Protestant doctrines. Probably all we can say with any certitude is that any religious stance was possible to thinking people in the reign of Elizabeth I. The turmoil of the half-century before Shakespeare's birth had thrown all questions of faith into the melting pot. Any religious unity that might have existed once was gone forever. There were those who accepted the 'settlement' of the Reformation conflict which obliged all subjects to worship in the (Protestant) Church of England. But there were large minorities who clung to the old Catholic faith or wished the official Church to go further along the Reformation path and espouse more radical forms of Protestantism.

The old unity may have gone but the government was not prepared to countenance dissent. Official Church and state were inseparable; no one could be a loyal subject of Queen Elizabeth and not a faithful worshipper at his/her parish church. In 1559, an Act of Supremacy named the queen as Supreme Governor of the Church in England and made it illegal to assert the authority of any foreign ruler, including the pope. Three years later, defiance of this Act was pronounced treason. Most people did not have to be dragooned into accepting this arrangement. In the quarter of a century that had passed since Elizabeth's father had had himself proclaimed Supreme Head of the Church, they had seen Protestantism steadily advance, stripping churches of statues, shrines and paintings supporting Roman Catholic dogma. They had moved from being passive observers at Sunday worship, watching the priest perform *his* office in Latin, to participants in vernacular services set out in an English prayer book. They were encouraged to read the Bible in their mother tongue. They heard sermons more frequently than their forefathers had done. In many churches they raised their voices in congregational singing of metrical psalms. These precursors of hymns were settings of the Psalms to simple tunes. (Elizabeth hated them; she dismissed them as 'Geneva jigs'.) They had lost several of the festivals and feast days that had given shape to the lives of earlier generations. We cannot imagine the shock these changes must have presented to ordinary parishioners. Then along came Mary Tudor and everything was suddenly 'as you were'. All the old rituals were reinstated and congregations which had paid to have their churches drastically changed now had to find money to undo the work which had been done. The government embarked on a savage regimen of persecution and throughout the country stubborn Protestants were arrested, interrogated and, in some cases, burned. Hundreds of people who could afford to do so fled overseas to reformed centres on the continent. Then, in 1558, the Protestant Elizabeth became queen and there was a reaction against the reaction. Most of Mary's bishops and clergy who refused to accept the Elizabethan settlement were sacked. Their places were taken by Protestant clergy, some of whom returned from exile, more extreme in their opinions than they had been when they left. They were now dubbed 'Puritans'.

It was now the turn of the more ardent Catholics to seek foreign havens. Some joined seminaries in centres such as Louvain and Douai, from where they planned the reconversion of England. They had the full backing of Pope

Pius V, who excommunicated Elizabeth and absolved all English Catholics from their allegiance to the 'heretic' queen. This placed English Catholics in a very difficult position. Most of them were loyal to the Crown but were being urged, as a matter of conscience, to defy the government. Some became 'recusants', i.e. people who refused to attend Anglican worship. Most of these tended to come from the wealthier sections of the community, who could afford to pay the fines imposed for non-compliance. Such individuals were targeted by the foreign instigators of the Counter-Reformation crusade. They sent priests across the North Sea to set up a network of centres in country houses where the 'missionaries' were succoured, celebrated Catholic rites and taught the Roman faith. Some took up a more extreme stance, plotting the death of the queen and the overthrow of the government.

Meanwhile, Puritan zealots were presenting the authorities with another set of problems. Convinced that the Church of England was only 'half-reformed' they attacked the Elizabethan settlement in sermons and pamphlets, demanding changes to the new prayer book (published in 1559), refusing to wear 'popish' vestments and pressing for further purging of church decoration. The queen had a deep-seated dislike of Puritans. This created a particular problem for her, since several members of her Council and Parliament were Puritan sympathizers. Moreover, their grasp of the international situation was better than hers. Elizabeth persuaded herself that the rulers of Spain and France, though egged on by the pope, were not seriously interested in unseating her nor that they were providing aid and encouragement to Catholic intriguers. Only too aware of the crises provoked by her father and her siblings, she always preferred to defuse potentially dangerous situations. If her subjects could not be persuaded to live in unity, at least she would not use to the full the powers of coercion she possessed. Anti-recusancy laws were enforced only sporadically. Though she instructed her bishops to curb the activities of Protestant extremists, she seldom pressed matters on her own initiative. England's religious life, thus, consisted of a passive, if confused, majority who conformed to official policy, under pressure from different directions by extremists who were part of national and international networks. To see how these networks operated and their impact on day-to-day life, let us consider the troubled careers of three men.

Edmund Grindal was one of those who chose to spend most of Mary's reign outside England. He was among the country's leading scholars and in his mid-thirties, within weeks of the queen's death he returned, hoping to be chosen as one of those who would replace Marian bishops declining to accept the Act of Uniformity and be able to help steer the Church along a more progressive path. By the end of 1559 he had been appointed to the crucial diocese of London, where he was faced with two related problems: many benefices, rendered vacant by the sacking of recalcitrant Catholics, urgently needed filling, but many of the available candidates were extremists of various hues who were determined to hijack the established Church for their own versions of Christianity. Puritan activists looked to Grindal for a lead and were quick to criticize if they decided he was compromising. His conscience was torn between obedience to the sovereign and desire for further reform. 'You see me wear a cope or a surplice in St Paul's,' he responded to some zealots. 'I would rather minister without these things, but for order's sake and obedience to the prince.'[2]

Those campaigning for the abolition of the 'dregs of popery' were not slow to draw a moral from the tragedy that befell London's cathedral on 4 June 1561. During one of the most violent storms to sweep across southern England, the spire of St Paul's was struck by lightning. The fire spread downwards, 'like a candle consuming', according to one eyewitness. Soon the whole roof was ablaze, burning timber and molten lead falling into the church. Elizabeth saw the conflagration from her palace at Greenwich and despatched men to help citizens engaged in the attempt to extinguish the flames. None of her subjects doubted that the disaster was a sign of divine wrath. But what was God angry about? Catholic polemicists were as ready as their Puritan opponents to interpret the calamity as God's judgement on the Elizabethan settlement. As the stifling summer continued, such arguments rumbled on as persistently as the recurring tempests. When another great rainstorm lashed the capital on 30 July, 'everyone thought that the day of doom was come at hand'.[3]

For Grindal the ideological conflict came to a head in 1566. Goaded beyond endurance by contumacious extremists and with the queen breathing down his neck, he deprived thirty-seven of the more outspoken clergy. He knew there would be a backlash and may have hoped that it would demonstrate to Her Majesty that Puritans were not to be dragooned into defying their own consciences. Any such hope was vain. Elizabeth dug her heels in and was not to be shifted by Grindal, his episcopal colleagues or the queen's closest advisers. When the Archbishop of Canterbury pointed out that many Puritans would rather go to prison than abandon their principles, her reaction was, 'send them to prison, then'. For Grindal the results were distressing in the extreme. Several of the deprived ministers simply ignored the ban and continued to preach. When the bishop placed one of the offenders under house arrest he was besieged in his own palace by a noisy demonstration of sixty angry women. For months he could scarcely go about the streets without running the gauntlet of verbal abuse.

There was no stopping the extremist bandwagon. More clergy were imprisoned. Some died in captivity. All were revered as martyrs. When churches were closed to the extremists, they gathered in private houses, lay and

ordained Puritans encouraging one another to endure persecution and continue contending for 'truth'. Inevitably,
harsh treatment drove some reformists to even more exaggerated views. There emerged from within the ranks of
Puritanism a sub-group, known as 'Presbyterians'. They
wanted the Elizabethan settlement abandoned in its
entirety and advocated the abolition of rule by bishops.
In its place they proposed a polity that gave greater independence to individual ministers and congregations. Such
a change would, of course, have undermined the entire
Church–state establishment.

Fortunately for Grindal, relief was at hand. In 1570, he
was able to lay aside the poisoned chalice when he was promoted to be Archbishop of York. Puritans were far less
numerous in the northern province. Here it was recalcitrant Catholics who posed the major threat to the religious
settlement. This very year saw the rebellion of the northern
earls (see p. 12), encouraged by the recent excommunication
of Elizabeth by Pope Paul V (see p. 11). Some 5,500 men
took up arms to follow their traditional leaders and they
had the sympathy of large numbers of the queen's subjects
who felt bereft of their old religious customs and ceremonies. The rebels took possession of Durham and wasted
no time in making clear their opposition to the Elizabethan
settlement:

> They not only threw down the communion tables, tore in
> pieces the holy bible and godly books, and trod underfoot
> the printed homilies, but also again set up the blasphemous
> mass as a sacrifice for the living and the dead. And as fur-
> ther cloak for their pretended piety, they caused [to be set up]
> some crosses and some banners of certain saints, whom they
> believed to be their patrons and defenders.[4]

Grindal had no qualms about stamping out opposition
to the Protestant Reformation. This time he had royal

support. Elizabeth, usually reluctant to take extreme measures, was incensed by treason and bayed for blood. The archbishop had no part in the suppression of the revolt but he instigated a vigorous purge. Wherever old religious images still remained in churches he had them removed and destroyed. Grindal's agents assiduously sought out those who were hiding mass vestments or service books. Priests who persistently demonstrated papist tendencies or simply refused to preach reformed doctrine were removed, as were those who failed the archbishop's rigorous moral test. There were few who merited firm discipline, like the rector of Gosforth who was found guilty of 'drunkenness and whoredom', but the deprivation of such sent a clear message that the new archiepiscopal broom was intent on a clean sweep. During Grindal's tenure of office the last vestiges of medieval Catholicism vanished. This included the old mystery plays, performed on major festivals in various churches or open-air venues, such as the York cycle of forty-eight pageants representing Bible stories, which were performed on Corpus Christi Day (in early summer). What the new regime objected to was not popular drama, as such, but the admixture of legendary and even pagan themes with the biblical narrative. Religious plays were by this time losing ground to the performances of travelling professional players and it is more than likely that the suppression of the mystery plays gave a boost to the emergence of the new theatres. Be that as it may, Grindal and his colleagues were bent upon severing this and all other links with the Catholic past. They were concerned about the suspect content of many of the old scripts, but also about the way the plays were delivered. Each scene was traditionally performed by a different trade guild. This meant that the pageants had a permanent place in the commercial life of the towns, stretching back over many generations, and that their continuance was safeguarded by the leading citizens. The reformed clergy wanted to put an end to this rival source of Christian teaching and to safeguard their own monopoly of religious education.

And it was education that was at the top of Grindal's agenda. A religion based on legends, ceremonial and holy images was to be replaced by a faith securely anchored in the Bible, clearly expounded by well-trained ministers. By the end of his tenure in York, the archbishop could inform Elizabeth,

> I myself procured above forty learned preachers and gradu-ates, within less than six years, to be placed within the diocese of York, besides those I found there; and there I have left them: the fruits of whose travail in preaching your majesty is like to reap daily, by most assured, dutiful obedience of your subjects in those parts.[5]

Grindal had completed the work of reform and left behind him churches that had changed out of all recognition in the eyes of older parishioners. Stone altars decked with ornate crucifixes and candlesticks had been replaced by wooden communion tables. Side chapels had disappeared. Stained glass had been replaced with clear glass in many windows. Rood screens had been dismantled. Pulpits and lecterns now took pride of place, for preaching was to be a regular rather than an occasional feature of worship. Naves were filled with pews, to accommodate congregations who were now expected to sit and listen to learned expositions of Scripture.

Grindal might have ended his days with a happy sense of achievement had he been allowed to remain in the northern province but, in 1575, he returned to the South – and to trouble. He was elevated to the position of Archbishop of Canterbury and Primate of all England. He was not Elizabeth's choice; it was the reformists of the Council who secured his appointment, against the queen's better judgement. She had, by now, become even more distrustful of political extremists and her disapproval was focused upon the one feature of reformed religion that Grindal believed to be absolutely crucial – preaching. Elizabeth's concept of Christian worship was the observance of Prayer Book rituals with the occasional addition of homilies from collections approved by the hierarchy. This formalized observance matched the ordered ceremonial of court life and of those organs of the state which made for cohesion at regional and local levels. Puritan religion was altogether more dynamic and open-ended. Preachers were prone to stir up enthusiasm – and enthusiasm was dangerous.

It took little time for the convictions of queen and archbishop to clash explosively. What Grindal strongly encouraged and what Elizabeth deplored was the 'exercises'. These began as regular meetings of local clergy, who assembled for Bible study and mutual encouragement. Grindal and his supporters considered them essential for the education of incumbents. However, in some areas they developed into radical enclaves outside the control of the bishops. When prominent lay people began to attend these gatherings and listen to sermons, not infrequently critical of the ecclesiastical status quo, it seemed clear to the queen that she had a subversive movement on her hands that might grow into something like the northern rebellion. There were, indeed, occasional demonstrations sparked off by the exercises; groups of zealots demanding, if not all-out Presbyterianism, at least greater freedom for local clergy and congregations to decide for themselves such issues as clerical dress, excising parts of the Prayer Book and the banning of officially approved ceremonies. By giving priority to Puritan assemblies pledged to strengthening Protestantism (by now under dire threat from enemies within and without), Grindal could not avoid clashing with a queen who demanded unity – at any price.

In this case the price was the archbishop's job. Elizabeth

ordered the suppression of the exercises. Grindal's reply was such as the queen had never received before:

> ... because I am very well assured, both by reasons and arguments taken out of the holy Scriptures and by experience ... that the said exercises ... are both profitable to increase knowledge among the ministers and tendeth to the edifying of the hearers, I am forced, with all humility, and yet plainly, to profess that I cannot with safe conscience and without the offence of the majesty of God give my assent to the suppression of the said exercises ...

If this disobedience raised Elizabeth's ire, worse was to follow:

> Ye have done many things well; but except ye persevere to the end, ye cannot be blessed. For if ye turn from God, then God will turn away his merciful countenance from you. And what remaineth then to be looked for, but only a terrible expectation of God's judgements, and an heaping up of wrath against the day of wrath?[6]

In May 1577, Grindal was sequestered – i.e. he was forbidden to exercise his office. An incandescent Elizabeth wanted to go further and have the archbishop deprived but there were legal difficulties about that. She had to be content to blackball him and know that he would spend his declining days in debilitating idleness. He had been in office less than two years.

In the year that Edmund Grindal made his journey from York to Canterbury (1575), another Englishman in his mid-twenties was on pilgrimage from Douai, in the Spanish Netherlands, to Rome. His name was William Weston. He had studied at Oxford, where there was a significant reactionary element, and probably became a Catholic convert there during his adolescent years. He went on to study at Paris before moving to the Catholic seminary at Douai founded by William Allen, one of the religious exiles unwilling to live under Elizabeth's Protestant regime. The Douai college was established with only one goal in mind – the reconversion of England. Here dedicated Catholic men were trained for the dangerous mission of infiltrating English society to encourage their co-religionists to resist all efforts by the heretical regime to induce them to accept the Church settlement. A vital element in sustaining secret adherence to the pope and his religion was the provision of priests who could, clandestinely, maintain banned rites and preach Catholic dogma.

Weston was committed to this programme. Having completed his basic theological studies, he travelled to Rome in 1575 to enrol in the Society of Jesus. This order, usually known as the Jesuits, comprised the storm troopers of the Catholic Church, totally dedicated to unquestioning loyalty to the pope and to recovering by evangelistic activity the ground lost to Protestants. In 1579, Weston was ordained priest and, having spent some time in Spain, was ordered to England where he arrived in August 1584. Within a year, the existing head of the Jesuit mission was expelled from the country and Weston took over.

The attitude of the government and the mood of the majority was becoming ever more hostile to what was seen as a fifth column, working in the interests of Spain and the papacy. The presence of Mary Queen of Scots as a prisoner in England provided some Catholics with hope that somehow a change of regime might be brought about. Several zealots were involved in schemes to rescue her. In the nearer continental countries religious strife continued and when, in 1584, the leader of the Dutch Protestants, William of Orange, was assassinated, fears for Queen Elizabeth's safety spread. In 1585, Parliament passed an 'Act against Jesuits, seminary priests and such other like disobedient persons'. Any priest entering the country henceforth would be deemed a traitor and liable to capital punishment.

Anyone who might 'willingly receive, relieve, comfort or maintain' such a priest would also find himself in the shadow of the gallows. Two years later, the anti-recusancy laws were tightened. Absence from Anglican worship carried a fine of £260 per annum and failure to pay would, henceforth, make the offender liable to the confiscation of two-thirds of his property.

Harsh though these laws sound, they did not become the basis for savage persecution. There were two reasons for this. The first was a sensitivity on the part of legislators to be seen as being no better than their Catholic counterparts on the continent. For example, when the government introduced an even more draconian anti-recusancy bill in 1593, Parliament toned it down considerably. The other was that public opinion managed to make a distinction between the machinations of popes and Catholic monarchs on the one hand and individual Catholics on the other. Throughout the country local justices were far from diligent in enforcing laws against their neighbours and friends. In 1592, 800 accused recusants were brought before the Lancaster assizes but only 200 were indicted and, of these, a mere 11 were actually fined. Shakespeare, who, by and large, steered clear of religious controversy, demonstrated the distinction between resentment of papal politics and sympathetic treatment of individuals. In the play *King John* he has the monarch assert,

Though you and all the kings of Christendom
Are led so grossly by this meddling priest . . .
Yet I alone, alone do me oppose
Against the pope, and count his friends my foes.

King John, III. i. 162–71

By contrast we might cite the example of Friar Laurence in *Romeo and Juliet*, who is presented as a wise and caring adviser to the tragic lovers, a man motivated by a desire to reconcile the feuding families of Montague and Capulet.

Weston's misadventures seem to endorse the dichotomy between severity at the top and generosity of spirit among ordinary people. Weston's strategy was to seek the support of leaders among rural society. Several 'old' families were temperamentally inclined to preserve traditional patterns of social and religious life and were uncomfortable about the changes being forced on the nation. He was introduced to the unstable Philip Howard, Earl of Arundel, whose father had been executed for plotting against the queen. Unable to establish himself in royal favour, Arundel had retired to his country estates and there he was received by Weston into the Catholic faith. He was subsequently arrested while trying to flee the country and spent the rest of his life in the Tower (he died in 1595). Weston, meanwhile, moved around the houses of various prominent gentry, creating a network of supporters prepared to gather co-religionists together for forbidden rituals and to conceal priests from the authorities. One of the rites carried out in these months was exorcism. Weston cast out demons from several people. All of his subjects seem to have been servants in the households where he stayed. In an age which believed that the material world was shot through with the spiritual such manifestations made a considerable impact. One observer reported seeing 'the devils gliding and moving under the skin. There were immense numbers of them, and they looked just like fishes swimming here, there and everywhere.'[7] Weston, himself, described sufferers who, 'let out violent and raucous shrieks during the ceremonies'. He affirmed in his autobiography that, 'Out of many persons demons were cast. The intervention of heaven was undoubted, and incredulous onlookers were astounded.'[8] Such demonstrations were certainly impressive and resulted in several conversions, though Weston's estimate of five hundred men and women brought into the Catholic fold may be questioned.

One reason for caution over the figures is that the

exorcist was not at liberty for very long. A dramatic campaign covering only a few months but attended by miracles which diverted many people from their obedience to the Elizabethan settlement could not have failed to attract the attention of the authorities. Weston was arrested in August 1586 and spent the rest of the reign in prison. It was his suspected connection with another plot against the queen's life that proved his undoing. The leader of the conspiracy was another young man of good breeding whose zeal exceeded his intelligence (or, at least, his skill as a conceiver and executor of conspiracy). This Anthony Babington found himself embroiled with agents from Spain and France who had grandiose plans for assassinating the queen, freeing Mary Stuart, raising widespread rebellion and re-establishing the Catholic faith with the aid of a Spanish invasion. He had serious reservations about the willingness of English Catholics to overthrow the government and see their country overrun by foreign troops, and turned to Weston for advice. The gentle Jesuit was impressed with Babington, as he later recalled:

> He was young, not yet thirty, good-looking with a fine presence, quick intelligence, enchanting manners and wit ... When in London he drew to himself by the force of his exceptional charm and personality many young Catholic gentlemen of his own standing, *gallant, adventurous and daring in defence of the Catholic faith in its day of stress*; and ready for any arduous enterprise whatsoever that might advance the common Catholic cause.[9]

There is no indication that Weston tried to dissuade Babington from his desperate enterprise, though he, 'judged it wiser not to join him'.[10] Probably his prudence was matched by that of the majority of English Catholics, who would not have subscribed to the view that the religious end justified the violent means. Few of them would have participated in the insurrection if Babington and co. had got it off the ground. In 1604 a Spanish envoy assessed the attitude of most Catholics in these words: '. . . they could not and would not dare to attempt anything. While a foreigner's strength might encourage them, it is much more likely after a landing that the interests of other princes would become apparent. They do not want foreigners . . .'[11]

A substantial number of Catholic laity actually subscribed to a written declaration of loyalty to Elizabeth and her successors. But they were in a difficult – not to say impossible – position. Obedience to the queen entailed attending worship in their parish churches. Obedience to their priests forbade such apostasy. Inevitably, people solved this dilemma in various ways. Some remained staunch in their recusancy, maintained the network which sustained a growing number of immigrant priests and paid the resulting fines. Their determination has left permanent marks in several country houses where secret chambers were created, many by the legendary Nicholas Owen. This skilled carpenter and later Jesuit lay brother had a positive genius for devising places of concealment within walls, under floors and behind staircases where priests and mass paraphernalia could be hidden. Several of these refuges were so cunningly concealed that they defied the most prolonged and persistent searches. Some Catholics attended church on Sunday and went to mass in their own homes later in the week. A few, who could afford to do so, avoided the choice by taking themselves into exile. The remainder, little by little, drifted into acquiescence to the Protestant regime. They continued to worship in the churches where their forebears had worshipped for generations, and kept their real beliefs to themselves. For all English Catholics the launching of the Spanish Armada in 1588 heightened their dilemma. Prominent leaders of their religion, such as William Allen, urged native Catholics to grasp the opportunity for rebellion. There was no response; many recusants actually volunteered to fight against the Spaniards. The crisis helped them to decide where their real loyalties lay. Whether the lax enforcement of the anti-recusancy laws was a sign of weak control over local courts or a calculated government policy not to provoke resistance, it certainly helped to maintain peace within the realm.

The treatment of Weston and his colleagues seems to suggest that the government wished to control potential troublemakers while not agitating Catholic Englishmen by overly harsh punishments. The Privy Council had infiltrated Babington's cell and were only waiting for the appropriate moment to pounce. When they did so, in August 1586, Weston was among those taken into custody. He was not charged with complicity in the Babington Plot but he remained in prison after the conspirators had been executed. For seventeen years he was held in various jails without indictment or trial. Throughout that period the nature of his confinement varied widely. Sometimes he had to endure long periods of solitude. At others he was allowed the company of fellow Catholic detainees.

Being permitted the company of other priests was not always a balm and a solace. The most trying period of his captivity occurred between 1592 and 1598. He and several other priests were in Wisbech Castle, the principal prison for Catholic activists. Here a bitter rivalry developed between the Jesuits and the secular clergy – i.e. those who belonged to no religious order. Each party believed that the other was trying to dominate the conduct of the English mission. The Wisbech Stirs, as they were called, were symptomatic of wider divisions within Catholicism which caused further splits among English Catholics, who, as we have seen, were already at odds over the degree of conformity with the Elizabethan settlement. Such discord goes some way towards explaining why Weston and many of his colleagues were not brought to trial. The government calculated that depriving recusants of their priests was one way of breaking their resistance, especially if those priests could be shown to be at war among themselves.

The last attack on Weston came in the closing years of the reign. He was now in solitary confinement in the Tower of London, sick, partially blind and mentally disturbed. The Bishop of London, Richard Bancroft, decided to rake up the controversy over Weston's exorcisms of 1585–6. This was part of a campaign against both Puritan and Catholic practitioners accused of fraudulent practices. Sensationalist pamphlets stirred widespread interest in a man who had, by now, been long forgotten. However, his trials were almost at an end. As soon as James I came to the throne Weston was given a choice between taking the oath of allegiance to the new monarch or going into exile. He chose the latter and died in Spain twelve years later, but not before writing his own, one-sided account of his tribulations.

Throughout the whole of Elizabeth's reign 183 Catholics were executed. They were claimed as martyrs by the leaders of their church, though, as the queen and her advisers were at pains to point out, all the victims were tried and found guilty of treason by due process of law. Disagreeable though this fact is, it must be weighed against the vastly greater numbers of men, women and children (both Catholics and Protestants) who perished for their faith in mainland Europe during the same period and, indeed, against the three hundred or so English 'heretics' who went to the stake during the brief reign of Mary Tudor. The persecution of dissidents (both Catholic and Protestant) who could not accept the Elizabethan settlement was, by the standards of the day, mild. The objective of the queen was to ensure that the realm had one official religion and only one. The policy failed; there were significant minorities that could not be contained within the Anglican fold. Yet the majority of Elizabeth's subjects now belonged, quiescently, to a church that had its own distinct identity and had shrugged off its Catholic heritage. This state of affairs had been achieved by stripping from the churches all relics of the 'papistical' past and by the softly-softly approach on which the queen had insisted.

Our third example of Elizabethan church life is a man who prospered by 'going with the flow'. Andrew Perne was not cast in a heroic mould. He did not nail his colours to the mast, like Grindal or Weston. He did not have convictions for which he was prepared to suffer. He tuned his flute to the official pitch and lived as a stalwart establishment figure. Perne was born, about 1519, into a Norfolk family of minor gentry and completed his education at Cambridge University, where he stayed for the rest of his life. Swimming cannily in this small pool throughout the turbulent mid-century years, he became, by cautious degrees, a large fish. By the end of Henry VIII's reign he was well ensconced as a fellow of Queens' College and by commending himself to wealthy patrons he had begun to accumulate parochial livings. This means that he was appointed as rector, drew the stipend that went with the job, and employed a curate to do the actual work. This was standard practice among clergy in government service and those following an academic calling.

At this stage of his career Perne was a steady, middle-of-the-road churchman. When Edward VI came to the throne, supported by a rigidly Protestant government, determined to purge the Church of every vestige of 'popery', he discovered that he no longer believed in those Catholic doctrines reviled by the regime. He was appointed a royal chaplain, often preached at court and was a friend of reformers such as Edmund Grindal. Government favour won him the mastership of Peterhouse and the first of five terms as vice chancellor of the university. The religious volte-face enforced by Mary Tudor (1553–8) did not trouble Perne. He pledged the university's loyalty to the restored Catholic faith and served on a royal commission set up to unmask

Protestant heretics in Cambridge. When the bones of the reformer, Martin Bucer, sometime Professor of Divinity in the university, were disinterred and solemnly burned, Perne presided over the gruesome ceremony and delivered a sermon denouncing Protestant teaching. According to the martyrologist, John Foxe,

> . . . the said Dr. Perne himself, either immediately after his sermon, or else somewhat before he went to it, striking himself on the breast, and in manner weeping, wished (at home at his house) with all his heart, that God would grant his soul might even then presently depart and remain with Bucer's. For he knew well enough that his life was such, that if any man's soul were worthy of heaven, he thought his in especial to be most worthy.[12]

Less than two years later Cambridge had a new Protestant queen. Would Perne be able to perform yet another about turn? The answer was 'Yes'. In many ways, he was a churchman after Elizabeth's heart: one who did not allow issues of doctrine – or even of conscience – to stand in the way of his allegiance to the Crown. When, at another university assembly, the condemnation of Bucer was reversed, who presided? No prizes for correctly answering that question. Perne took every opportunity to commend himself to the new monarch. In 1564, Queen Elizabeth was planning a state visit to Cambridge. Edmund Grindal, then Bishop of London, was in charge of making the arrangements. He had long since parted company with his erstwhile friend and wished to ensure that Perne played no significant part in the festivities but the turncoat's friends had been hard at work and it was Perne who was chosen to preach the welcoming sermon – on the subject of loyalty to the sovereign.

Grindal wanted the Master of Peterhouse to be kept in the background because permitting him the celebrity he craved might comfort 'all dissemblers and neutrals and discourage the zealous and sincere'.[13] But it was Perne whose attitude chimed most closely with that of the archbishop's royal mistress. She distrusted 'the zealous and sincere'. She declined to probe too closely into the theological niceties of her subjects' beliefs, as long as they dutifully trooped to church on Sunday mornings and did not gather together to hear Puritan preachers or Catholic priests. English Christianity had come to embrace a wide range of beliefs and practices. As well as the divisions we have already noted within the Anglican and Catholic bodies, there were groups and sects beyond the fringes of both. The attitude of authority towards them depended in no small measure on their own discretion. If they kept themselves to themselves and did not challenge the established Church/state order they were, by and large, unmolested.

Perne had good reason to know about potentially disturbing religious groups. Cambridge was, outside London, the most active centre of religious radicalism. And beyond Cambridge, in the low-lying East Anglian lands where he grew up, lay the most radical region in England. Here were to be found not only congregations under the tutelage of ardent Puritans, but also cells of Anabaptists, who rejected the rites that were traditional to both Catholic and Protestant churches. They practised adult, 'believers' baptism. More importantly as far as the law was concerned, they shunned all oaths. Since this was an age in which the majority of contracts were sealed with an oath sworn on the Bible and in the presence of lawyers, government officials or other interested parties, non-compliance was a threat to the established order.

There were also Brownists. Robert Browne studied at Cambridge in the 1570s and became a preacher in one of the local churches. He became notorious as a noisy critic of the religious establishment and spent several brief periods in jail. Probably his sufferings would have been greater had his family not had close connections with William Cecil,

Elizabeth's closest adviser. He formed his own separatist church and spent much time on preaching tours in East Anglia. He seems to have been much influenced by Anabaptist groups settled in Norfolk, though he did not accept some of their more extreme tenets. By 1582, groups of Brownists existed over a wide area, but opposition had become too persistent for their founder. He and some of his followers moved to Holland. But within a couple of years he was back, still seeking followers of his idiosyncratic and still-evolving religious views. Eventually, he was reconciled to the Anglican Church and accepted appointment (through family connections) to a Northamptonshire parish (1591). Browne lived on for many years but was seldom a stranger to controversy and when he died, in 1633, he was, once again, in a prison cell. Perne will have viewed him as an example of what happens when religious enthusiasts accept only the authority of the Bible, or rather their interpretation of the Bible, and reject the rule of bishops and all other human leaders.

Yet Perne, for all his personal dedication to the religious establishment, was no persecutor of dissidents, preferring, it seems, to let sleeping dogs lie. Only this can explain his refusal to take action against the Familists, otherwise known as the Family of Love. This eclectic, mystical sect had its origins in the Low Countries. Its members, like the Brownists, considered themselves free from the authority of bishops but also regarded the Bible as little more than a guide for beginners on the path to perfection. Holiness was achieved by the indwelling of the Spirit of God and those who had achieved this state were exempt from all human laws and rules of conduct. Outsiders often accused Familists of polygamy and other sexual offences but no evidence for such practices has survived. This is because, unlike Anabaptists and Brownists, Familists did not challenge the religious establishment. They attended Anglican worship and conducted their own rituals in secret. The largest Familist commune was in the Cambridgeshire parish of Balsham. And the rector of Balsham was Andrew Perne. Under his benignly blind eye the clearly heretical sect continued unmolested.

Within the narrower confines of the university Perne was less tolerant. It was natural that all the rival theologies and disputes about church order should be argued vigorously among the students. Each faction had its heroes and for some years the prominent spokesman for the more radical element was Thomas Cartwright, fellow of St John's College and an eloquent and forceful preacher who drew crowds to his sermons. Cartwright was an enemy of episcopacy and a forerunner of the Presbyterian movement. His views brought him into conflict with another up-and-coming scholar, John Whitgift, fellow of Peterhouse. Whitgift's mentor and friend, to whom he was partly indebted for his advancement, was Andrew Perne. He came to the attention of Queen Elizabeth, who took an instant liking to his unyielding adherence to the ecclesiastical status quo. Whitgift was a conservative politique, with no time for ideologues who disturbed the peace of the Church. In 1567, royal patronage helped him to gain the mastership of Trinity College. He soon gained a reputation as a rigid disciplinarian and a persecutor of any he suspected of harbouring unconventional opinions. He was a powerful figure within the university and when, in 1569, Cartwright was appointed to a professorship he was determined to oust this troublesome Puritan.

This was no easy matter. The radical party was strong in the ruling councils of the university and Cartwright had many followers among both senior and junior members. He was also supported by Lord Burghley and the Earl of Leicester. After months of bitter conflict, the Whitgift clique resolved upon a draconian solution to their problem. If they could not oust Cartwright under the existing rules, they would change the rules. Whitgift obtained the queen's ready assent to a new set of statutes. This placed power in the hands of a smaller body of college heads, which the conservatives were able to manipulate. One of the new rules made it an offence to criticize the government of the Church and it was for breach of this rule that Cartwright was duly sacked from his professorship and later stripped of his fellowship (1571). After some years on the continent he returned and was granted by his old patron, the Earl of Leicester, the sinecure appointment of Master of the hospital in Warwick which had been set up for the care of a community of old soldiers. In 1583, when the Archbishopric of Canterbury became vacant, Elizabeth was in no doubt who she wanted in that position. John Whitgift, the hammer of the Puritans, was duly installed.

The new archbishop's uncompromising purge inevitably provoked a reaction. Warfare between the rival partiers was intensified, fanned by furious blasts from pulpit and press. The most celebrated contribution to the war of words came to be known as the 'Marprelate Tracts'. This was a series of vitriolic pamphlets attacking, 'that swinish rabble of petty antichrists, petty popes, proud prelates, intolerable withstanders of reformation, enemies of the gospel, and most covetous wretched priests'.[14] This extreme language was not typical of the Puritan opposition and actually did the radical cause more harm than good but it indicates the divisions within the Church which continued to the end of the reign and beyond.

And Andrew Perne? He did not escape vilification. Marprelate dubbed him 'Old Andrew Turncoat' and even the prominent poet, Edmund Spenser, lampooned him in his poem *The Shepheardes Calendar*. He remained at Cambridge to the end of his days, prospering mightily and dying a rich man. He was often the guest of his old friend, John Whitgift, and it was in the archbishop's palace at Lambeth that he died suddenly in April 1589, an establishment man in the very centre of the religious establishment.

5

A CLUTCH OF VILLAINS

POINS: *My lads, my lads, tomorrow morning, by four o'clock,*
early at Gadshill! There are pilgrims going to Canterbury
with rich offerings, and traders riding to London with fat
purses: I have vizards [masks] for you all; you have horses
for yourselves... If you will go I will stuff your purses full of
crowns; if you will not, tarry at home and be hanged.

Henry IV, Part 1, I. ii. 137–47

'The rich get richer and the poor get poorer' is an aphorism that may be applied with reasonable accuracy to most societies at most times. Those born to wealth have the opportunity to make their capital work for them and can also use it to cushion themselves against dearth in hard times. Their less fortunate neighbours, being embroiled in the struggle merely to keep alive, have little chance to improve their lot – honestly. That is why many desperate people who have the necessary wit and courage turn to a life of crime. Of course, there will always be those who cannot claim the excuse of poverty; the minority who prefer a life of bullying, cheating or trickery to doing an honest day's work for an honest day's wage. The criminal underclass of Elizabethan England comprised both kinds of 'rogues' and that stratum of society was large.

In the second half of the sixteenth century at least thirty per cent of the population existed at or below subsistence level. There were many reasons for this. The birth rate was rising. Inflation was steadily pushing up the cost of essentials. Bad harvests made an immediate impact on food prices. When old estates were broken up or changed hands, traditional tenants and servants sometimes faced eviction. New landlords were concerned to exploit their lands more efficiently, i.e. with fewer workers. Soldiers and sailors returning from foreign service found it difficult to integrate into civilian society. Add to these such age-old problems as artisans incapacitated by illness or injury, women rendered destitute by the loss of husbands or parents, and younger sons who had no expectations of inheriting wealth and it is easy to see why there was a large 'floating' population of rootless people who could not support themselves through regular labour or trade. Such 'vagabonds' of no fixed abode were regarded with suspicion or fear by honest house-holders. The government was well aware of the problem and made sporadic attempts to deal with it. The difficulty was always that of distinguishing between what Victorian legislators would later categorize as the 'deserving' and the 'undeserving' poor. Elizabethan poor law, therefore, always vacillated between harsh punishment and charitable relief.

Professional criminals were to be found everywhere in Elizabeth's England. The reasons for their existence were, as in most ages, twofold: they were driven either by poverty or by disregard for the rights of others in society (frequently a combination of the two). The law was only beginning to come to grips with the related issues of poverty, vagrancy, mental and physical disability and felony. Punishments for condemned offenders were harsh but their deterrent effects were considerably offset by the inadequacies of the system of law enforcement. If the nettle of lawlessness was never firmly grasped by central government it was for a reason which, with the benefit of hindsight, we can see clearly. The leaders of Church and state worked on the principle that the basic structure of society was God-given and that all the queen's subjects should be encouraged or, if necessary, coerced into accepting their lot. If masters and servants, landholders and tenants, tradesmen and apprentices, craftsmen and labourers, husbands and wives stuck to what they were good at, social dislocation which encouraged crime could be largely avoided. So, for example, sumptuary laws laid down regulations regarding dress, so that men and women of humble station might not pose as their betters by wearing silks and high-grade furs. More seriously, the basic treatment of vagrants was to send them back to their own villages so that the local authorities could deal with them and, if necessary, provide for them.

Stability was the prime concern of government and the most obvious way to maintain it was to make potential offenders fear the terrible punishments which awaited them if they transgressed the law. Every town had its wayside gibbet where the rotting corpses of executed criminals were displayed. Visitors to London crossing the bridge were presented with the sight of up to forty severed heads stuck on poles. The law exacted the maximum penalty for a wide range of crimes and few people questioned the right of the state to defend respectable citizens from their less well-intentioned neighbours. Crown court records provide abundant evidence of the kind of capital sentences handed down on a regular basis for a variety of crimes. For example, at the sessions held in London on 16 April 1591, we read that Elizabeth Arnold, an 'unmarried woman' was found guilty of stealing from 'Thomas Collier of Turnhill Street' and 'John Smythe of Limehouse' jewellery to the value of £28 as well as other unspecified items. Two other women, 'Mrs Elizabeth Hawtrey' and 'Miss Elizabeth Johnson' were indicted as accomplices and receivers of stolen goods. Miss Johnson pleaded guilty and was sentenced to be hanged. The other women asked for sentence to be set aside on the grounds that they were pregnant. At this point, 'a jury of matrons being empanelled both were found not pregnant and sentenced to be hanged'. Whatever time may have been taken by these proceedings, the court was still able to consider the case of Edmund Chapman, who was 'found guilty of having seized and raped a girl of nine years old, and sentenced to be hanged'.[1]

Custodial sentences were virtually unheard of, jails being primarily used for holding suspects awaiting trial or execution. Municipal authorities lacked the resources for keeping prisoners for months or years with a view to their reform. This goes a long way towards explaining why execution was not kept as a last resort. Rather, it was a means of exterminating those of whom society was well rid. The only punishment that might be deemed to have been 'corrective' was being locked in the pillory or the stocks. This public shaming meant that offenders were identified, so that their neighbours would be aware of their misdeeds. It was always about exposing the moral distance that existed between good citizens and the criminal underclass, whose members were frequently denounced as too lazy or too perverted to seek an honest living.

There was, however, a more humane side to Elizabethan law and order. High on the list of philosophical fashion was the definition and advocacy of the 'godly commonwealth'. By this was meant the desire to bring society into line with the ethical principles laid down in the Bible. Books were written, sermons preached and broadsheets distributed urging the need for a drastic overhaul of the existing system. Holy Scripture demanded the highest moral standards in personal and public life, but it also

spoke of responsibility for the poor. The best way to eradi-
cate crime, according to the commonwealth men, was not
to threaten offenders with death but to enable them to live
respectably without recourse to robbery, violence or fraud.
The responsibility was shifted from the 'have-nots', who
had no way to help themselves, to the 'haves'. It was the
rich who were denounced from pulpit and printed page,
rather than the poor.

> The rich worldling makes no conscience to have ten or twenty
> dishes of meat at his table; when in truth the one half might
> sufficiently satisfy nature, the rest run to the relief of the poor
> . . . Some will not stick to have twenty coats, twenty houses,
> twenty farms, yea twenty lordships and yet go by a poor
> person whom they see in great distress, and never relieve him
> with a penny, but say 'God help you; I have not for you.'[2]

Sermons, such as this by the Puritan preacher, Henry
Smith, frequently challenged Elizabeth's well-to-do subjects. Such exhortations certainly found sympathy among
the lower orders of society who could well identify with
the outcasts who could only survive by preying upon their
betters.

Who, then, were these predators of the open road, par-
odied by Shakespeare? Edward Poins, who made his only
appearance in *Henry IV Part 1*, seems to have been a rec-
ognizable type in popular literature of the period. Several
ballads and broadsides featured the witty, fun-loving
highway robber. (The word 'highwayman' was not in cir-
culation until early in the next century.) Falstaff was in
awe of him. 'This is the most omnipotent villain,' he says,
'that ever cried "Stand" to a true man'(I. ii. 105). Poins is
certainly a cut above Falstaff and his cloddish companions and it is he who organizes the attack on travellers at
Gadshill, near Rochester (a notorious haunt of robbers).
He also plans the trick that turns the tables on the other

members of the gang, despoiling them of the loot they have just taken from the pilgrims and merchants they have way-laid. Such 'gentlemen of the road', well-bred villains, not to be confused with common or garden thugs, certainly existed. They were the cream of underworld society and were known, in the thieves' vernacular, as 'upright men' or 'high lawyers'.

One such was Gamaliel Ratsey. He came of a good Lincolnshire family but first appears in the records as having been arrested for stealing £40 from an inn at Spalding and subsequently escaping 'in his shirt'. We next find him serv-ing in the army of the Earl of Essex in Ireland. It may be that he volunteered for the expedition as a means of distanc-ing himself from the agents of the law or he might have been offered the choice of enlisting or facing trial (and certain death). Many of Elizabeth's armies were made up of 'gaol house dregs' (see above, p. 134). We may guess that military life appealed to him, for he was a bold fellow who deliber-ately courted danger. When this upright man returned to civilian life it was as the 'captain' of a little band of ruf-fians. In this mirror-image world of Elizabethan society Ratsey posed as a swaggering officer leading a troop or even as a haughty nobleman accompan-ied by a band of retain-ers. He was always well horsed and accoutred and armed with pistols. The availability of the easily portable wheel-lock sidearm was one of the more sinister developments of criminal life and was responsible for an escalation of vio-lence. These weapons had first appeared in England in the 1530s and by the end of the century were standard issue to the queen's armies. Ratsey may well have learned how to handle such a pistol while in Ireland.

He became a legend in his own lifetime and his exploits (some apocryphal) became the subject of popular ballads. He was described as a master of disguise who particularly enjoyed wearing a hideous mask. By popular repute Ratsey was something of a Robin Hood figure who occasionally shared his ill-gotten gains with the poor. Like Poins, he enjoyed playing tricks on other members of the criminal fraternity. Perhaps this asserted his own superiority within the wider network of rogues and vagabonds. Having robbed two clothiers, he solemnly proceeded to knight them as Sir Samuel Sheepskin and Sir Walter Woolsack. On another occasion he obliged a clergyman to preach an impromptu sermon for himself and his companions, extolling their courage and affirming that 'God delighteth in thieves'.

A more elaborate blag is reminiscent of Poins's exploit and may have inspired Shakespeare's story. Ratsey encountered a band of strolling players at an inn. They claimed to be under the patronage of a local magnate whose name they were using to obtain engagements. When the upright man met up with the same troupe again a little later he discovered that they had changed the identity of their benefactor and were now claiming to be in the employ of a noblemen more respected in their new location. Ratsey applauded them and demanded a private performance. The following day, he caught up with the players on the road and relieved them of all their takings, throwing in for good measure a moralizing speech denouncing their dishonest way of life.

Ratsey eventually met his end on the scaffold in March 1605 but this was only the beginning of his fame. His supposed exploits were immediately published in two popular pamphlets, *The Life and Death of Gamaliel Ratsey, a Famous Thief of England* and *Ratsey's Ghost Or, The Second Part of his Mad Pranks and Robberies*. Violent as such unsavoury ruffians were, there was a ready market for their romanticized adventures and it is not surprising to find that Falstaff and co. were Shakespeare's most popular creations. Given the enormous disparities of wealth in Elizabethan England, stories of larger-than-life desperadoes who preyed on the rich and had their own means of social levelling were always sure of a good audience.

With the exception of messengers on urgent business

who used post horses and spent long hours in the saddle, travellers moved slowly along England's roads. To cover fifty or sixty kilometres in a day was to make good progress. Everyone therefore – criminals included – made use of resting places, of which there were many. Hospitality fell into two categories – inns and alehouses. If we can rely on the comments of foreign visitors, English inns, for the most part, compared favourably with their continental counterparts. Competition induced proprietors to provide reasonable standards of food and accommodation; most towns of any size contained several inns. It was, therefore, good business to offer other attractions. Wandering players were hired to perform in the courtyards. Rooms were provided for gambling. Prostitutes were allowed to ply their trade discreetly. Inns offered many opportunities to the upright men and their associates. The wise traveller kept a wary eye out for cutpurses and cardsharps. He was also well advised to guard his tongue. Highway robbers had their informants among inn staff. In *Henry IV, Part One* the villain, Gadshill, has a nocturnal meeting with the chamberlain (the man responsible for the allocation of guest rooms) of a Rochester inn, who assures him, 'It holds current that I told you yesternight: there's a franklin in the Wild of Kent hath brought three hundred marks with him in gold; I heard him tell it to one of his company last night at supper . . .' (II. I. 52–3). Gadshill thanks him for the information and promises that the unwary traveller will meet with 'St Nicholas' clerks' on the road. 'St Nicholas' was a euphemism for 'Old Nick', i.e. the devil and, in their vernacular, the 'gentlemen of the road' acknowledged that they were his 'clerks'.

Alehouses were much more modest establishments, usually nothing more than wayside cottages with a sign outside offering passers-by refreshment that was home-brewed or bought in from wholesale suppliers. Ale was the staple drink for most people because supplies of uncontaminated water were hard to come by. A traveller passing through unknown country would be unwise to sample what came out of any well or stream. During Elizabeth's reign tastes were changing. Beer increasingly became the beverage of choice. It was more difficult to make but it tasted better and lasted longer than ale. Few peasant households possessed the necessary capital or expertise for beer production. The way was, thus, open for entrepreneurs to set up properly equipped brew-houses to supply rural and backstreet premises. Poor householders only had to set out tables and benches in their kitchens or barns. These premises frequently became the haunts of travelling criminals. The poor tenants or owner became confederates either willingly or under duress. They provided lodgings and meeting places. They received stolen goods. They concealed villains on the run. By the end of the reign there were more than twenty-five thousand such establishments throughout the land – vital hubs in the criminal network.

Among the denizens of the underworld there existed an identifiable pecking order. The upright man was not a feature of every stretch of highway but where his writ ran he was monarch of the road and he set the rules for the rough-and-ready gang culture operating in his area. Other rogues operated only by his permission. It was not unknown for him to formally 'license' his associates or others permitted to ply their trade in his territory. He might demand 'fees' for his protection. If an underling was accompanied by his woman, or 'doxie', he might have to grant to his superior the *droit de seigneur*. Of particular value to the upright man was the 'ruffler' and he would usually have some such in his company. Rufflers were soldiers returned from foreign service. Hardened by war and desensitized by the horrors they had seen, they were ready for any exploits. Men who had survived on campaign by breaking into farmsteads, helping themselves to livestock and demanding money with menaces had learned the rough science of survival and were not squeamish about continuing their military way of life. Rufflers often combined begging with their more violent activities. They paraded their battle scars and injuries (whether real or faked) before the public and were always ready with lurid tales about how they had come by their wounds.

There were other kinds of wandering beggars. What most of them had in common was a sob story designed to loosen the purse strings of charitably inclined citizens and the story might be supported by faked documents. The ruffler would, on demand, produce his discharge papers. Young men would offer evidence that they were apprentices who found themselves destitute because their masters had died. Women might show letters confirming that their homes had been destroyed by fire and that they were on their way to seek refuge with distant relatives. There were a hundred and one plausible tales told by these beggars to extort cash from the unwary. Several claimed physical or mental disability. 'Dummerers' produced certificates stating that they were bereft of the power of speech and, therefore, unemployable. 'Palliards' were experts in faking more visible ailments. Self-inflicted scars and lurid cosmetics applied to give the impression of sores gave their bodies a truly revolting appearance and when these were only partially covered with garments little more than bloodstained rags, the total effect could be appallingly convincing. These scoundrels were the equivalent of today's benefit fraudsters and their trickery was effective because there were thousands of unfortunates in England who really were deserving of the pity and assistance of their neighbours.

The 'patch' deserves special mention. He or she was a simpleton, idiot or dangerous lunatic. That such people were commonplace in Tudor society is evidenced by the number and variety of them who appear in Shakespeare's plays. They range from Touchstone, the professional court comedian in *As You Like It*, to Bottom, the cloddish country yokel in *A Midsummer Night's Dream*, and the heart-renderingly pathetic Fool in *King Lear*. In real life such unfortunates were regarded as freaks, objects of fun. For visitors to London the lunatic asylum of Bedlam was a major attraction where they could go to laugh at the antics of the pathetic residents. The audience at the Globe almost demanded that a new play should have a fool on the cast list. But counterfeit idiots did not only appear on stage. A good actor could pose as someone fallen beside his/her wits, and might carry documents purporting to prove that the carrier had been an inmate of Bedlam. The fake fool might wander among market stalls shrieking obscenities and picking fights, till someone paid him to go away. He might pose as an epileptic, dramatically falling down in the marketplace with soap in his mouth to produce a realistic foaming. One of the most famous of Elizabethan rogues was just such a man supposedly inflicted with the falling sickness.

His name was Nicholas Blunt, alias Jennings. He travelled much of south-east England, sparsely clad in a tattered cloak, with an old felt hat for a begging bowl. His head was bound with bloody cloths and his face smeared with blood and dirt. He told a good tale of inherited epilepsy and of a lengthy stay in the madhouse. In the early years of the reign, a Kentish gentleman, Thomas Harman, set himself the task of examining all the vagrants to be found in his part of the country. In some ways the ancestor of today's investigative journalist, Harman wrote up his findings in an exposé entitled *A Caveat or Warning for Cursitors Vulgarly called Vagabonds*. One of the rogues featured in his report was Blunt. Harman checked the beggar's tale and discovered it to be a pack of lies. He set men on Blunt's trail and had him apprehended. When stripped and searched, the 'poor madman' was found to be carrying the sum of fourteen shillings, many times the daily wage of an honest craftsman. On this occasion Blunt escaped but the tenacious Harman refused to be balked of his prey. Weeks later, he discovered the rogue in a suburb the other side of London but not now posing as a ragged fool. Now, he was 'Nicholas Jennings', and smartly dressed in the clothes of a respectable merchant. This did not mean that he had abandoned his career as con man. His story now was that he was a maker and seller of hats who, through no fault of his own, had fallen on hard times and was travelling the country seeking employment with other members of his craft – for which of course he needed a little money. This time Jennings was thrown into prison and interrogated very closely. What he revealed surprised and shocked even Harman. The criminal was exposed as a married man with a substantial house at Stoke Newington. This Walter Mitty character, it transpired, had a considerable repertoire of roles which he performed to sustain his substantial lifestyle. But the performance had come to an end. Blunt/Jennings spent several days in the Cheapside pillory in the very heart of London, before being whipped at a cart's tail all the way from there to his home. Was he chastened? Unfortunately the records do not tell us.

It was not uncommon to encounter on the road whole families of vagrants. From an early age children were brought up 'in the trade'. Clad in tattered garments and made to look pallid and undernourished, these 'kinchin coes' and 'kinchin morts', as they were known in thieves' cant (the underworld language) were tutored in the looks and demeanour intended to pluck the heartstrings of house holders. But when the charitably disposed citizen was talking with their parents, these little apprentice rogues might well be round the back of the house squeezing through a small window to see what they could filch while the owner was otherwise occupied.

Upright men were not uncommonly found in company with bawdy baskets. In many ways these women were the female counterparts of the kings of the road. They offered for sale trinkets, stolen items and, as their name suggests, sexual favours. The upright men were their protectors, abettors and pimps. If the impression has been given in the above paragraphs that the criminals who stalked the highways were poor people who only battened upon the well-to-do members of society, the following tale by a contemporary pamphleteer will dispel such notions. On a lonely lane, a disabled beggar was confronted by an upright man and his female companion. The woman claimed that the beggar had cheated her out of two shillings' worth of goods. When he protested his innocence, the poor man was set upon by the couple and robbed of what little he had on him, amounting to fourteen pence. There was certainly no honour among thieves in Elizabeth's England.

If life on the road offered many hazards to the unwary traveller, a visit to the city could be no less unpleasant. Here the cony-catchers lay in wait for their prey. These were the tricksters – cutpurses, cardsharps, brothel-keepers and their kin, all dedicated to parting the 'conies' (the mugs) from their cash. Any tourist arriving in London would make a beeline for its major attraction, St Paul's Cathedral. The Gothic edifice, which predated Wren's seventeenth-century masterpiece, was in a poor state and was made worse after the spire was struck by lightning in 1561. This disaster was seen as a visitation of divine displeasure by critics at the time and one of them provides an interesting word picture of what the visitor might expect to find within this hallowed space:

> God's house must be a house of prayer, and not the proud tower of Babylon, nor the pope's market-place, nor a stews for bawds and ruffians, nor a horse-fair for brokers; no, nor yet a burse for merchants, nor a meeting-place for walking and talking.[3]

The cathedral was very far from being the sacred place where people spoke in hushed tones. It was a magnet that attracted visitors for a variety of purposes: 'The south alley for usury and popery, the north for simony, and the horse fair in the midst for all kinds of bargains, meetings, brawlings, murders, conspiracies, and the fort for ordinary payments of money.'[4] On Sundays and holidays children played there, chasing each other round the pillars. Doors in the north and south walls allowed people to use the church as a short cut, not only for pedestrians but also for pack animals. The noise and clamour, even during divine service, were such that frequently 'suffereth not the preacher to be heard in the choir'.[5] Here criminals also gathered to pick pockets, to make assignations, to plan new villainies and to keep an eye open for potential victims.

Another such concourse was Whitehall, where the palace buildings and law courts constantly attracted crowds. Wherever people came together in large numbers and were distracted by their surroundings or their company one was sure to find the cutpurse and the pickpocket ('nip' and 'foist' in thieves' jargon). As well as simply jostling conies in the crowd, the thieves had many other ways of distracting their quarries. They might offer their services as guides to obvious visitors so that their accomplices could appropriate purses while their owners were gazing on a tomb or inscription. They might fall down, as though in some sort of seizure, in order to take the purse of a sympathetic stranger coming to their aid. In an age when strict dress codes distinguished the social classes, a cony-catcher might disarm his victim by posing as a wealthy courtier or nobleman's son. For some crooks there was little need for pretence. Many a gentleman ran through his fortune trying to cut a dash at the royal court. If he could not gain the hoped-for advancement or tied himself to a patron who fell out of favour, he would be left with little but his fine clothes and his familiarity with the personalities and fashions of high society. But these could be turned to advantage. A man up from the country would be flattered if he was taken up by a gentleman whose obvious importance was demonstrated by the silks and furs he was wearing. He would listen with fascination to stories about the queen and the life of the court. He would willingly go with his new 'friend' to some tavern where he would meet other 'leaders of society' and would feel privileged to join them in a game of primero or some other game using marked cards or loaded dice.

The most popular places of entertainment were the bull- and bear-baiting pits and the theatres. The animal show arenas were located in Southwark, outside the jurisdiction of the London municipal authorities. The City fathers were hostile to all these activities and especially to the theatres. For most of the reign the word 'theatre' indicated an inn yard or similar location where wandering players performed from time to time. These vagrant thespians had a dubious reputation and it was this which prompted the London Common Council, in December 1574, to take draconian action by banning all public dramatic performances from the city. It is often assumed by historians that this action on the very eve of the flowering of Elizabethan drama is proof that the government of the capital was in the grip of 'killjoy' Puritans but the preamble to the Act must be taken seriously. It avers that,

> ... sundry great disorders and inconveniences have been found to ensue to this City by the inordinate haunting by great multitudes of people, specially youth, to plays, interludes and shows, namely occasion of frays and quarrels, evil practices of incontinency in great inns, having chambers and secret places adjoining to their open stages and galleries, inveighing of maids, specially orphans and good citizens' children, to privy and unmeet contracts, the publishing of unchaste, uncomely and unshamefast speeches and doings. Withdrawing of the Queen's Majesty's subjects from divine service on Sundays and Holydays ... sundry robberies by picking and cutting of purses, uttering of popular, busy and seditious matter and many other corruptions of youth.[6]

This prohibition, as is well known, was to the immediate advantage of English drama, for it led to the establishment of the first purpose-built playhouses – the Curtain, the Theatre, the Rose, the Swan and the Globe – which were all erected, outside the jurisdiction of the mayor and aldermen, in Southwark, across the river, or in the northern suburbs. But they were not the only buildings dedicated to the dramatic arts. Other theatres sprang up in the last couple of decades of the reign which had only a brief life and have left little trace in the records. As well as these, there were private premises (usually under the patronage of noblemen or prominent courtiers) that were exempt from the 1574 Act. All this testifies to the immense popularity of this new form of entertainment.

But it would be a mistake to envisage all London theatregoers as being regaled with the masterpieces of Shakespeare, Marlowe or Greene. The plays that have survived stand head and shoulders above the run-of-the-mill items on offer.

> ... the popularity of the theatre lay in its direct appeal to the senses. Just as it was the rough and tumble at the bear garden, the 'biting, clawing, roaring, tugging, grasping, tossing and tumbling' of the bear, and the nimbleness of the dogs, that delighted spectators, so it was the vehemence of the pageantry, and the fine dresses of the actors that charmed the playgoers.[7]

Plays clothed vice in glamour. Some of the scenes and speeches performed on the Elizabethan stage would not be allowed on modern television screens, even in our liberated age. The audience was composed of people who derived pleasure not only from the cruel exploitation of animals but from public hangings, burnings and the branding of convicted criminals. The actors and impresarios who provided the entertainment the people wanted lived and worked beyond the fringe of respectable society and shared the criminals' underworld. For example, Edward Alleyn amassed considerable wealth from his operation of the Rose and Fortune theatres, but his principal income came from brothels, and he was not alone in plying this trade (see below, p. 227). He and his colleagues sold sex in premises adjacent to the playhouses, and the performances served to excite the lust of patrons and render them amenable to being propositioned. But that was only part of the 'goings-on' in the theatres. As the 1574 Act observed, back rooms were used for gambling, paedophilia, seduction and the corruption of children.

Involving boys and girls in a life of crime was a well-organized business. Sixteenth-century London had its Fagins. In 1585, William Fleetwood, Recorder of London and one of the great Elizabethan parliamentarians, drew the attention of the government to the activities of one Wotton, a London merchant who, having failed in business, had turned his premises into a thieves academy where he schooled small boys in the delicate arts of extracting coins from pockets, snipping the cords of purses, shoplifting and picking locks. Like Dickens's villain, Wotton acted as a receiver of stolen goods and, presumably, made a good living from his nefarious trade.

It will make a tidy end to this catalogue of villains to say something about Mary Frith, alias the 'notorious baggage, Moll Cutpurse'. Her story is almost a compendium of everything we have already said about the denizens of the criminal underworld. Her colourful escapades were so much romanticized during her own lifetime in ballads, plays and pamphlets that it is virtually impossible now to extricate fact from fiction. She appeared in the dock on numerous occasions charged with being a nip, a trug (prostitute) or a shaver (swindler or thief). Somehow, she avoided serious punishment, possibly because she was also useful to the authorities as an informer. Certainly, she was an underworld celebrity, 'well known and acquainted with all thieves and cutpurses'.[8] However, what really caught the public imagination was that she often went about dressed as a man (for a time she even ran a fencing school). On at least one occasion she appeared on stage – something completely forbidden to women. She survived well into the Stuart era, though it may be that her eccentricities eventually went too far. She spent some years in Bedlam.

So much for the army of multifarious villains. What arrangements were in place to protect society from them? The underworld, as we have seen, had its rules, its hierarchy and its procedures. Moreover, the readiness of crooks to use violence in the pursuance of their 'trade' made them an effective force for evil. Those charged with apprehending crooks and bringing them to justice were amateurish by comparison. In *Much Ado About Nothing* Shakespeare pokes fun at the guardians of law and order. The constable, Dogberry, instructs the members of the watch in their duties:

DOGBERRY: . . . This is your charge: you shall comprehend all vagrom men; you are to bid any man stand, in the prince's name.

WATCH: How if 'a will not stand?

DOGBERRY: Why, then, take no note of him, but let him go; and presently call the rest of the watch together, and thank God you are rid of a knave.

(III. iii. 21–6)

Keeping the queen's peace was the responsibility of all her subjects. Every parish was expected to ensure its own security and this task was invested in the constable, an elected, unpaid officer. He had the power to apprehend suspects, to detain them in jail, and to bring them before the magistrate. To him also fell the duty of inflicting minor punishments, such as flogging and branding. In urban areas he might empanel members of the 'watch' to assist him. The watch, as the name suggests, kept an eye on alehouses and other potential black spots and toured the streets at night. But, even if these officers were more committed and courageous than Dogberry and co., they could not be everywhere and vigilance was expected of every citizen. Thus, if, for example, someone was observed pilfering from a market stall, bystanders were expected to chase him, setting up the hue and cry. Any crime was regarded as an offence against the whole community, which is why punishments were carried out in public.

That, at least, is how the system was supposed to work. Its weakness was that it depended upon the man in the street. All too often he could not be bothered to do his civic duty. Taking up the hue and cry was an unwelcome distraction from his business. As for going to court to give evidence, that was much too much trouble. As long as the victim of robbery got his goods back he was often disposed to let matters rest there. In 1596, a Somerset JP reported that scarcely one in five offenders was ever brought to book. Another disincentive was the intimidation by local criminal gangs. The same magistrate cited an instance of a 'very sturdy and ancient traveller' who was condemned to be whipped, whereupon,

> in the face and hearing of the whole bench [he] sware a great oath that if he were whipped it should be the dearest whipping to some that ever was. It struck such a fear in him that committed him that he prayed he might be deferred until the assizes, where he was delivered without any whipping or other harm . . .[9]

The basic response of government to the outlandish behaviour of the criminal class was to meet terror with terror. All felonies, except petty larceny (theft of goods worth less than twelve pence) were punishable by death. This did not mean that capital sentences were automatically imposed, but lesser punishments were made as painful and unpleasant as possible in the hope that they might have deterrent value. Imprisonment before trial was, for those who could not afford to buy special comforts and privileges, a wretched ordeal. An appeal to the authorities by one group of prisoners is eloquent indication of jail conditions:

> . . . we the miserable multitude of poor distressed prisoners, in the hole of the Wood Street Counter, in number fifty poor men or thereabouts, lying upon the bare boards, still languishing in great need, cold, and misery, who, by reason of this dangerous and troublesome time, be almost famished and hunger-starved to death; others very sore sick, and diseased for want of relief and sustenance, by reason of the great number, which daily increaseth, doth in all humbleness most humbly beseech your good worship, even for God's sake, to pity our poor, lamentable and distressed cases; and now help to relieve and comfort us with your Christian and Godly charity against this holy and blessed time of Easter.[10]

Unsurprisingly, many unfortunates did not survive a stay in one of Her Majesty's prisons, of which there were a great number. London and its environs alone contained eighteen such establishments.

Despite the manifest failings of the system, deterrence continued to be the driving force behind legislation. Robbery on the highway, theft from private property, nipping and foisting, escaping from prison, rape, murder, 'unnatural acts' and a host of other offences were all classed as felonies and punishable by death. Gibbets and gallows were regular features in the landscape and were meant to serve as permanent incentives to Elizabeth's subjects to be law-abiding. Vagrancy, which lay at the root of many crimes, was not a capital offence. On first conviction a rootless man might be branded, pilloried or dragged through the streets behind a cart. Then he would be ordered (or taken) back to his own parish, where the officials would be charged with seeing that he found work or assisting him from local charity. If the offender absconded again and was arrested far from his town or village, he was classed as a felon and faced the ultimate penalty. This draconian regimen seems to have produced contradictory reactions from the population at large. Many, perhaps the majority, were desensitized by the frequent spectacle of hanged malefactors or decaying corpses on roadside gibbets, and public executions never failed to draw a crowd. But there were also people who were appalled at the law which regularly meted out death, with little or no regard for the circumstances which lay behind crimes. Broadsides enjoined readers to pity for the poor mother who stole to feed her children or the unemployed tradesman driven to larceny because, despite his efforts, he could not find work. Sporadic bread riots in various parts of the country focused the attention of government on the underlying problems. Many victims of crime declined to support the legal process because they did not want someone else's death on their conscience.

The problem seemed intractable. The legislature revisited it no less than five times during the reign (1563, 1572, 1576, 1579 and 1601). Elizabethan poor laws began the process of dealing comprehensively with the related problems of poverty, vagrancy and crime. They differentiated, for instance, between the impotent poor, such as orphans, widows and the infirm; the injured, notably old soldiers; and the wilfully unemployed, who preferred to live by their wits. There was a limit to what the Council and Parliament could do; implementation relied upon local authorities. To help parish officials to meet their responsibilities a poor tax was imposed. The money raised was to fund almshouses and houses of correction. The latter provided accommodation and food for the destitute. In return they did a variety of jobs from carding wool to making nails. The best known of these institutions was Bridewell, once a royal palace in London, which had been converted to its new use as early as the reign of Edward VI.

Sadly, such provisions only nibbled at the problem. There was still a considerable need for private charity. Preachers and magistrates urged parishioners to do their Christian duty of relieving the poor and reducing the level of crime. And not without results. Many Elizabethan wills made provision for alms to be distributed to the poor and for money to be provided for the maintenance of houses of correction. Occasionally those in power were moved to give a lead.

It is agreed in the House of Lords that there shall be a charitable contribution made towards the relief and help of soldiers maimed and hurt in the wars of France, the Low Countries and on the seas. To this end every archbishop, marquis, earl and viscount shall pay 40s. and every baron 20s. . . . and if any lord spiritual or temporal should refuse or forbear to pay (which it is hoped in honour none will) the ordinary means to be used to levy the money.

This initiative in 1593 had a knock-on effect. Within days the lord mayor and aldermen of London had organized a similar fund.[11] Unfortunately, such generous impulses were only drops in the ocean of penury and crime which encroached remorselessly upon the uplands of Elizabethan respectability.

6

THE LAWYER

The first thing we do, let's kill all the lawyers.
Henry VI Part 2. IV. ii. 73

A curious paradox about Elizabeth's subjects (though the same could probably also be equally said of their later descendants) is that they had a reputation for litigiousness coupled with a profound mistrust of the legal profession. When, in *Henry VI Part 2*, Jack Cade's rebellious rabble appear, intent on overturning the government and establishing the rule of the 'common man', one clause of their manifesto is doing away with the exponents of the law. It is not difficult to imagine a roar of approval going up from the groundlings in Shakespeare's theatre at the words 'let's kill all the lawyers'. Judges and barristers were widely believed – not entirely without reason – to be mere agents of the state. There was a strong coercive element to the workings of the judicial system. Evidence of this was obvious to any of the queen's subjects going about his/her daily affairs. Gibbeted corpses swung in the breeze. The heads and body parts of executed felons adorned town gateways. Every village had its stocks or pillory, which was often occupied. A stroll through any marketplace would, sooner or later, bring into view an ex-offender minus an ear or bearing a brand mark on his cheek. It was quite common to see a condemned beggar or vagrant being whipped through the streets behind a cart or a cheating stallholder made to carry a placard announcing his crimes. Justice was public; it was just as important for it to be seen to be done as to be done. This was a principle to which the authorities were, quite unashamedly, committed. In a society when there was a wide gulf between the 'haves' and the 'have-nots' and where no efficient police force existed, fear was an important deterrent. Without it anarchy might prevail and there was nothing queen and council were more apprehensive about than anarchy. Thus, although the law was, theoretically, even-handed it was, to a large extent, weighted in favour of the social status quo.

And yet, the law courts never wanted for business. Claimants were not inhibited about pursuing their rights through the courts, whether contesting a will or charging a neighbour with defamation. There were several layers to the legal system, from the courts which operated in village communities and town markets, all the way up to Queen's Bench, solemnly sitting in Westminster Hall, and the more sinister royal court which sat in the nearby Star Chamber.

For generations English people had had a passion for fairness, for asserting their rights, for 'justice' and, though the judicial system operating in the late sixteenth century was far from perfect, Elizabeth's subjects had a respect for the common law because it was *common* law, the law of the people, which had evolved over the centuries and was founded on precedent. This was the way English common law differed from Roman law, as practised on the continent. The famous legal conflict at the basis of *The*

Merchant of Venice turns on rigid interpretation of statute. Venetian law permits Shylock to pursue his claim to one pound of Antonio's flesh in settlement of a debt. So much is clear from the statute. *But* that statute does not entitle the claimant to any blood. Therefore his claim fails on strict application of the law as written. English law by contrast, had been built up, case by case, over the centuries. It was equity law, which might almost be translated as 'common sense law' resting on the decisions of generations of judges, giving their interpretations in real cases. It allowed scope for defence and prosecution counsels to argue their cases in the hope of swaying a judge or jury. This concept of law as the accumulated wisdom of the ages was woven into the fabric of community life and was a vivid part of the pattern from the bottom to the very top. At her coronation the queen had vowed to rule according to 'the laws and customs of the realm'. Lawyers were, therefore, vital, both as interpreters of the tradition and contributors to that tradition.

The obvious advantage of going to court to settle disputes was that it removed the temptation to seek redress by more violent means. In the strange Induction (opening scenes) to Shakespeare's *The Taming of the Shrew*, the drunken tinker, Christopher Sly, is berated by the hostess of an inn for breaking some of her glasses. Later, servants of the local lord claim to have heard Sly continuing the quarrel while in his drunken slumber:

> Yet would you say ye were beaten out of door;
> And rail upon the hostess of the house,
> And say you would present her at the leet,
> Because she brought stone jugs and no seal'd quarts.
>
> Induction. ii. 82–6

'You would present her at the leet.' It was a fundamental assumption in Elizabethan England that everyone belonged somewhere. In the interests of social stability individual mobility was discouraged. Every manor, village or estate was expected to look after its own affairs. The court leet was a neighbourhood assembly, usually presided over by the steward of the lord of the manor and responsible for the peaceable and efficient running of everything concerning the local population, from the repair of roads and bridges to the quality of ale. Because everyone was accountable to his/her community the court leet was where all minor disputes and offences were dealt with by a jury of residents. In fact, during the course of the reign, the importance of the court leet diminished. Despite the efforts of the government to impose *stasis*, society was changing. Harsh economic reality as well as personal ambition drove people to travel in search of work or in pursuit of fame and fortune (see above, p. 5). Alleged minor offenders were more likely to find themselves brought before the magistrate's court (see below).

However, the delay involved in confining someone in the local lock-up until the JP could convene his court was not appropriate to all situations. When disputes arose in a market it was essential that justice was meted out before stallholders had taken down their booths and visiting tradesmen had packed their wagons and moved on. Hence, the court of pie powder. In all probability this strange title derives from the French *pieds poudrés*, dusty feet, referring to the travellers who moved from fair to fair and market to market. The town bailiff or manorial steward was on hand, assisted by chosen 'justiciars', to hear complaints about false weights, drunken brawls, theft, etc. The court was empowered to impose punishments such as fines and placing in the pillory.

The real workhorses of the English judicial system were the justices of the peace (or magistrates). These unpaid officials were appointed every year by the government to each shire. During the course of the reign their numbers increased, as did their duties. In some counties there were three times as many JPs by 1603 as there had been in 1558. This increase was made necessary by the hugely increased workload these men had to shoulder. No less than 309 current statutes concerned magistrates' responsibilities and 77 of them had been added during the queen's reign. They covered a wide range of activities from organizing military musters and administering the poor law to the licensing of alehouses and the maintenance of highways and bridges. They provided the regime with a system of local government that had the enormous advantage of being cheap. We might wonder why anyone would want to take on such an onerous, unrewarded task. The answer is prestige and power. Magistrates were chosen almost exclusively from the ranks of the county gentry. By proving themselves useful to the Crown they placed themselves in the way of deserving royal favours and they increased their own authority locally. According to Sir Thomas Smith 'There was never in any commonwealth devised a more wise, a more dulce and gentle, nor a more certain way to rule the people, whereby they are kept always as it were in a bridle of good order, and sooner looked unto that they should not offend than punished when they have offended . . .'[1]

The core of the magistrate's work was judicial. Their major courts were the quarter sessions, held four times a year. If urgent matters cropped up in between times there would be a petty sessions, usually presided over by two JPs. They had competence to consider all cases of 'theft, robbery, manslaughter, murder, violence, complots, riots, unlawful games, or any such disturbance of the peace and quiet of the realm'.[2] The scope of sentences available was wide and to some extent at the magistrate's discretion. For all felonies, which included theft of goods to the value of more than a shilling, the death penalty was mandatory. By some reckoning more than eight hundred convicted offenders were sent to the gallows every year, half of them consigned thither by the magistrates. To put this figure in true perspective it should be recorded that it did not include all those who, after conviction, were pardoned or had their sentences commuted. The law was harsh, but one reason for that was the hope that it would have a deterrent effect. Also, all cases that might end in the convicted offender facing a capital sentence had to be tried before a jury. Even so, the hard-headed lawyer, Sir Edward Coke, whose career we shall be considering shortly, was moved to comment,

> What a lamentable case it is to see so many Christian men and women strangled on that cursed tree of the gallows; insomuch as if in a large field a man might see together all the Christians that, but in one year, throughout England, came to that untimely and ignominious death, if there were any spark of grace or charity in him, it would make his heart bleed for pity and compassion.[3]

With so much work being done by magistrates who were, in reality, amateurs at the law, one might wonder whether anything was left for the professionals to do. In fact barristers and Crown judges were kept very busy. They served the central law courts in Westminster and regularly toured the English shires on commissions of *oyer and terminer* ('to hear and determine'). Cases that were particularly serious or complex or that involved wealthy and influential members of society were referred by magistrates to the assize (sitting) courts held by the travelling judges.

The legal profession was very popular with those seeking a lucrative career. For many men it was a golden pathway leading to wealth, position and political influence. To understand something of how justice was administered in the higher courts and by whom, we will follow the career of the pre-eminent lawyer of Elizabeth's reign, Edward Coke (pronounced 'Cook'). Like other prominent and successful subjects he came from wool-rich Norfolk, where his father was a busy barrister with a large client base among the gentry families of East Anglia and a secure place in society. He studied at Norwich Free Grammar School before moving to Trinity College, Cambridge in 1567. He took no degree at the university because his sights were firmly fixed on a legal career and, after three years, he went on to Clifford's Inn.

The inns of court – the lawyers' university – were housed in a collection of buildings beyond London's western wall, between Holborn and Fleet Street. This suburb between England's mercantile centre and the seat of government at Westminster, as well as housing the lawyers' quarter, was also graced by the town houses of the *haut monde*. Its denizens had at their disposal all the facilities of the capital and proximity to the royal court. If a few terms at university were recommended as the best way for a young gentleman to round off his classical education, time spent at the inns of court was valuable for obtaining a smattering of law which would be helpful in the running of an estate and in performing the duties of a local magistrate. It was also helpful as a means of getting to know the right people. Coke, however, was there with more serious intent.

There were two kinds of tutorial establishment. The inns of Chancery, like Clifford's Inn, provided the necessary basics in preparation for the more detailed instruction given at the four senior inns – Middle Temple, Inner Temple, Lincoln's Inn and Gray's Inn. After his initial year at Clifford's Inn, Coke enrolled at the Inner Temple. What now faced him was an exacting seven- or eight-year course of study, consisting largely of lectures, known as 'readings', and 'moots', which were exercises in arguing hypothetical cases. In keeping with the solemn profession for which they were preparing, the students were governed by strict rules. Regular attendance at chapel was enjoined, as was sobriety of dress – no silks or furs or extravagant ruffs. They even had to shave – at least once every three weeks.

But students, then as now, were not very good at subjecting themselves to regulations. The fleshpots of London Southwark (the red-light district not controlled by the city fathers – see below, p. 230) were strong magnets, especially to well-to-do young men with money in their purses.

To absorb the surplus energies of students and to foster fellowship, the inns had developed a vibrant social life. Highlights of the year were the plays presented at major festivals. Acted and, usually, written by members of the inns, these productions attracted audiences from the elite of city and court. *Garboduc*, the first tragedy written in English, was created by two members of Inner Temple, and staged there during the Christmas festivities of 1561. It was such a hit that the queen ordered a repeat performance in Whitehall Palace. In 1566, *Supposes*, a comedy translated from the Italian, was presented at Gray's Inn. There were certainly others, for drama at the inns of court was a fixture of the capital's social calendar. Later in the reign, professional playwrights were sometimes called upon. Shakespeare's *The Comedy of Errors* was presented at Gray's Inn in 1594 as part of an evening's festivities, which included 'dancing and revelry with gentlewomen'.

Such frivolity was, apparently, little to the taste of Edward Coke. He was so industrious and determined that, after only six years, he was deemed to have satisfactorily concluded his studies. The senior members of the inns, the benchers, decided, in 1578, that this conscientious and bright young man (he was twenty-six) was ready to be 'called to the bar'. This meant that in any court he could take his place among the professionals who sat within the area separated by a barrier from the public. Coke was appointed as a reader in one of the inns of Chancery but, though recognized by his fellows, the new barrister had to commend himself to potential clients. It is not surprising that he began practising in his native county where he was already known to the local gentry. Social contacts were as important as courtroom skill. His family had connections with the Howards, the great East Anglian magnates, and Coke was soon representing members of this powerful clan in courts as far afield as London and Cardiff.

However, his first major coup came when he was defending a Norfolk clergyman *against* an influential county magnate. Lord Henry Cromwell, a Puritan sympathizer, had sent some radical preachers into Northlingham, the parish of Edmund Denny. This had led to an altercation during which Denny had shouted at his adversary, 'You like those that maintain sedition.' Cromwell claimed that this was a case of *scandalum magnatum*, slander of a peer of the realm. He brought a case in Queen's Bench against the cleric. Coke ferreted among all the legal precedents and discovered flaws in Cromwell's case and forced a settlement. This enhancement of Coke's reputation clearly made an impact in his own shire. This may well have been instrumental in his securing an advantageous marriage. Within months he had taken to wife Bridget Paston, an eighteen-year-old heiress and member of an ancient Norfolk family. As well as bringing considerable wealth and a fine house, Bridget was an excellent partner for a man of soaring ambition. She managed Coke's domestic life and produced ten children. The couple became the founders of a major Norfolk dynasty.

Coke rapidly became a celebrity in the central courts. He may have shown little interest in student drama but there was no doubting his acting ability in the courtroom. Indeed, his performances would not have disgraced the most accomplished tragedian.

> Coke's courtroom manner was histrionics and bombast and abuse . . . [but he] had a quiet manner which he could also call upon, something that went with his bookiness and draftsman's precision . . . he could let fly single phrases, cool or corrosive . . .[5]

The stage on which he gave some of his finest performances was Westminster Hall. The huge medieval edifice was home to the courts of Queen's Bench, Chancery and Common Pleas. One end of the building was partitioned off by high wooden screens and it was behind them that the judges and lawyers conducted their business. The rest of the space had the appearance of a shopping arcade. From booths on each side people sold books, stationery, hats, clothes, etc., and, inevitably, there were 'eateries' from which customers could buy cakes and ale. The general public, then, could wander around the hall, meet friends, do their shopping and, if they felt so inclined, pop into the law courts to hear the latest cases being argued. But if justice was administered in a popular, everyday setting, the professionals took other measures to differentiate themselves from ordinary people and to surround themselves with the mystique of their craft. The officials wore garments that easily marked them out. Judges were clad in scarlet or purple. Sergeants-at-law (senior barristers) wore particoloured robes of blue and green, and covered their heads with a white coif. Other counsel were enjoined to wear gowns of a 'sad' (sombre) colour. Men of the law were also much given to the use of jargon. Though there was a need for specialized language to describe the technicalities of judicial process, the employment of unfamiliar, antiquated terminology – in a mixture of English, Latin and Norman French – also had the effect of erecting an impressive barrier between the experts and the uninitiated.

The central courts were in something of a state of flux in the reign of the first Elizabeth. Queen's Bench was the senior common law court. Common Pleas existed to hear cases between private individuals which did not affect the Crown. Chancery was a court of equity, i.e. it existed to review decisions and procedures in lower courts to ensure that judgements which were in accord with precedent, in fact, met the requirements of justice or fairness. Much of

Chancery's work dealt with issues that, in later centuries, were the province of the Court of Appeal. There were, thus, areas of overlap between the concerns of the three courts. This led to rivalry. Court officers shamelessly competed with each other for business. There was, for example, the notorious Bill of Middlesex. Suppose Plaintiff A was bringing an action in Common Pleas against Defendant B over an alleged offence in Gloucestershire – a case that might prove potentially lucrative for the law officers involved. Queen's Bench, by long-established tradition, held the monopoly of criminal cases in the county of Middlesex. Someone would now be found to accuse B of a fictitious felony supposedly committed in Middlesex. Queen's Bench officers would then arrest B on a Bill of Middlesex. Once in custody, B was liable to answer for all misdeeds he stood accused of committing – including that for which he had been indicted to appear in Common Pleas. The mythical offence would then be forgotten and A would be summoned to appear in Queen's Bench to press his charge against B. One court would, thus, have successfully stolen business from another. This was the ruthless world in which Coke was proving himself to be a hard-headed master.

His ambition was boundless. His Howard connections provided him with an easy path to a place in the House of Commons. He was returned as member for Aldeburgh in 1589. He applied himself to this new role with his accustomed energy. So much so that in the next Parliament (1593), when he was returned as one of the knights of the shire for Norfolk (see above, p. 41 for patronage in parliamentary elections), he was selected as Speaker. In this role he seems to have gone out of his way to demonstrate his loyalty to the queen. He kept a close eye on the councillors sitting on his right and did his cunning best to steer debate so that the results satisfied them. He went further in his dealings with members of the house. He became a finger-wagging pedagogue, telling them how they should behave. On at least one occasion he reprimanded members for whispering. 'It is not the manner of this house that any should whisper or talk secretly,' he admonished in school-masterly tones. 'Here only public speeches are to be used.'[5]

In Coke's defence it should be pointed out that the Commons was in need of a disciplinarian. Issues of religion and parliamentary privilege raised powerful emotions and, without firm control by the Speaker, the atmosphere in the chamber could easily degenerate into that of a bear-garden. Two Puritan bills on church reform were brought in during this session. In order to drown out opposition speeches the promoters resorted to a chorus of coughing and spitting. Coke was eventually obliged to resort to similar tactics. Rising in his seat to speak, he treated the house to a filibuster which continued until business for the day was closed.

Coke's courting of the government brought him the rapid promotion within the legal profession that he craved. It also involved him in a bitter rivalry that was to dog him for several years. In 1594, the position of Attorney General (principal prosecutor for the Crown) became vacant. Coke used his influence with Lord Burghley and with Sir Robert Cecil, who was being groomed to step into his father's shoes as leading adviser to the queen, to obtain the post. But someone else interested in the post was Francis Bacon, second son of Sir Nicholas Bacon (see below, pp. 257–61) and another lawyer and parliamentarian of note. Bacon's champion was Robert Devereux, Earl of Essex, an adventurer and favourite of the queen. Essex had just been admitted to the Privy Council and was engaged in a struggle for supremacy with the Cecils. He was utterly determined to obtain the Attorney Generalship for his protégé, as he made clear to Sir Robert:

> . . . the Attorneyship for Francis is that I must have, and in that will I spend all my power, weight, authority and amity and with tooth and nail defend and procure the same for him

against whomsoever ... For if you weigh in a balance the parts
every way of his competitor and him, only excepting five poor
years of admitting to a house of court before Francis [Coke
had joined the Inner Temple in 1571. Bacon entered Gray's
Inn in 1576], you shall find in all other respects whatsoever no
comparison between them.[6]

For all Essex's bluster it was Coke who won the preferment.
He and Bacon were destined henceforth to cross swords
several times. Some of their clashes occurred in the law
courts over issues which, to outsiders, could occasionally
appear quite arcane. Such was Slade's Case, which occupied
the best legal brains from 1596 to 1602. John Slade, a Devon
farmer, agreed to sell for £16 a crop of wheat and rye growing at Halberton, near Tiverton. When harvest time came
Morley backed out of the deal. Slade, therefore, brought
an action against him in the local Assizes. There were two
courses open to the plaintiff: he could claim payment of
the debt (£16) or he could proceed by *assumpsit* (meaning
'he has undertaken'). The latter covered any kind of verbal
or written (but not sealed) agreement, non-performance of
which entitles the offended party to seek financial com-
pensation. Clearly, Slade was claiming damages to cover all
the costs involved in storing the grain and seeking another
buyer (and, perhaps, losses arising from the late harvest-
ing of the crop). Morley claimed, *non assumpsit modo et
forma* (there was no undertaking in the manner and form
alleged). Before judgement could be given, Lord Chief
Justice Popham ordered the case to London because a more
fundamental point of law was involved, namely whether
Slade was allowed to bring a case of *assumpsit* when a
simple claim for debt was available to him. Meeting period-
ically in Sergeants' Inn, the top legal experts argued points
of law back and forth as year succeeded year. Coke represented Slade and Francis Bacon was on the defence team.
Not until November 1602 was the Lord Chief Justice ready

to give his definitive determination, which was that every contract implies an undertaking and that, even if an action for debt is appropriate, a plaintiff is at liberty to proceed upon the basis of *assumpsit*.

It is not difficult to see why lawyers' (potentially lucrative) procrastination was listed by Shakespeare among the 'thousand natural shocks that flesh is heir to':

> The oppressor's wrong, the proud man's contumely,
> The pangs of despised love, the law's delay,
> The insolence of office and the spurns
> That patient merit of the unworthy takes
>
> *Hamlet*, III. i. 71–4

In defence of the men of law it could well be argued that such lengthy and weighty deliberations were the stable foundations upon which English common law rested.

Coke was, as chief Crown prosecutor, involved in all the major state trials, including those of Catholic activists. Among the most prominent of these was the Jesuit, John Gerard. After a long search the missionary was arrested and eventually lodged in the Tower. There, in April 1597, he was interrogated by Edward Coke. In this confrontation between two great intellects – one trained in theology and the other in law – it was ultimately not the prisoner but the legal system that was on trial.

Coke was a devoted servant of the law. The law existed to safeguard both the rights of the individual and the rights of the state. But suppose those two could not be held together? Suppose there were people in England who had committed no felony and who protested their loyalty to the queen but who yet needed to be silenced in the interests of the state? This was the case with Catholic proselytizers. In a world where politics and religion were inextricably intertwined believing the wrong things and persuading other people to believe the wrong thing tended to undermine the state and had to be suppressed. But England had no Inquisition (a fact upon which the governors of this Protestant kingdom prided themselves) and this meant that alleged offenders had to be dealt with by the common law courts. Even when a suspect was found guilty of a capital offence under the recusancy laws the government was reluctant to carry out the death sentence. Elizabeth and her ministers knew that martyrdom was a powerful propaganda weapon for the enemy. A series of statutes had been enacted that progressively limited the movements of Catholic activists without resorting to the ultimate deterrent. The latest (1593) provided for the permanent imprisonment of any suspected Jesuit or seminary priest. This was why Gerard was in the Tower facing England's most formidable cross-examiner (see above, p. 112).

The object of his interrogation was to gain information about the whereabouts of other Catholic troublemakers. Gerard maintained a stubborn silence. At this Coke, perhaps reluctantly, sanctioned the use of torture. The prisoner had his wrists manacled and was then suspended by them from a hook in the wall. Two days of this treatment did not break him. At a later session the Attorney General returned to verbal attack. The exchanges between the two men became, at times, highly philosophical. Both men were trained rhetoricians and Coke acknowledged the intellectual calibre of his adversary. He tried to point out to Gerard that his equivocation was, in fact, lying. This is how the conversation continued:

Gerard: A man cannot deny a crime if he is guilty and lawfully interrogated.
Coke: What do you mean by lawful interrogation?
Gerard: The question must be asked by a person who has authority or jurisdiction and it must concern an action in some way harmful to the state . . . In general equivocation is unlawful save when a person is asked a question . . .

> which the questioner has no right to put, and where a
> straight answer would injure the questioned party.[7]

It was an answer that indicated the pointlessness of the whole situation. Elizabeth had been deposed by the pope. Therefore, according to Gerard, her government was not lawfully constituted.

In this situation it was the 'quiet' Coke who was to the fore. He knew his man and, therefore, knew what tactics were likely to be effective.

> Coke did not bully or threaten. He did not cuff the priest
> across the table. He did not call in warders to beat the pris-
> oner. He derided Gerard's colleagues . . . denounced Gerard's
> methods but never attacked the prisoner by name. His inter-
> view with Gerard is one with other moments in which Coke
> scored his points with understatement and innuendo.[8]

He was to be spared the need for further interrogation. Days later, Gerard became one of the few prisoners ever to escape from the Tower of London.

Coke was familiar with what the regime required thanks to his appearances in Star Chamber. This was the senior court of the land, which took precedence over common law courts. Technically it was the Privy Council sitting as a judicial body and it took its name from the room in Whitehall where it met to adjudicate on matters considered potentially dangerous to the Crown and the security of the realm, such as riotous assembly, slander and libel of the queen or her officers, bribery of judges and corrupting of juries. Just as Chancery acted as a court of equity for redressing any imbalances in the civil law, so Star Camber ostensibly oversaw the workings of the criminal law. It had begun its life in the fifteenth century as a means of checking the power of overmighty subjects who imposed their will on lesser mortals, interfered with the impartial pursuit of justice and, in so doing, held the authority of 'the Crown' in contempt. In order that witnesses could give evidence without fear of reprisals the court often held its sessions in camera. The accused were not allowed to hear the evidence against them or to speak in their own defence. The court could impose whatever punishments it saw fit, short of deprivation of life or property. The usual penalties imposed were fines. Coke described Star Chamber in glowing terms: 'This Court, the right institution and ancient orders thereof being observed, doth keep all England quiet.'[9] Keeping England quiet meant, in the last analysis, subjugating the judiciary to the executive. Star Chamber was a tool waiting to fall into the hands of a tyrannical government, which it did in the next century.

Yet, during Elizabeth's reign the proceedings of the common law courts were quite draconian enough. Every time Parliament adjudged that a gap in the existing law needed to be filled, they plugged it with a statute designed to strike terror into the hearts of would-be offenders. For example, a law was enacted to deter people from exporting sheep and thus harming the native wool trade. Upon conviction, an offender was to be taken to the local marketplace and there have his left hand cut off and nailed to a post. If he survived this ordeal he was to be imprisoned for a year and suffer the forfeiture of all his goods. If he repeated the offence – and it seems scarcely credible that he would be so stupid – only the gallows awaited him.

In June 1598, Edward Coke's wife died and he lost no time in making a second, very advantageous, marriage. His bride was a young widow, Elizabeth, Lady Hatton, granddaughter of the late Lord Burghley and niece of Sir Robert Cecil, who had stepped into his father's shoes as principal adviser to the queen. This prize was a rich one, not only in terms of the wealth Elizabeth brought with her but also because it brought her husband into the most powerful family in the land. Coke was not alone in desiring this match. Another contender for Lady Hatton's hand was none other than Francis Bacon. Not only did Coke act swiftly and secretly to gain the prize, he also acted unlawfully. The wedding took place in a private house, without banns or licence, which was against ecclesiastical law. The couple were duly prosecuted in the archiepiscopal court but the Church's sanction had no real teeth and, after making humble submission, the Cokes were absolved. The eager bridegroom may soon have discovered that there was a downside to the marriage. The feisty Elizabeth was very different from the first Lady Coke. As Coke's biographer observes, 'if she and Coke were not compatible, at least they were well-matched'.[10]

A little more than a year later Coke again found himself at odds with Francis Bacon – though only obliquely. Bacon's patron, the Earl of Essex, smarting from his rebuff by the queen, gathered a group of armed friends around him at his London house. Coke and Cecil were determined not to wait for the coming storm. John Hayward, another of Essex's protégés, had written a book which Elizabeth regarded as seditious. Coke carried out his own investigations, aimed at implicating the earl in the book's publication. In the event, this counter-plot proved unnecessary. Essex went on to launch his pocket rebellion. When it failed, Coke had the satisfaction of leading the prosecution in the House of Lords which led to the earl's being found guilty of treason. He had the rare distinction of being the last person beheaded in the Tower of London.

When Queen Elizabeth died Edward Coke still had thirty years of active life ahead of him – years marked by fresh achievements and political controversies. But by 1603 he had both made law and used law to become one of the richest men in the land. The previous decade alone had seen his annual income rise from £100 to £12,000 and his second marriage brought him another fortune. He invested in more than a hundred properties, mostly in Norfolk. The law had made him. But, in no small measure, he had made the law. Not only did he establish precedents himself; he left posterity lawbooks that listed and analysed hundreds of cases. His *Reports* covered about forty years of judicial activity and gave detailed accounts of law in the reign of Elizabeth I and James I. His *Institutes* was a monumental historical treatise in four parts, providing future generations of law students with an account of the development of English law and a means of finding a way through its intricacies.

7

THE SOLDIER

England, impatient of your just demands,
Hath put himself in arms . . .
His marches are expedient to this town,
His forces strong, his soldiers confident . . .
And all the unsettled humours of the land,
Rash, inconsiderate fiery voluntaries,
With ladies' faces and fierce dragons' spleens,
Have sold their fortunes at their native homes,
Bearing their birthrights proudly on their backs,
To make a hazard of new fortunes here . . .

King John, II. i. 56–71

Warfare in Shakespeare's plays is a brave and noble enterprise – at least for those whose cause is just. It is not surprising that this should be so. By the time that his works were being performed, in the last decade of Elizabeth's reign, England was locked into a long-running conflict with Catholic Spain. Nationalism and religious fervour could easily be aroused and playgoers loved to cheer on patriotic exploits which mirrored those of their contemporary military heroes. The groundlings at the Globe were stirred by the rousing speeches in *Henry V*, first performed in 1599. Their spirits were fired – just as patriotic fervour is whipped up by the singing of 'Land of Hope and Glory' at the last night of the Proms. And they did have contemporary heroes to cheer. Among the queen's prominent subjects there were bold spirits who were dedicated to the military life. Not only did they see it as a pathway to personal fame and fortune, they also learned from their continental counterparts and tried to bring innovation and efficiency to England's fighting machine.

One such was an adventurer who added as much lustre to Elizabeth's reign as Drake, Raleigh and Hawkins. Like them, he was certainly a flawed figure. His biographer has described him as being motivated by 'greed, religious bigotry, family ambition and the simple hunger for glory',[1] but, in the pursuance of his own career he fought for the modernization of his country's military machine. His name was John Norreys.

John was born, about 1547, into a family that could boast a history of loyal support to the Tudor family. His great-great-grandfather, Sir William Norreys, was among the gentry who rebelled against Richard III, threw in his lot with Henry, Earl of Richmond (later Henry VII), fought at the Battle of Bosworth and, in other military engagements, helped Elizabeth's grandfather to consolidate his regime. The family's loyalty was rewarded with extensive lands in Berkshire and Oxfordshire and one of William's sons became a leading member of Henry VIII's court. This Henry Norreys was particularly close to Anne Boleyn. In fact, he was too close; when Anne fell, Henry fell with her, being executed as one of her supposed lovers. In the long term this disgrace acted in the family's favour; having shared the shame of Anne's fall from grace the Norreyses became warm friends of Anne's daughter, the future

Queen Elizabeth. John's father, another Henry Norreys, received Elizabeth at Rycote, his Oxfordshire home, on several occasions and also took part in court tournaments, an entertainment of which she was very fond.

Tournaments, like archery, had by this time become a sport, rather than a valuable means of military preparation. Frequent extravagant tiltyard displays were things of the past (see below, pp. 236–7). Elizabeth enjoyed the manly spectacle of mounted knights belabouring each other with lance and mace but they featured less often in the entertainment offered at her court or at the estates of prominent subjects whom she visited.

When Henry Norreys demonstrated his tiltyard skills before the queen it was not as someone thirsting for a military vocation, although he certainly maintained his family's fascination with warfare. Elizabeth had another career in mind for him. In 1566 she knighted him and appointed him as her ambassador to the French court. Accordingly, Sir Henry moved to Paris, taking with him his wife and his two older sons, William and John. The work of a diplomat included reporting back to the government what was happening in the land of England's closest neighbour. The most important thing happening in France was the Wars of Religion. Political power was contested by aristocrat-led armies which identified themselves as Catholic or Calvinist (Huguenot). Norreys sent his sons to watch military engagements and gather information for his reports home. The fate of their Protestant co-religionists was a matter of vital concern to the government at Westminster. If the Huguenots were crushed, France would be in a position to make common cause with Spain against 'heretic' England, something frequently urged by successive popes.

Young John Norreys was captivated by the clash of arms and, particularly, by the generalship of the Huguenot leader, the Prince de Condé. It was a comparatively short step for John to become a volunteer in the Protestant army.

He served under another Calvinist general, Gaspard de Coligny, in the campaigns of 1567–8 and 1569–71. He was not unique in this. Many young Englishmen of prominent families sought in foreign conflicts the thrill, adventure and camaraderie denied them in the staid life of England. For some, and certainly for John, such commitment had a distinctly religious element. Western Europe was in the grip of Reformation and Counter-Reformation. People took sides in the ideological confrontation that divided nations, regions and local communities into 'papist' and 'heretic' camps. John, like his father, was decidedly of the reformed camp and believed that he was engaged in a holy crusade against the Romish forces of Antichrist. He decided that, since his government was not prepared to take up arms in this holy war, he would do so on his own initiative. His religious commitment can only have been reinforced by the experience, because the armies were accompanied by preachers who fired up the combatants with zealous exhortations. Thanks to his years spent in France, Norreys became a member of an international fellowship of Protestant captains, for he formed relationships not only with French leaders, but also with Dutch and German professionals.

What he learned about tactics and strategy formed the basis of his own generalship. There were basically two kinds of engagements fought in the sixteenth century – pitched battles and sieges. Norreys had little time for the latter. He was by nature hot-headed and short-tempered. Settling to the lengthy bombardment of a town or castle held little appeal for him. He also disliked sieges on professional grounds. Static armies easily fell prey to disease and desertion. They were also difficult to keep victualled. A force on the move stood some chance of being able to live off the land. When it was pegged down for any length of time the possibilities of plunder steadily diminished. The strategy Norreys developed largely involved techniques for maintaining communication and discipline within relatively small and mobile military units.

In 1571 Henry Norreys was recalled. Soon afterwards he was raised to the peerage as Baron Norreys of Rycote and thereafter devoted much of his energy to local government (including reforming the muster system). However, his court influence was kept very much alive thanks largely to the efforts of his wife, Marjorie (dubbed by Elizabeth 'my black crow'), who was a great favourite with the queen. They were well placed to gain for their sons, William and John, roles in an army that set out in 1573, under the leadership of the Earl of Essex, to pacify eastern Ulster. The arrangement was that investors (including the queen) should contribute cash or soldiers to the enterprise in return for estates in the newly conquered territory. The Norreys boys were hopeful of establishing personal fortunes by joining the expedition.

Ireland had long been notorious as the destroyer of reputations and would continue to be so long after Elizabeth's unsuccessful attempts to establish effective English rule. The terrain was difficult for campaigning. Much of the land was of poor quality and hard to make agriculturally productive. The majority of the people were Catholic. Petty warfare was endemic – not only between the indigenous population and the settlers, but also between the Irish clans and between different groups of settlers. Militarily, John Norreys found himself on a sharp learning curve. His enemies knew the swamps and woods of their own land and used them effectively to harass Essex's forces. Norreys now had his first encounter with guerrilla warfare. On one occasion he had to rescue his brother from certain death when they were caught in an ambush and William had his horse shot from under him.

But he was a quick learner. After a few months he returned home to raise his own company of troops, equipped (especially with firearms) and trained for the particular conditions of Ireland. Now he learned at first hand the logistical problems of maintaining his own combat force. His victuallers short-changed him over the supply of food, and chandlers sent him gunpowder adulterated with coal dust. However, he acquitted himself well, impressed his commander and was entrusted with increasing responsibility. But the difficulties of the campaign, the stubbornness of the foe and financial worries caused by protracted fighting, which cost lives and yielded little reward undermined Essex's character. He became increasingly brutal and unreasonable. Norreys, never the most even-tempered of men, shared the failings of his general. Their plundering and their savage reprisals against prisoners alienated the population. Their most notorious act was their treatment of Sir Brian MacPhelim O'Neill. This local magnate had been playing a double game but was currently wooing the English commanders, whom he invited to a feast. After three days of enjoying O'Neill's hospitality, Essex ordered the arrest of his host and all his followers. Norreys entered the hall with a body of soldiers and massacred two hundred men, women and children. Small wonder that the Irish came to believe that 'Black Jack Norreys' was in league with the devil. This demonstration of ruthless slaughter was not the only one given by Norreys during a savage and ultimately fruitless campaign. When the London government ordered Essex's army to withdraw, Norreys returned home considerably out of pocket. One thing he had yet to learn was how to play the system to his personal advantage.

But Norreys and his ilk are only one part of a very complex picture. At the same time as Shakespeare's actors were fighting their mock battles on the stage of the Globe, Sir Henry Knyvet, who had seen action in Scotland, and possibly the Netherlands, and been wounded in the queen's service, offered Elizabeth a pamphlet in which he expressed his concerns about the state of military affairs:

'all private soldiers have been so lightly regarded, yea so uncharitably and cruelly used, as, were it not for their extraordinary obedience and loyal love which they bear to Your Most Sacred Majesty, they would more willingly be hanged at their doors than abide shameful martyrdom with many extremities abroad.'[2] The bravado of swaggering captains should not deceive us into thinking that all Englishmen were gung-ho, that they were led by an expansionist government, intent on taking the field to champion an aggressive Protestantism or that the queen had at her disposal a well-trained army ready to make conquests and win glory in foreign fields.

War was unpopular at all levels of society. Queen Elizabeth loathed the very idea of it. Her father's involvement in continental conflicts had been disastrous. When her sister had been inveigled by her Spanish husband into providing troops for his army in France, the results had been the loss of Calais and also the loss of her people's affection. Despite the provocations offered by Counter-Reformation enemies and the urgings of her own councillors, the queen stubbornly resisted the bloody – and expensive – expedient of sending English armies abroad. Peaceable regimes do not enjoy spending money on armaments and no one was more peaceable and parsimonious than Elizabeth Tudor. When urged by her more impatient councillors to take a positive stance backed by the threat of force, she fell back on diplomacy and prevarication. For most of her reign her instincts proved sound. France, the traditional foe, was too rent by internal divisions to be a realistic threat and skilful diplomacy prevented Scotland being a nuisance. Spanish ambassadors threatened intervention and intrigued with Catholic sympathizers among her subjects, but Philip II's long-expected 'Enterprise of England' did not materialize. Indeed, the Spanish king's problems seemed to vindicate Elizabeth's inaction. His attempts to back with force his authority in the Netherlands gobbled up his precious resources, including the mineral wealth flowing from the New World, without putting an end to the rebellion of his Protestant subjects. It was not until 1585 that the queen was prevailed upon – very unwillingly – to send troops across the North Sea to aid the Protestant states in their struggle against their Habsburg master. There was, of course, Ireland, that continual thorn in the flesh of English governments. Elizabeth was obliged to despatch small royal armies to keep the peace in that corner of her realm. But, apart from service in Ulster, any young man desiring a military career (and there were some) had no option but to become a mercenary soldier, selling his sword to a foreign prince or general.

Most of the queen's subjects shared her disinclination for foreign entanglements. In *Henry IV Part 2*, Peter Bullcalf is among those offering money to recruiting officers to escape being pressed into the army. He roundly states, 'I had as lief be hanged, Sir, as go' (III. ii. 216). His reluctance is not surprising. Campaign conditions were appalling. Death rates from disease and privation, as well as battle wounds, were high. Those returning from war were left to fend for themselves and were often reduced to beggary or crime. By comparison with foreign forces, English armies were ill-equipped and poorly trained. Moreover, the running of the war machine was a corrupt racket. The fundamental problem lay in England's geographical position. The Channel, as Shakespeare pointed out, had long served England well, '... in the office of a wall/Or as a moat defensive to a house' (*Richard II*, II. i. 47–8). Englishmen had not been called upon to fight a defensive war on home soil since Henry VII's invasion in 1485. As a result they had become complaisant.

In peace there's nothing so becomes a man
As modest stillness and humility

Henry V, III. i. 3–4

But 'stillness' had, for many of the queen's subjects, become negligence. Great lords, shopkeepers and farm labourers alike all had things to do which, to them, were more pressing than preparing for the unlikely eventuality of war. Yet, like all responsible governments, Elizabeth's held firmly to the classical adage, 'If you desire peace, be prepared for war'. England had no standing army. The country's security and commitment to foreign campaigns rested on the militia system, an inefficient method of conscripting and training a citizen army. All able-bodied men between the ages of sixteen and sixty were – technically – liable to be ordered to arms as and when necessary. If troops were required for action in Ireland or Scotland or on the continent instructions would be sent from the court to local officials outlining the government's requirements. What this normally meant was that the lieutenants or JPs of the counties nearest to the proposed conflict were instructed to have the requisite number of armed men ready for despatch. Sometimes private commissions were given to major landowners to raise fighting units but this last vestige of military feudalism was rapidly disappearing. Elizabeth's father and grandfather had been careful to remove the potential threat of overmighty subjects with their own private armies.

If ordinary subjects were to be transmuted into soldiers they had to be trained. The mechanism for this was the muster system. Shire officials were expected to summon men for regular sessions where they would learn military drill and the handling of weapons. That all looked very well on paper. In practice, the system had two flaws: (a) neither muster-masters nor militia members were enthusiastic about training, and (b) the training that was provided was not such as to create an army capable of meeting on equal terms the professional forces that could be put into the field by England's potential enemies. We can have some sympathy for the muster-masters. Most of them were drawn

from the ranks of the already overworked justices of the
peace. As well as organizing the musters they had to cope
with a prodigious amount of paperwork. The accurate and
up-to-date records required by the government meant that
muster-masters had to note the names of those who had just
reached recruitment age, those who had turned sixty and
were no longer eligible, those who had died or moved and
any who had become incapable as a result of injury or illness. They also needed to keep on good terms with their
social equals and superiors in the shires. These were the
members of the 'officer class', who would be required to
lead their contingents if ever active service became a reality.
Many of these captains, as we shall see, were only intent
on turning the system to their own advantage by drawing
pay for non-existent soldiers and other corrupt practices. A
muster-master would have to be a very strong-willed royal
servant to stand up to the pressure of his compeers. When
it came down to it, he was just as much open to temptation. The unwillingness of men to appear on his list meant
that he had what amounted to a licence to print money. He
accepted or, more probably, actually solicited bribes from
those who could afford to buy their way out of liability for
conscription. He then filled the resultant gaps in his shire
company with individuals who lacked the means to evade
their duty. Shakespeare had clearly in his sights the reluctant
soldiers who made such profiteering possible when he gave
Henry V these lines in his famous speech before Agincourt:

> . . . gentlemen in England now a-bed
> Shall think themselves accurs'd they were not here,
> And hold their manhoods cheap whiles any speaks
> That fought with us upon Saint Crispin's day.
>
> *Henry V*, IV. iii. 64–7

It was frustratingly difficult for the government to know
the state of national readiness. When crisis struck in 1569

in the form of a rebellion led by the Earls of Westmorland and Northumberland, the official muster rolls received by the Council indicated that Elizabeth had more than half a million trained subjects ready to take the field. The French ambassador, who presumably passed on the best intelligence to his superiors, reported that a more realistic tally was nearer 120,000. An act of Parliament in the last year of Mary's reign reveals that the muster system was a shambles. It imposed fines on any able-bodied men who absented themselves from the musters or who turned up without the proper equipment. Any muster-master detected taking a bribe was obliged to pay ten times the amount received. Similar penalties were prescribed for captains who received payment in lieu of service or withheld pay from their troops. The same act encouraged whistle-blowing by detailing rewards for informers. But the government was fighting a losing battle. It proved impossible to have a clear picture of just how many properly equipped fighting men were available for national defence.

Internal peace had sapped not only the willingness of Englishmen to be ready for war, but also the effectiveness of their preparations. Unlike their counterparts in mainland Europe, the officer class had not kept well abreast of changes in military science. In continental conflicts, firearms had been replacing bows and crossbows before Elizabeth came to the throne, but the basis of English training was still the longbow and all able-bodied men were required to practise regularly in the butts. The 7,000-strong royal army that set out to quell the northern rebellion in 1569 had about sixty matchlock muskets (arquebuses). Fortunately, the rebels were no better provided for, and, as a result, the skirmishes that took place were very much old-fashioned engagements. Elizabeth's generals would not be so lucky when they were called upon to face continental foes.

European field armies consisted of cavalry and infantry. The former were, traditionally, the elite, drawn from the upper echelons of society, men who, from their earliest years, had learned to be fine horsemen. But increasingly armies were supplemented by contingents of mercenaries, men who made a profession of war. Cavalry dominance of the battlefield was now being seriously challenged by ranks of infantry armed with pikes and the most proficient troops in contemporary Catholic armies were Swiss mercenary pikemen. They were well led, well trained and well disciplined. Rarely could a cavalry charge break their ranks and, in close encounters, their vicious six-metre long weapons played havoc with horses and riders. But more long-lasting in its impact on warfare was the introduction of firearms. This was still in its infancy at the beginning of the reign. Arquebuses were cumbersome (about 140 centimetres in length) and not very accurate. They also had the disadvantage of being difficult to operate in wet weather, when keeping the powder dry became a problem. But they required far less strength and skill than longbows and the terrifying noise they made was a bonus. Foreign tacticians (prominent among whom was Maurice of Nassau) devised new ways of deploying them on the battlefield, but, by the end of the century, the English were still playing catch-up.

Spanish success depended heavily on siege warfare. The Spanish general the Duke of Parma was well supplied with cannon. If he could manoeuvre his cumbersome machines into position he could, and did, deploy them to devastating effect. The enemies' best chance of frustrating him was to open the sluices and turn the surrounding terrain into quagmire. In 1585, the siege of Antwerp, a city of 100,000 souls and the centre of Dutch resistance, was in full swing. Parma went about his work patiently and industriously. He constructed an enormous and heavily defended bridge over the Scheldt. But the defenders were not without their own innovative engineers. One of them devised an updated version of the fireship. It was a vessel observers described with some accuracy as a floating volcano. Gunpowder packed deep in its bowels was covered by a stone cone filled with cannonballs, scrap metal and lumps of marble. The powder was ignited by a time fuse worked by clockwork. When it was sent against the bridge, the diabolical device erupted with what has been described as 'possibly the largest man-made explosion in history up to that date'.[3] Debris and bodies were thrown several miles and the Spaniards lost over a thousand men, many of whom were never recovered.

War has always proved to be the mother of invention and there were not lacking ingenious technicians who offered their services to Elizabeth's government. Two brothers by the name of Engelbert demonstrated their long-range mortar which, according to the inventors' description, would discharge 'shot of such bigness that nothing would be able to resist their violence, and every such shot would discharge every way round about, above 2,000 musket shots, with such force that every one of them would be death to man and horse'.[4] Her Majesty could not be pre-vailed upon to invest.

The general lack of preparedness extended to every element of an army's requirements. Soldiers have to be protected as well as armed and there is evidence that the provision of armour (harness) left much to be desired. Generals in the field frequently complained that they were ill supplied by the commissariat. The government kept a supply of harness, mostly stored in the Tower of London, but much of it was rusting and antiquated. In 1584, the Lord Deputy of Ireland returned 300 sets of armour, for which he was being charged forty-two shillings apiece, on the grounds that he could buy better imported items at twenty-five shillings each. In any case, heavy armour was going out of favour. The elaborate plate armour, tailor-made for mounted knights, was a thing of the past and foot soldiers often complained of the ill-fitting harness with which they were issued. Manoeuvrability was prized more than cumbersome and heavy armour designed to protect most parts of the body. In 1593, Sir Richard Hawkins reported that he had provided good-quality 'proof armour' (i.e. armour tested for its effectiveness) but that his men 'esteemed a pot of wine a better defence than an armour of proof'. Common soldiers wore a variety of protective coverings. There was no uniform. As well as helmets some wore steel breastplates, others had 'jacks', linen surcoats to which overlapping strips of steel were attached. Some preferred thick leather jerkins. Defensive armour for the limbs had almost disappeared by the end of the century.

If the muster system was riddled with incompetence and corruption, these failings became much more pronounced when men were summoned to active service. The irregularities accompanying recruitment for Ireland indicate the degree of sharp practice that was common. A captain in, for example, Leicestershire might set off at the head of his contingent en route for the army's assembly point at Chester. He would have received sufficient travelling expenses for himself and his men. When they had gone a few miles he would offer his company their freedom, and receive from every member who wanted to go home whatever he was willing to pay for his discharge. Arrived at Chester, the captain would, of course, have to account for the men on his muster roll. No problem; he had a prior arrangement with an agent on site who rounded up enough locals to fill the gaps. The company was then paraded before government officials and found to be all present and correct. As soon as the review was over the stand-ins were paid off and the captain continued on his way. If there were further inspections in Ireland the deception was repeated by temporarily enlisting willing Ulstermen. Throughout the ensuing campaign our ingenious captain would claim pay for every soldier on his, by now, fictitious list, including those who had died, deserted or never actually set foot in Ireland. Pocketing the wages of dead soldiers was the

biggest scandal perpetrated by their captains. Knyvet was
enraged by it:

> If the killing or robbing a man by the highway side deserve
> death what punishment are they worthy to have, that by
> diminishing their companies for gain, and robbing the prince
> of dead pay to maintain their licentiousness, are the cause
> of lingering wars to the great destruction of a multitude of
> valiant men, the unjust wasting of the prince's treasure, and
> betraying of the actions they take in hand. Truly, ten deaths
> were too little for them and the penalty of treason their true
> reward of their desert.[5]

Chicanery and thuggery were endemic at every level of
military life. The conflict between chivalric idealism and
the brute facts of war is an important theme in Shakespeare's
Henry V. The little band of petty crooks who set off with
the English army are in no doubt about their motives: 'Let
us to France; like horse-leeches, my boys,/To suck, to suck,
the very blood to suck' (II. iii. 54–5). So urges Pistol, and
his companion, Bardolph, is later hanged for stealing from
a church. The king indignantly denounces this desecra-
tion and orders that his followers are not to exact money
or goods from the civilian population, but this does not
disguise the fact that plunder was one of the compensations
many soldiers sought for risking life and limb in the service
of the Crown. As for Pistol, he has another means of lining
his pocket during the campaign: 'I shall sutler be/Unto the
camp, and profits will accrue' (II. i. 108–9). For any old soldiers watching Shakespeare's play, those words would have
evoked bitter memories. Sutlers were private victuallers
who followed the army providing from their wagons food
of dubious quality at exorbitant prices. Troops on campaign had to feed off the land but their scavenging soon
laid waste to the country they crossed. Their only recourse
then was to the profiteering sutler. The biggest curse of

camp life was the inadequate supply system. Keeping an army equipped and provisioned far from coast ports was difficult enough. It was rendered much more so by human incompetence and opportunism. It was 'so riddled with inefficiency and corruption at every point that disease caused by malnutrition and even starvation were major contributors to casualty rates that often reached ninety per cent'.[6]

Was military life in Elizabeth's England, then, nothing but a sordid morass of misery, exploitation and self-seeking, under a glistening sheen of patriotism? No; there were, of course, brave men, willing to risk all for what they believed in. There were adventurers 'seeking the bubble reputation even in the cannon's mouth' (As You Like It, II. vii. 152–3). There were honourable administrators and leaders in the field who took seriously their obligations to queen and country.

Henry Norreys is an example of the professional commander who was as careful as possible about filling the ranks of his companies with experienced soldiers or novices who could be licked into shape, but the pool of such men he had to draw on was not large. When the crisis years came and England needed to recruit as many men as possible for service overseas, the quality and commitment of the average soldier left very much to be desired. Even if it had been efficient and free from corruption the routine muster system would have been hard pressed to deal with the demand. Between 1585 and 1602, London (by far the largest contributor to the army) provided nine and a half thousand citizen-soldiers, the vast majority of them for service in the Netherlands and France.[7] Francis de Vere, writing from Ostend in 1601, spoke for many fellow captains when he complained that the reinforcements sent out to him were 'the very scum of the world'. In addition to the dubious methods of making up the numbers already referred to, the recruiting authorities resorted to any and every stratagem to make up their allotted quota. Forcibly enlisting prisoners was a useful way of emptying the jails. Another device was waiting outside churches on Easter Sunday, when all the queen's subjects were obliged by law to attend divine service, and literally grabbing all men of fighting age as they emerged. Falstaff could boast that he had assembled a rabble of 'discarded unjust serving-men, younger sons to younger brothers, revolted tapsters and ostlers trade-fallen, the cankers of a calm world and a long peace; ten times more dishonourable ragged than an old faced ancient . . . No eye hath seen such scarecrows. I'll not march through Coventry with them, that's flat' (*Henry IV, Part 1*, IV. ii. 31f). The fact that Shakespeare could have this proclaimed from the theatre stage indicates that these abuses were common knowledge.

England's crisis years began in July 1584. In that month William the Silent, the leader of the movement for Dutch independence from Spain, was assassinated. There now seemed to be every prospect of Philip II's general, the Duke of Parma, rapidly winding up the rebellion. Once the Netherlands had been brought to heel, he would undoubtedly turn his attention to England. Elizabeth's ministers were frantic. There had already been attempts on the queen's life and two elaborate plots had been foiled. The death of William rang loud alarm bells in London. Elizabeth was ardently pressed by her Council to send an army across the North Sea to keep Dutch independence hopes alive. Within months John Norreys had been recalled from duties in Ireland to form a regiment for the Netherlands.

The conflict, which a previous Spanish general had described to his king as 'a war such as never before was seen or heard of in any land on earth', had already been running for almost twenty years. What made it particularly difficult for soldiers was the terrain. One commentator called it 'the great bog of Europe. There is not such another marsh in the world . . . Indeed, it is the buttock of the world, full of veins and blood, but no bones in it.' The Netherlands comprised walled towns and cities scattered across a landscape of marsh and water meadows, intersected by rivers, dykes and canals which, by the opening of sluices, could flood the land. The harshness of the landscape was matched by the ruthlessness of the contenders. Sieges lasted weeks or months and took a great toll on defenders and attackers alike. When a citadel fell Spanish fury was vented on its inhabitants. It was the norm for thousands of defenceless men, women and children to be put to the sword, *pour encourager les autres*. In fact, the ferocity of the attackers, fed by their intense hatred of Protestants, only made the rebels more determined. If they could expect no mercy from the Spaniards, they had no incentive to negotiate. This was the atmosphere into which English soldiers – many inexperienced in the normal hazards of warfare – were thrust.

The campaign of 1585–7 could never have been a success, in terms of delivering the Netherlands from Spanish control. The difficulty of the terrain made military victory unlikely. The bitterness of the principal contenders was such that neither side could have been brought to a negotiated settlement. But what made the situation worse for the English participants were the divisions in the allied ranks. The freedom fighters looked to their friends for wholehearted support. That was something Elizabeth was determined not to give. She was anxious that aiding rebels against their lawful ruler would provoke Philip into that very invasion that her intervention had been designed to prevent. When Norreys took part in a raid on Arnheim, the queen rapped him over the knuckles for defying her instructions to 'stand upon a defensive war'. Then, to make matters worse, he fell out with the man she had appointed to overall command, her personal favourite, Robert Dudley, Earl of Leicester.

Their relationship began well enough. In a gruelling

battle fought on the banks of the Maas against superior odds and in driving rain, Norreys impressed the commander and was knighted for his bravery and tactical skill. However, instead of building on this foundation of mutual trust Dudley antagonized his subordinate by replacing several of his officers with captains newly brought from England. Most of them were Leicester's court friends, men with little or no field experience. From this point, every disagreement over policy was exaggerated into a major dispute. When – inevitably – discontent over non-payment of soldiers' wages flared up, each officer faction blamed the other, while discipline broke down and desertions became frequent. Unsurprisingly, Elizabeth preferred Dudley's version of events and, when Norreys was recalled in July 1587, he was, if not in disgrace, certainly in disfavour. But the long-feared Spanish invasion was under way within months and the government could not afford to leave a soldier of Norreys's stature in mothballs. He was admitted to the council of war charged with organizing national defence.

We know, of course, that Philip II's grand strategy was foiled by a combination of Channel storms and the harassing tactics of the English fleet. The fact that, once again, the realm was spared a defensive war on home soil makes it difficult for us to analyse just how ready England was for its potential ordeal by fire. Demands for reform, aided by mounting concern over Spanish preparations, had begun to create some semblance of an effective army. England now had a two-tier militia: in addition to the general muster there were shire-based 'trained bands'. As the name suggests, these were men selected, equipped and trained for modern warfare. Particularly, they were instructed in the use of firearms. Norreys was assigned to oversee the readiness of the south-eastern counties – the area where the Spaniards were expected to attempt a landing. He threw himself into the work. By the end of the year, he was personally drilling the London troops twice a week and, early in 1588, he set off to tour the coastal fortifications from Hampshire and the Isle of Wight to Kent. Armed with the Council's mandate, Black Jack exercised firm and authoritarian control and did not allow himself to be diverted by local power politics. For example, he did not hesitate to transfer men from one county to another where he observed gaps that needed to be filled. This 'overbearing' attitude towards the great men of the shires was a novel experience for them but it was essential if a truly 'national' defence force was to be established.

Norreys had witnessed at first hand in the Netherlands how a powerful invader could be harassed, impeded and even checked by determined defenders, and laid down a detailed strategy for the protection of the realm. It embraced harassing the invaders at their landing points, destroying standing crops and removing stock, horses, wagons and anything else that might be of use to the enemy, and the selecting of suitable locations at which to confront them in pitched battle. As soon as it was known (in early June) that Philip's massive fleet of 151 ships had left their Iberian harbours, the government anxiously awaited news of their progress, in order to calculate when to order mobilization. Leaving it too late would be disastrous. Initiating it too soon would be a considerable waste of money. The army was to be concentrated at three points – a main force at Tilbury under Dudley's leadership (much to Norreys's chagrin); another in London to safeguard queen and capital; and a third south of the Thames to be ready if and when the enemy made landfall. Norreys spent his time with the third force, keeping well away from Tilbury. It was there that Elizabeth made her famous address to the troops, defying Philip to do his worst. What commentators rarely mention about this speech is its peroration. Elizabeth gave a ringing endorsement of her lieutenant general – 'than whom never prince commanded a more noble or worthy subject'.[8] It was Dudley and not Norreys who received this public expression of royal confidence.

Within weeks, the earl was dead. Black Jack Norreys survived until 1597, living a soldier's life to the end. A raid with Francis Drake on the Portuguese coast was followed by bravado expeditions in Brittany and won him acclaim without achieving much in military terms. In 1595, he was ordered again to Ireland. The exhausting and intractable problems of that province would have taken their toll on any commander but Norreys was beset by old and familiar problems – inadequate supplies, inefficient organization and opposition at court (for which he bore some share of responsibility). One of his last letters indicates that few of the fundamentals of military life had changed during the course of his career:

> I lament that I am trodden to the ground with bitter disgrace and the memory of my former desert disgraced and this upon mistaken information . . . I am now set to an impossible task, whereat my enemies do laugh in their sleeves.[9]

Sir John Norreys died on 3 July 1597.

8

SHIPS AND SHIPMEN

... the sea being smooth,
How many shallow bauble boats dare sail
Upon her patient breast, making their way
With those of nobler bulk!
But let the ruffian Boreas once enrage
The gentle Thetis, and anon behold
The strong-ribb'd bark through liquid mountains cut;
... Where's then the saucy boat
Whose weak, untimber'd sides but even now
Co-rivall'd greatness?

Troilus and Cressida, I. iii. 34–44

England's coast dwellers understood well the changing moods of wind and wave in waters that were unpredictable. The North Sea, English Channel and Irish Sea were perilous but excellent training areas for succeeding generations of fishermen, boat-builders and coastal traders. If the beginnings of a great mercantile empire were established during the reign of the first Elizabeth it was because centuries of experience, skill and courage had created a firm foundation.

From communities huddled in sheltered bays, villages on the banks of navigable rivers and towns overlooking wide estuaries, the fishing fleets had, from time out of mind, sailed forth, season after season, in search of the fish that formed a major part of the nation's diet. Most fishermen did not limit their activities to local waters. The men from Brighton (then spelled 'Brightelmeston'), for example, followed an annual schedule. As soon as winter had released its grip, the smarter vessels trawled along the Kent coast in search of plaice, while the larger boats ventured further out in the Channel for mackerel. From June to November the more seaworthy craft (between 15 and 40 tons) made their way to Scarborough for cod and Yarmouth for herring. During their time away from home, the fishermen sold their catch in northern markets, where foreign merchants as well as local buyers congregated.

The pattern was very different along the west-facing coasts of England and Wales, due to long connections with markets in the Iberian Peninsula and along the Biscayan coast, as well as the possibilities of transatlantic voyages. By the 1570s, vessels of 40 tons and more were making annual trips to Newfoundland and bringing home cargoes of cod and 'train oil' (oil extracted from marine creatures – in this case, cod). Devon mariners sold these commodities in markets as far north as Chester and there are records of large consignments of salt-preserved fish being sent to London. The western fishermen had the advantage of being less bothered by the political confrontations that often bedevilled trade through the Narrows. French and Spanish merchants, frustrated by the conflicts of their governments with the Netherlands and the piracy rampant in the English Channel were only too ready to do business with the men who came from Devon and Cornwall, even when their respective governments were at war. As well as the centuries-old trade in wine from Bordeaux, shipmasters of the English south-west brought in from Spain and Portugal cargoes of more essential commodities such as salt, indispensable as the only means of keeping fish and meat edible and palatable. Traditional fishing harbours could easily develop into thriving trading ports, providing they were linked, by sea and land, with an efficient infrastructure.

What was good for fishing and good for commerce was inevitably good for shipbuilding. The development of the North Devon economy provides an excellent example of the symbiosis of various trades. The first half of Elizabeth's reign was a boom time for this area. Merchants were bringing in a variety of cargoes – salt, wine, dried fruit, iron, oil, pitch – to ports such as Torrington, Bideford and Barnstaple, sheltered from the worst of the weather but enjoying easy access to the Atlantic. This created a demand for ships and men to man them. Shipyards at Bideford, Northam and Appledore had full order books. Their prosperity stimulated a wide hinterland. Young men came looking for work on shipboard or in the shipwrights' yards. Gloucestershire clothiers brought their woollens here instead of to the eastern ports. General merchants built warehouses on the quays and moored their own ships there. As early as 1565 an Exeter merchant ordered a 250-ton vessel from Bideford builders. This was extremely large by the standards of the day (few North Devon ships exceeded 40 tons) but, by the end of the century, it was not much out of the ordinary. By then ventures to Newfoundland and other parts of the American seaboard were becoming routine, and government spokesmen referred to these voyages as the 'nursery of seamen'.

Thus, the emergence of England as a leading maritime nation was based on skills and experience passed on from father to son for generations. But that alone does not fully explain the phenomenon. What provided the stimulus for Elizabeth's mariners to venture far beyond their traditional trade routes was rivalry with Spain – a rivalry spurred on by desire to share in the profits of long-distance commerce – especially with the New World – and also by religious conflict. To many of the queen's Protestant subjects, the major Catholic powers of Spain and Portugal (united under one crown from 1580) assumed an exclusive right (granted by the pope in the Treaty of Tordesilas as long ago as 1494) to explore and exploit all those parts of the earth which might yet be discovered. Such an assumption was like a red rag to the bull of English maritime pride.

Yet we must not idealize the captains and crews who operated out of English ports. They were men hardened by their constant struggle with the elements and driven by their need to keep their families above the breadline. Out at sea there was only the finest of lines drawn between law and licence and no magistrates on hand to enforce law. Strict morality was a frequent victim of the harsh conditions of shipboard life.

> LUCIO: Thou conclud'st like the sanctimonious pirate that went to sea with the Ten Commandments, but scrap'd one out of the table.
> 2ND GENTLEMAN: 'Thou shalt not steal'?
> LUCIO: Ay, that he raz'd.

> *Measure for Measure*, I. ii. 7–11

Such offhand cynicism is a fair indication that piracy was an accepted aspect of marine life and that few crews were above it. Given the opportunity, ships' masters of all nations were ready to prey upon vulnerable vessels, remove the cargo, then scuttle the ship with its unfortunate mariners to destroy any evidence. Piracy was a capital offence but prosecutions were few. One good reason was that wealthy and influential backers of sailing ventures expected to take their share of the profits – however those profits were achieved. To see how maritime enterprise developed during the early years of the reign, how it involved all ranks of society and how it impacted on international relations at the highest level we can do no better than consider the career of a leading sea captain-cum-businessman-cum-naval administrator.

John Hawkins was born in 1532 into a seafaring family. His father was a successful shipowner and merchant and a prominent member of Plymouth society. He could afford to give his second son a good education and by the time John was in his mid-teens he was able to take his place in the family business alongside his elder brother, William. Business was good, especially during 1557–8, when England was at war with France. This gave piracy a veneer of patriotism. Merchant ships attacked each other while their respective governments looked on. By the time he was in his mid-twenties, Hawkins was a rich man – rich, independent and ambitious. He sold up his share in the family business and established himself in London, where he could find influential backers ready to support his grandiose plans. He was thinking transatlantic, by which he meant not voyages to Newfoundland or Iberia, but to the Portuguese and Spanish settlements on the coasts and islands of West Africa and South America. These precarious trading posts owed loyalty to their home governments and were not supposed to do business with 'interlopers' but the reality was that they were isolated colonies, far from their homelands and in need of a more vigorous exchange of imports and exports than the fleets from Seville and Lisbon could guarantee them. The world's two greatest maritime empires had serious flaws and Hawkins was intent on exploiting them.

Between 1562 and 1569 he led three extremely profitable trading expeditions. To Hawkins must go the credit for inventing what a later age would know as the notorious 'triangular traffic'. He sailed to the Guinea coast, calling en route at ports where the Portuguese agents were prepared to do business. Reaching Africa, he went ashore and raided the immediate hinterland for human cargo – slaves (sometimes aided by the Portuguese and their allies among the local rulers). These he shipped to the New World plantations, whose owners were desperate for workers more robust than the indigenous people. The authorities in Seville and Lisbon could not but regard with mounting indignation what Hawkins claimed as 'honest trade'. Whenever possible they impounded his ships, imprisoned his crews and confiscated his cargoes. Hawkins complained and was backed by his own government. But Elizabeth and her council were in no position to assume the moral high ground. In November 1568, four Spanish merchantmen took refuge from storms in Plymouth and Southampton. They carried £85,000, which was urgently needed by the Duke of Alba to pay his troops in the Netherlands. Elizabeth, always haunted by money problems, simply could not ignore this windfall. Despite angry protests from King Philip, she appropriated the money. Along with the Earl of Leicester, the Lord Admiral and other members of the Council, the queen was already among Hawkins's financial backers. Despite the losses he had incurred, he and his patrons made substantial profits from the three slaving ventures. Unofficial support for maritime adventures of dubious moral and legal probity were becoming second nature to the government as relations with Spain worsened.

Because neither side could afford open hostility a state of cold war persisted between England and Spain but, while the two governments maintained the niceties of diplomatic etiquette, feelings in the maritime communities reached white heat. One incident above all others inflamed passions among those who 'went down to the sea in ships' – the 'massacre' of San Juan d'Ulúa. In February 1568, Hawkins, homeward bound with six ships already badly mauled by storms, put in at the island of San Juan d'Ulúa, near Vera Cruz, to carry out essential repairs and rest his men before the Atlantic crossing. Within hours of his arrival, a heavily armed Spanish fleet arrived, also seeking safe anchorage. Aboard was the new Viceroy of Mexico, Don Martin Enriquez. According to Hawkins, the two captains agreed to share the haven, but the next morning Enriquez launched an attack. Battle raged all day and only with the coming of night were the English able to escape seawards. By then they had lost ninety men and four of their ships. Worse trials awaited them in the open ocean. By the time Hawkins sighted the Cornish coast on 25 January 1569, he had only one leaking ship left of his original flotilla, manned by fifteen exhausted men of the five or six hundred with whom he had set out (one other vessel, similarly stricken, had limped home separately). Hawkins had paid the price for 'trespassing' in waters the Spanish government regarded as its private domain and Enriquez felt fully justified in dealing harshly with the 'poachers'. That, of course, was not how ordinary Englishmen saw the matter. Throughout the South-west there was scarcely a family not mourning the loss of a loved one in 1569. There was a groundswell of hatred for Catholic Spain and a clamour for reprisals. Legitimate trade with the Iberian nations now all but ceased and overt piracy grew.

The government was in a dilemma. While anxious to maintain normal diplomatic relations, it had to contend with a hostile public opinion *and* it was still furtively profiting from the proceeds of piracy.

International tension reached a new level in 1580. That was the year the crowns of Spain and Portugal – and, therefore, their respective empires – were united. Now the treasures of the Orient would be poured into Philip II's coffers, along with those of the New World. These would not prove adequate for his needs; the conflict in the Netherlands and the losses to pirates ensured that his government descended further and further into debt. But to other maritime nations, seeking a share in world trade, this massive monopoly was a threat which had become intolerable. For England an even more significant event occurred on 12 October 1580. At Greenwich Palace on that autumn Sunday, the queen spent six hours in private conversation with a mere sea captain. He was a kinsman of John Hawkins who had been brought up in the mariner's Plymouth household and had learned about ships and ship-men on voyages under his relative's command. His name was Francis Drake and he had just returned from his his-toric circumnavigation of the globe. Elizabeth had been one of his principal backers and she now gained a substantial tranche of the voyage's profits, much of which had come from Drake's plundering of ships and settlements along the Pacific seaboard of the Americas. The queen now had a choice: she could either make a terrible example of the pirate, 'El Draco' (the 'Dragon', as Spaniards called him), as Philip's ambassador insisted, or she could gratefully pocket her £160,000 share of his loot (roughly equivalent to one year's government expenditure). There was no contest, as Elizabeth demonstrated a few days later when Drake was knighted on the deck of his own ship.

In that same year, Robert Hitchcock, a Buckinghamshire gentleman and expert on matters military, wrote a pam-phlet for presentation to the queen. He was one of a number of commentators on the contemporary political scene who were offering the government advice on prepa-ration for the bloody showdown with Spain, which they saw as inevitable. Hitchcock's answer was, in a word, 'fishing'. He suggested that money should be raised for the building of four hundred fishing boats of seventy tons each. They should be sent into England's traditional fisher-ies, but especially into the Newfoundland waters. As well as the obvious commercial advantages (he advocated that Wednesdays should be made compulsory 'fish days', like Fridays), this endeavour would stimulate shipbuilding and all the trades connected with the equipping and victualling of sea-going vessels and solve the vagabondage problem, since all idle men would be liable to be pressed into becoming crew members. Hitchcock's clinching argument was that his scheme

> Will breed such store of mariners that, whensoever the noble navy of England shall be set to the seas for the safeguard of this land, there shall be no want of mariners to serve in the same, whereas now they be but scant and hard to be found.[1]

What did the writer mean by 'the noble navy of England'? The government kept only a few fighting ships as a charge on the national coffers. Traditionally, when an emergency arose the royal fleet was augmented by commandeering merchantmen. In 1560, Elizabeth's navy consisted of twenty-two vessels fit for service. There was little change over the next twenty years, but 1580 began a prodigious surge in shipbuilding. This was partly as a response to the concerns of activists such as Hitchcock, although there was no question of the queen sanctioning his grandiose scheme. If any one man was responsible for putting the royal navy in a state of preparedness for the Spanish onslaught of 1588, that man was John Hawkins.

In 1577, he became Treasurer of the Navy and a member of the Navy Board. He brought to his task both business acumen and first-hand experience of handling ships and men, and his reforming zeal was felt in two areas: bureaucracy and ship design. Hawkins attacked the corruption of the previous regime, which extended from the top right down to the dockyard operators. When money was provided for maintenance, repair or new building, everyone along the contract chain creamed off profit. That was the system. Hawkins could not change it but he did considerably tighten up controls. He made sure that the funds went further than previously. That meant that when expenditure increased, because of the new-build programme,

government got more for its money. The annual sum spent
on the navy rose from around £10,000 in 1580 to more than
£90,000 in 1588.

By the time Philip's invasion fleet set sail, England was
able to muster thirty-four royal fighting ships, half of
which were of 300 tons or more. To this were added 192
privately owned vessels, either commandeered or offered
for service. Two-thirds of the queen's ships had been built
or rebuilt during the previous decade in accordance with
revolutionary design concepts. Older vessels had carried
tall fore and aft superstructures ('castles') making them
imposing and offering more space for armaments. The new
fighting ship was narrower, sleeker and – most importantly
– more manoeuvrable. Less wind resistance enabled it to
turn more easily and to position itself either at a distance for
firing its cannon or alongside the enemy for grappling and
boarding. Much thought and invention had also gone into
the design of naval ordnance. English artillery weapons
were acknowledged as the best in Europe. This was largely
thanks to the development of iron foundries in the Kentish
Weald. Another innovation from which England's mariners
benefited was the development of efficient gun carriages.
Cannon were cumbersome weapons and this, coupled with
their powerful recoil, made them difficult and dangerous
to handle in the confined space of a ship's deck. Experts
at Chatham and Portsmouth, by now established as the
major royal dockyards, invented a lighter, more stable gun
carriage, with four wheels instead of two, which made
the guns easier to handle and quicker to reload. This
did not totally eliminate the risks involved in carrying
explosive devices on wooden ships, as an incident in 1595
demonstrates:

> The gunner being careless, as they are many time of their
> powder in discharging certain pieces in the gunroom, set a
> barrel of powder on fire, which blew up the admiral's cabin,

slew the gunner with 2 others outright, and hurt 20 more, of which 4 or 5 died.[2]

Firepower in the sixteenth century had still a long way to go before it reached the destructive potential it achieved at the time of Nelson. There was little chance of sinking an enemy vessel; the missiles were not heavy enough, nor were the gunners skilled enough to inflict fatal damage. Cannon were used to kill and maim crews, cripple ships and thus make them vulnerable to boarding.

In battle any ship was only as good as its crew. As in land armies, numbers were made up of a large percentage of vagrants, criminals and pressed men. In 1585, John Hawkins drew Burghley's attention to this situation and, as a solution, suggested that professional seamen should be paid more.

By this means her Majesty's ships will be furnished with able men, such as can make shift for themselves, keep themselves clean without vermin and noisomeness which breedeth sickness and mortality ... There is no captain or master exercised in service, but would undertake with more courage any enterprise with 250 able men than with 300 of tag and rag, and assure himself of better success. The wages being so small causeth the best men to run away, to bribe and make mean to be cleared from the service, and insufficient, unable and unskilful persons supply the place, which discourageth the captains, masters and men, that know what service requireth.[3]

Hawkins knew well the difficulties of commanding men in the small space of a ship at sea. Disease and injury were trials that had to be endured but the incompetence and insubordination of inexperienced and unwilling sailors raised other problems which Hawkins, like Hitchcock, looked to government to circumvent.

In an age when differences of social ranking were clear-cut we would expect strict hierarchy to exist on board a ship of war and that is exactly what we find. Every crew member had his place, determined by experience, function and social standing. At the bottom of the heap were the boys and younkers (youngsters). These children and teen-agers were the fetchers and carriers of the ship. They were the equivalents of trade apprentices, learning by experience the workings of a great ship. Some of them were designated as grummets or cabin boys, assigned, permanently or tem-porarily, to the officers. If the ship was carrying troops, they came under the command of the provost martial. His equivalent among the seamen was the boatswain. Since he was in charge of all the 'tackle' – ropes, sails, rigging, anchors, cables and boats – he was obviously the man on whom the minute-to-minute manoeuvring of the vessel rested. He controlled the teams who raised and lowered anchors, took in and let out sail, lowered longboats, etc. He stalked the deck, enforcing prompt obedience with his knotted rope. More drastic punishment included whipping and ducking. Discipline was necessarily harsh, bearing in mind the quality of the average seaman and the fact that every man on board was, in his own small way, responsible for the safety of the entire ship's complement. Mishaps were common and could have very serious consequences. Lord Admiral Howard reported to Burghley one such incident that led to the *Elizabeth Bonaventure* suffering severe fire damage:

> There were two poor knaves that came from Chester that strived for a place to hand up their netting [hammocks] for to lie in, and one of them had a piece of candle in his hand, and in striving, the candle fell down where there lay some oakum ... I hope to make them a warning to others to beware.[4]

The officers, who had varied responsibilities, are easily identifiable by their titles. The swabber kept the ship clean. The purser looked after the accounts and supervised the stores of tools, materials and food. The quartermaster oversaw the cook and saw to the feeding of the crew, but he also steered the ship. The coxswain was in charge of the longboat when launched and of training the oarsmen. The duties of the master gunner are self-explanatory. The master was the navigating officer. On his skills with astrolabe, cross-staff, back-staff and quadrant depended the vessel's maintenance of a true course, as set by the captain.

Victualling the queen's ships was a constant problem. It was vital to maintain the health and strength of crewmen and nothing was to be served by keeping them on short rations. However, storing sufficient food and keeping it fresh for days or weeks at sea was difficult. Officially the allocations for royal navy personnel were: a gallon of beer and a pound of biscuit per day, supplemented by a pound of salt beef or pork on four days a week and fish, cheese and butter on the other three. How much of this actually reached the mariners is doubtful. Obtaining supplies and eking them out sensibly taxed the brains of pursers and quartermasters. And even of their exalted superiors. In another letter of Lord Howard to Burghley, the admiral explains the stratagems necessary to keep the fleet fed as it waited in harbour for news of the Spanish Armada in May 1588:

> I have received your lordship's letter, where in you desire that a certain ship, called the *Mary* of Hamburg, stayed at Plymouth, may be suffered to pass with her lading of rice, almonds and other goods, to London, whither she is bound. Your Lordship shall understand that we have barely three weeks' victuals left in our fleet, being bound in by the wind, and watching the first opportunity of the same to go forth unto the seas; and that therefore, for our better provision and prolonging of our victuals, I have caused the said rice to be stayed and taken for her Majesty's use, paying for the same as it is valued at. And for the ship, and the rest of her lading, I will give orders that she may pass hence to London . . .[5]

Sailors in the queen's ships were just as much prey as soldiers in her armies to the ubiquitous menace of corruption. If they could get away with sharp practice, victuallers over-priced and under-supplied provisions. Pursers pocketed some of the money that had been allocated for food. Quartermasters worked hand-in-glove with victuallers for their mutual profit. It is scarcely surprising that, as one commentator observed, men were as willing to serve in the royal navy as they would have been to be prisoners of war, set to work in enemy galleys.

But Elizabeth's England boasted a few brave – or foolhardy – spirits whose imaginations were fired by the exploits of men like Drake and Hawkins. Piratical raids on Spanish ships and settlements continued unabated now that England was formally at war with Spain. Humphrey Gilbert and Walter Raleigh both made unsuccessful attempts to establish North American colonies to solve England's overpopulation problem and provide bases for further intervention in King Philip's monopolistic commercial activities. But the real prizes were to be found, not on the Atlantic seaboard, but in the lands and islands of the Pacific. The pioneer adventurers had brought back mouth-watering tales of the wealth of the Indies. Astronomical profits were within the grasp of any captain who could gain access to the Orient and bring back cargoes of silk, gems, ivory and spices (pound for pound, pepper was more valuable than gold). An exciting spirit of enterprise gripped the commercial community. Trading enterprises such as the Muscovy and Cathay companies were set up and encouraged exploration by bold captains. Martin Frobisher made three failed attempts to locate a north-east passage around America to the lucrative Indies. Such expeditions attracted a number of young men looking for fame and fortune.

To succeed in sailing to the other end of the world through mountainous seas along trade routes patrolled by Spanish and Portuguese men-o'-war demanded of a captain more than courage; he had to be strong-willed and ruthless in driving his crews to the end of their endurance – and beyond. Hawkins and Drake were commanders of that stamp. Others were not.

Thomas Cavendish was the third son of a well-to-do Suffolk squire. He was possessed of ambition, self-belief and youthful arrogance. When Drake returned from his round-the-world voyage, Cavendish was twenty and newly established among the fashionable elite at the royal court. He was a compulsive gambler, often in debt. His imagination was fired by the leading maritime adventurers and he invested in some of their exploits. As a member of Walter Raleigh's entourage he studied navigation in the unofficial 'academy' which met in the courtier's house. His first taste of life at sea was in a voyage to Raleigh's Virginia settlement in 1585, in which he acquitted himself well and won the respect of senior mariners. What Cavendish now dreamed of doing was repeating Drake's circumnavigation. He was impatient to embark on this grand adventure and, to this end, he poured money into acquiring ships and men. This drove him to the brink of bankruptcy, a fate only staved off by the profits brought in by sending his little fleet on pirate raids. Drake had established trading contacts with oriental merchants and princes and, in so doing, had laid down a challenge to other captains to follow his lead and reap the rewards of regular trade with the Indies. Early attempts to take up this challenge had come to grief. Cavendish's bid for fame and glory began in July 1586, when he sailed out of Plymouth with the *Desire* (120–140 tons) and two small vessels. He had prepared as well as possible for the expedition, talking with men who had accompanied Drake and obtaining backing from some of the nation's leaders. Forward planning and reliable crews gave Cavendish a good advantage and the first phase of the voyage went well. Landfalls on the coasts of Sierra Leone and Brazil enabled him to revictual with freshly hunted meat and fruit. By the end of the year, the voyagers had safely reached the southern Patagonian coast.

They safely located the Straits of Magellan and thus avoided the furies of Cape Horn. Halfway through they were met with a dismal sight. The Spanish government had set up a little colony there to guard the straits and prevent any other foreign captain repeating Drake's passage. By the time Cavendish arrived, the original complement had been reduced to a handful of weak, half-starved survivors of the harsh climate and the unfriendly indigenes, surrounded by the unburied corpses of their comrades. They begged the English for safe passage to Peru but Cavendish, having helped himself to twelve abandoned cannon, took advantage of a favourable wind to sail on into the Pacific. Cavendish's men had negotiated their biggest natural challenge and received a lesson in the harsh realities of colonial life.

But they were now entering a zone dominated by their Spanish and Portuguese rivals from their bases in Peru and Indonesia. The potential peril was made very clear the first time Cavendish's ships stopped for fresh water. His landing party was attacked by Spanish troops. Twelve men were killed and others were taken prisoner before the longboat could pull away from the beach. Cavendish more than repaid this hostility. He continued up the coast indulging in an orgy of vengeance. He and his men burned every undefended settlement and unguarded ship they came across. Reporting to his backers after his return, Cavendish exulted in the death and destruction he had meted out – proof of his Hispanophobia, ratcheted up by the ordeal of his long journey. At Arica he captured four merchant vessels and held them to ransom, demanding the return of his captured men. When his ultimatum was rejected, Cavendish sent his prizes to the bottom of the harbour.

King Philip's subjects were not his only problem. Scurvy and ship fever were decimating his crews. One ship had to be scuttled because he did not have enough men left to handle her. This manpower shortage cost him dear when he was presented with the best opportunity of the entire expedition. He fell in with and captured the 700-ton *Santa Anna*, a merchantman laden with gold, silk, pearls and civet (used in perfumes). By now Cavendish did not have hold space for all his prize's valuable cargo. He spent two weeks sorting through the *Santa Anna's* treasures, took what he could carry, then sank her. Worse was to follow. His crew insisted on an immediate share-out of the spoils and Cavendish gave in to them. Now all his men could think of was getting home as quickly as possible to spend their loot. Some took the *Desire's* sister ship and tried to return the way they had come. They were never heard of again.

Having given evidence of weakness, the young captain demonstrated his immaturity by behaving with intolerable arrogance towards the friendly people of Samór in the Philippines where he next dropped anchor. The outraged local bishop described him as, 'an English youth of about twenty-two years, with a wretched little vessel of about a hundred tons' who dared to 'come to my own place of residence, defy us, and boast of the damage he had wrought'.[6]

The Orient, with all its commercial possibilities, now lay open before the English pioneers, but they could not exploit its commercial possibilities. The vision of direct trade with the East had to be abandoned. The voyage of the *Desire* had become just another example of piracy on the high seas. She left Java on 16 March 1588, enjoyed a providentially calm crossing of the Indian Ocean, rounded the Cape, still enjoying good weather, which persisted till she was lashed by storms in the English Channel. The *Desire* finally dragged herself into Plymouth on 3 September, in the aftermath of the victory over the Armada.

From a commercial point of view, the voyage had been a moderate success. Cavendish's patrons were well rewarded for their investment, but if they had expected rewards on the scale of those that had been gained from

Drake's circumnavigation they were disappointed. Few potential backers were falling over themselves to support another expedition led by Thomas Cavendish. He, with his usual bravado, made every effort to cash in on his voyage. Emulating Drake, he took the refurbished *Desire* to Greenwich where he entertained the queen and lavished gifts upon her. This, however, did not net him the hoped-for knighthood and the establishment was decidedly cool about supporting the more ambitious expedition Cavendish now tried to organize. He was frantic to complete his work, based on the lessons learned on the 1586–8 voyage, the more so because rival mariners, English and Dutch, were also looking to the Orient. But Cavendish was his own worst enemy. Few people could see beyond the boastful, arrogant exterior of this thick-skinned young 'wastrel'. But, by sheer determination and invincible self-belief, he succeeded in assembling a fleet of four capital ships and a pinnace, manned by 350 sailors and soldiers.

Such a large undertaking, facing the challenges of natural hazards, divided counsels, enemy action and disease, demanded leadership of the highest calibre. Cavendish did not possess it. His problems began even before his ships left port. Problems over equipment and manning delayed embarkation. To make up lost time – and thus to reach Magellan's Strait during the southern summer – Cavendish decided to head directly for Brazil, without stopping on the African coast to replenish supplies and make necessary repairs. This led to arguments with senior crewmen, some of whom were more experienced than him. When he encountered disagreement, Cavendish was unable to find the line between firm discipline and violent bullying. Off the South American coast, the flotilla was subjected to, first, doldrums and, then, severe storms. It was here that the desertions began. One ship turned for home. Cavendish recorded in his journal that his men were 'the most abject minded and mutinous company that ever was carried out of England'[7] but he was unable to impose his will on it. Instead, he became a raving paranoid, who saw personal treachery in everyone who ventured to express an opinion at variance with his own.

Battling through the Straits at the worst time of year and losing scores of crewmen to exposure and fatigue, the ships were forced to turn back. Now arguments broke out between those who wanted to return to Brazil for rest and refitting and those who proposed making an attempt to reach the Orient by sailing eastwards, round the Cape of Good Hope. They settled on the former course but, almost immediately, the fleet was split up by foul weather. Cavendish, in his flagship, never saw the other vessels again and was convinced that their captains had deserted. The inevitable showdown occurred sometime in March or April 1592. In a last attempt to assert his authority Cavendish made a 'death or glory' speech to his 'cowardly' crew. He urged them to, 'Cheerfully go forward to attempt either to make themselves famous in resolutely dying, or in living to perform that which [would] be to their perpetual reputations.'[8] It was a challenge that might have stirred hearts and stiffened wills had it been uttered by a more inspiring leader, but Cavendish's men had lost all confidence in their captain. His next action confirmed their disdain for him. When they refused to continue the voyage, he grabbed one of the ringleaders and tried, single-handedly, to hang him. Devoid, now, of any clear purpose, the ship zigzagged the Atlantic and, when no haven was found, course was finally set for home.

For Cavendish that meant failure and humiliation. These he could not face. He skulked in his cabin, made his will and contemplated death.

> . . . rather than thus basely to return home again . . . had I found an island which the charts make to be in 8 degrees southwards of the line, I swear to you I sought it well with

diligence, meaning, if I had found it, to have there ended my unfortunate life.[9]

The rest is silence. Sometime in May or June 1592, Thomas Cavendish died at the age of thirty-two. Suicide? Murder? Or, as the received story had it, death from a broken heart?

Whatever the truth of the matter, Cavendish's story does provide us with a corrective to the heroic legend of Elizabeth's brave 'sea dogs'. Life for England's sixteenth-century mariners was hard. From the fishermen who plucked a living from the inshore waters, to those who espoused a life of crime on the high seas and the pioneers who determined 'to boldly go' where none of their countrymen had gone before, Elizabethan seafarers were a rough, unscrupulous breed, toughened by their calling. Their success against the Armada and their plundering of Spanish treasure ships were the bright episodes in a narrative that was harsh, black and, for much of the time, dreary. The vision of lucrative trade in eastern waters persisted, however, and in 1600 Elizabeth granted the charter to a new commercial enterprise, destined, in the fulness of time, to be the engine of English colonial expansion – the East India Company. With the coming of peace under James I, the royal navy was downsized. Without reformers of the stamp of Hawkins its organization became riddled with corruption. It would be a century or more before it could be claimed that Britannia ruled the waves. But the actions of Elizabeth's mariners had provided later generations with legends to inspire, an infrastructure of dockyards to improve the quality of ships, and a Navy Board (or Admiralty) to oversee the wellbeing of men and vessels. The only other ingredient needed to give England ultimate domination of the oceans was a vibrant seagoing community. And that was already in place.

9

MERCHANTS AND MERCHANDISE

*. . . my meaning in saying he is a good man is to have you
understand me that he is sufficient; yet his means are in
supposition: he hath an argosy bound to Tripolis, another to
the Indies; I understand, moreover, upon the Rialto, he hath
a third at Mexico, a fourth for England, and other ventures
he hath squander'd abroad. But ships are but boards, sailors
but men; there be land-rats and water-rats, water-thieves
and land-thieves, I mean pirates; and then there is the peril
of waters, winds and rocks. The man is, notwithstanding,
sufficient.*

The Merchant of Venice, I. iii. 14–23

Commerce, as Shylock well knew, was a risky business and
assessing a prospective client's creditworthiness was an
essential part of a merchant's professional life. European
banking as a separate operation that oiled the wheels
of commerce was in its infancy. Major banking houses,
like those of the Medici in Florence and the Fuggers in

Augsburg, were few and no such institutions existed in England. Wealthy merchants doubled as bankers, lending out surplus cash on interest to each other and to reliable clients, including the government. Prominent merchants in London and other cities led multifaceted lives: as well as trading in specific commodities, they provided credit facilities, owned property and were the leading figures in the social and political life of the municipalities. They were, in effect, the urban equivalents of the landed nobility, in many cases richer than the aristocracy and, through the vigorous role they played in the House of Commons, a community of growing political influence.

It was during Elizabeth's reign that London became the trading centre of northern Europe and we can attach a precise date to this development – 27 January 1571. On that day the queen formally opened the London bourse and ordained that it should be henceforth known as the Royal Exchange. Hitherto, Antwerp had dominated the region's commercial activity but its ascendancy was brought to an end by the Spanish Fury of November 1576. Spanish troops, angered by non-payment of their wages, went on a violent rampage through the Netherlands' city. Antwerp never recovered from this devastation because the commercial agents of other nations now relocated to the safety of London.

The building, which was henceforth the hub of England's mercantile life, was an impressive edifice, standing on ground between Three Needle Street and Cornhill. It consisted of a large open area (the trading floor), with covered walkways, like a monastic cloister, enclosed by four-storey buildings given over to shops (it has been called England's first shopping mall). It was the brainchild of one of the age's more remarkable wheeler-dealers. Thomas Gresham was born into a prominent London merchant family. His father was Richard Gresham, member of the Mercers' Company and sometime Lord Mayor, a wealthy citizen who enjoyed close relations with the royal court. Thomas was apprenticed to his uncle (also a mercer) and became a freeman mercer in 1543, at the age of about twenty-five.

He was now a member of an exclusive club whose senior officers, as well as regulating the standards and operating practices of their own trade, formed the aristocracy of the City. The term 'livery company' denotes the distinctive ceremonial dress proudly worn by members on major occasions and when participating in public processions. The companies of London originated, like their counterparts in other commercial centres, from trade guilds, some of which could trace their descent back to pre-Conquest times. Their prime function was to ensure the maintenance of high standards within their particular 'mystery' (profession). They regulated weights and measures, disciplined members whose behaviour threatened to bring the craft into disrepute, set regulations for apprenticeship and operated a closed shop which kept at bay unlicensed competitors. But, as elite bodies within urban society, they also performed various religious and civic functions. Before the Reformation they had maintained chapels and chantries and funded masses for the souls of past members. They were important channels of charitable activity. When a wealthy member made provision in his will for the founding of a school, the building of a bridge or the distribution of annual doles to the poor, it was usually his company that oversaw the execution of the benefactor's wishes. But the companies had become major landholders in their own right. Their portfolios extended from tenements let out to city dwellers to country estates worked by tenant farmers. The funds of these wealthy corporations were expended for the benefit of members, especially those who, through sickness or other misfortune, had fallen on bad times. But the liverymen also used their financial resources to influence society. For example, when, in 1561, the Merchant Taylors established a grammar school in Suffolk Lane, it was largely at the instigation of the current master, Richard

Hilles, a Protestant activist determined to see future generations brought up in the Reformed faith.

The London corporations also had to shoulder obligations placed upon them by the government. Thus, we find in their records charges demanded for 'cleansing the city ditch', 'setting the poor in Bridewell to work', selecting and equipping 'men of honest behaviour to serve the queen' in the army, and to fund the building of 'six ships of war and one pinnace'.[1] The companies were, indeed, the major building blocks in the edifice of municipal life. From them were drawn London's aldermen, city council members and lord mayors. Being a freeman of one of these bodies was an honour and a mark of distinction. Such status was occasionally conferred on prominent men (much as universities confer honorary degrees). For example, Thomas Becket and Thomas More had both been members of the Mercers' Company. Belonging to such an elite band was also a matter of *fellowship*. A company's calendar was punctuated by ceremonial events, feasts, religious observances and rituals at which members – and occasionally their wives – met to enjoy one another's society. The number of companies grew during the reign and there existed a definite ranking system among them. There were twelve companies that made up the 'first division' and, of those twelve, the Mercers' Company was the richest and most important.

The word 'mercer' derives from the Latin for merchandise and a mercer was a general merchant. However, in effect, members of this distinguished company dealt almost exclusively in luxury goods, especially textiles. Thomas Gresham brought into the country exotic silks and velvets, Flemish dressed cloths and tapestries, as well as what was for him something of a speciality – arms and armour. The basis of his export trade was woollen cloth. This had been long established as England's most valuable commodity but, by the 1570s, it was going through changeable and difficult times.

For more than a century the basis of England's overseas trade had been the various types of cloth produced in the major centres of East Anglia and the West Country (and, to a lesser extent, the uplands of Yorkshire and Lancashire). From the sheep to the shop business passed through several hands and, over the years, the various interested parties had formed power groups in their efforts to achieve greater control and, thus, secure higher profits. Internally, trade was dominated by regional entrepreneurs (clothiers), who had gradually drawn into their own hands the supply of raw product to the spinners and weavers and so were able to set the prices paid to the suppliers of cloth. Gloucestershire, Somerset and Devon supplied heavy, white broadcloth to the market, while the eastern producers sold a variety of lighter textiles, many of which, like Kersey and Lindsey, took their names from their villages of origin. The 'fustians' of the Pennine region were coarser cloths, largely destined for the home market. By the mid-sixteenth century several clothier dynasties had emerged – immensely rich families whose power and wealth are still in evidence in the fine houses they built for themselves and the 'wool churches' of Suffolk and Somerset whose construction they helped to finance. Cloths were sold undressed and undyed because continental craftsmen were more skilled in these techniques and had access to a variety of natural dyes. The men in control of external trade were the dealers (principally the mercers) of London and Bristol. They had formed themselves into monopolistic bodies in order to wrest control from the clothiers. The Company of Merchant Adventurers of London was, by charter, the only body whose members were allowed to export from the capital to mainland Europe and a similar body controlled the trade through Bristol. The Merchant Adventurers effectively prevented the clothiers shipping from other ports, some of which went into serious decline. The suppliers to London were obliged to bring their cloths to Bakewell Hall, in the heart of the City, next to the Guildhall, for the merchants to buy at their own predetermined prices.

Until the accession of Elizabeth mercer families like the Greshams had grown wealthy as a result of their unchallengeable position in the cloth market. But economic times were changing. There was underlying inflation, which had many causes and which was not understood by government. Merchants trading in non-essentials were faced with increasing rents and wage demands, while finding it difficult to put up their own prices. This, in itself, had little impact on men as wealthy as Thomas Gresham. What disrupted his commercial life was the worsening of relations with Spain, which made trade through the entrepôt of Antwerp more and more difficult. Gresham's response was to change the balance of his activities. Thanks to his overseas contacts and to his proven financial skills, he had become the Crown agent at Antwerp. His principal responsibility was arranging government loans with the leading European banking houses. In this capacity he was brilliant. After decades of mismanagement, which had seen the government debt soar and interest rates rise, Gresham negotiated more favourable terms with the German finance houses. Between 1560 and 1565, borrowing fell from £280,000 to £20,000. Elizabeth was not slow to recognize and reward Gresham's abilities. She conferred knighthood on him in 1559, appointed him temporary ambassador to the Spanish regent in the Netherlands and employed him as a major consultant in all things financial, such as the issue of new and purer coinage, which did much to restore confidence in the currency, confidence which previous administrations had squandered by debasement. The beginnings of mechanized currency manufacture were seen in 1561. Hitherto coins had all been hand struck. Now a screw press worked by horse-power was installed in the Tower of London mint, which resulted in items of greater uniformity.

Gresham's already large fortune grew exponentially as a result of his varied activities. He built himself an impressive city mansion on Bishopsgate Street and acquired country residences in Sussex and Middlesex, in addition to the family estates he had inherited in Suffolk and Norfolk. He extended his Lombard Street business premises and his organization expanded in line with his varied activities.

Meanwhile, the difficulties experienced by the textile trade were becoming critical. Market disruption occasioned by political friction, the dictates of fashion, energetic foreign competition and the impact of inflation combined to threaten the livelihood of workers, clothiers and mercantile corporations. Between 1567 and 1571, some 18,000 Calvinists were executed in the Netherlands. In France an estimated 10,000 Huguenots suffered a similar fate in the St Bartholomew's Day massacre and its aftermath. The trickle of men and women fleeing from religious persecution now became a torrent. Inevitably, they wanted work and they brought their skills with them. Others of their countrymen had already arrived – for a different reason. They had been brought over by enterprising English entrepreneurs who realized that the way to overcome foreign competition in the textile industry was to set up alien craftsmen in England in their own premises. Their impact was explosive. They gave rise to what soon became known as the 'new draperies'. These were very diverse kinds of lightweight cloths, woven from wool, silk and linen, with names like 'says', 'bays', 'serges', 'carrels' and 'oliots', and were created largely with the warmer lands of the Mediterranean in mind. Because the most profitable element in the production of finished cloth was fulling and dyeing, English merchants brought skilled artisans over from Germany and the Netherlands and paid farmers to grow the plants that produced the vegetable dyes. The new draperies rejuvenated the flagging traditional market and saved several English towns from terminal decline.

The impact of the influx of foreigners extended beyond the cloth trade. The men from the Low Countries and France set themselves up as printers, goldsmiths, shoe makers, tapestry-weavers, paper manufacturers and lace-makers, among other vocations. They introduced new fashions to England, such as Dutch-style gardens, and it may well be that it was these immigrants who changed native drinking habits. This was the time that Englishmen developed a taste for beer rather than ale. By adding hops to the recipe, brewers produced a more long-lasting beverage, which rapidly gained in popularity. As one historian has observed, these alien immigrants were 'the main factor in an industrial renaissance which had as much importance for the economic development of England as the literary and artistic renaissance had for its intellectual development'.[2] For the most part they established their premises outside the areas where local trade companies and guilds held sway, such as in the suburbs and villages around London.

English people have always had an ambivalent attitude towards immigrants and our sixteenth-century ancestors were no exception. In a report prepared for Parliament as early as 1559, Lord Burghley deplored the import of trifles such as pins, hats and gloves (prominent status symbols) by which foreigners 'filch from us the chief and substantial staples of the realm, where the people might be better employed in making them'.[3] He identified an ever-present ironical fact that as people become richer, their demand for possessions to express their wealth increases, thereby contributing to a trade imbalance which has the effect of diminishing the nation's overall wealth. Burghley approved of any new craft established in the country that would reduce England's dependence on imports. Such new crafts could only be taught by foreign experts.

Those whose livelihoods were at stake did not display the same detachment. Commercial companies and guilds petitioned the government for restrictions on immigrants.

Some instituted their own restrictive practices against the foreigners. They wanted to force new arrivals to channel their activities through the existing organizations. Their concerns found their way into the Statute of Artificers (1563), which imposed seven-year apprenticeships on everyone wishing to join a trade body, even if they were already fully trained craftsmen in another country. However, the growing foreign community was developing a power base of its own. When an attempt was made to give the law stronger teeth, in 1599, immigrant workers in London petitioned the queen to ban such restraint. As a result, the merchant community was instructed to desist from such discrimination. Government protection did not prevent bands of protestors taking direct action. In 1593, a notice was pinned to the door of the Dutch church (the old church of the Austin Friars which had been given to the Netherlanders for their worship), warning that if the strangers were not all gone by July, 'apprentices will rise to the number of 2,336. And . . . they will down with the Flemings'.[4] This was only one of several sporadic outbreaks of persecution. However, such xenophobia was only the expression of frustration with a situation that could not, realistically, be changed. When a group of London printers urged the Stationers' Company not to employ foreigners, the pragmatic reply was that if they sacked the immigrants, customers would simply take their business to independent alien printers because they appreciated the quality of their work.

Economic change invariably sorts the business men from the business boys. There are those who concentrate their efforts on trying to protect and sustain the status quo and those who embrace the new ways and try to turn them to their own advantage. Complaints poured in to the government from cloth workers, municipal corporations and tradesmen, urging the nation's leaders to do something to put an end to the lengthening list of bankrupt dealers and out-of-work artisans. In 1586, for example, the Council tried to resolve a dispute between West Country clothiers and the Merchant Adventurers. They concluded,

> . . . as matter most necessary in this time, for many respects, and especially for keeping of a great multitude of poor people in work by continuance of drapery in the aforesaid counties, that the clothiers should not lack the ordinary vent of their cloths at London for default of reasonable sales thereof to the merchants; and thereupon it was determined that the clothiers should be commanded to recontinue their former trade, and that they should ordinarily bring to the merchants at Bakewell Hall such sorts and numbers of cloths as they were in former seasons . . . to do, and in like manner the Merchant Adventurers should also buy the same at such reasonable prices as they were accustomed to do without any fraud or delay . . .[5]

But Elizabeth's ministers could not buck economic trends any more than Canute could have commanded the tide to turn. The difference between the two monarchs was that the king knew the limitations of royal edict and the queen did not. The monopolies system provides a telling example of the conflict between government power and economic forces. It was not just members of commercial corporations who sought to make a profit from trade. Acquisitive people from the queen downwards wanted their 'cut'. Government guarded jealously royal revenue from customs duties but another source of income was the granting of monopolies. Always strapped for cash, Elizabeth was open to appeals from courtiers and other favoured individuals offering to buy from her licences to control production or importation and sale of various commodities.

A cautionary tale about monopolies has as its central characters Sir Walter Raleigh and the vintner, John Keymer. In 1583, Raleigh, the queen's latest favourite, was granted the farm of wine – i.e. the right to sell retail licences to wholesale importers. One of the merchants the courtier now proceeded to enter into contract with was John Keymer, who obtained the right to sell wines in Cambridge. Unfortunately for him, this infringed the existing arrangement whereby the university grandees supplied the town with imported alcoholic beverages. The vice chancellor protested to the Council but his students took more direct action, ransacking Keymer's premises and assaulting his wife. When the merchant refused to yield to either kind of pressure, he was arrested, tried before the vice chancellor's court and imprisoned. There he stayed for eighteen months and was only released on providing assurances that he would abandon his attempt to operate in Cambridge.

Thomas Gresham was not among those who buckled under the weight of commercial inevitability. When cloth dealing became difficult, he supplemented his core export commodities with tin from Cornwall and lead from Derbyshire. He enjoyed the income from his property holdings in the capital and the provinces. But his major enterprise, and the one for which he is remembered, was the founding of the Royal Exchange. London merchants had long dreamed of having a permanent meeting place and Thomas's father had tried to make it a reality. What inspired them was the impressive Antwerp bourse, a custom-built edifice opened early in the century, which brought together in one place all the facilities traders needed to do their deals efficiently and comfortably. London merchants, by contrast, had to meet in each other's premises or congregate in groups on Lombard Street. Gresham's vision was, like everything else he undertook, composed of commercial ingenuity and self-interest.

What he could clearly see, and what he impressed upon the city fathers was that, if London could offer facilities that rivalled those of Antwerp, foreign merchants would readily make England's capital the centre for their commercial activities. He persuaded them to give permission for the compulsory purchase of existing buildings in return for which he promised to build a splendid business centre at his own expense. In fact, he did not employ only his own capital; he formed a consortium to buy property on Cornhill and clear the site. That done, construction began in the summer of 1566 and was completed thirty months later. The benefactor was in a hurry to launch the project because he wanted to get tenants into the shops that formed part of the complex in order to start collecting rents. Gresham took care to blazon his own importance in the new structure. At several points, it was adorned by his badge – a grasshopper – and a statue of Gresham himself was prominently placed. Early in the next reign, the dramatist Thomas Heywood wrote a play in which Gresham's achievements were eulogized. A contemporary described Venice's Rialto as 'but a bauble' by comparison. 'The nearest that which most resembled it,' he observed 'is the great bourse in Antwerp, yet not comparable either in height or wideness, the fair cellarage or goodly shops above . . . This Gresham hath much graced your city of London. His fame will long outlive him.' However, the building's success was not immediate. It took all of Gresham's entrepreneurial skill to find tenants for all the shops. He realized he needed the endorsement of an important patron. And who more important than the queen? Elizabeth loved men who loved money and knew how to acquire it. Thus

In the year 1570, on the 23 of January, the Queen's Majesty, attended with her nobility, came . . . to Sir Thomas Gresham's in Bishopsgate Street, where she dined. After dinner, her Majesty returning through Cornhill, entered the Bourse on the south side, and after that she had reviewed every part thereof . . . she caused the same Bourse by an herald and a trumpet, to be proclaimed the Royal Exchange, and so to be called from thenceforth, and not otherwise.[6]

But Gresham's beneficence (or, perhaps, his ego) was not satisfied with this accomplishment. He was determined to immortalize his name. In his will he stipulated that, after the death of his widow (their only son had died young), his residence in Bishopsgate should become a college where professors, paid for out of the Royal Exchange rents, would lecture on the seven sciences. He thus initiated Britain's first and still-existing adult education college. Among other benefactions initiated by Gresham was a row of almshouses.

He was certainly a man who loved to flaunt his wealth. When he was not entertaining royalty, he was entertaining royally. No expense was spared in dining and accommodating important friends and clients from Elizabeth's court and the grandees of the City. If ever the term 'merchant prince' could be applied to any man, that man was Thomas Gresham.

There were businesses that were beyond the scope of individual merchants to establish and develop. They required large injections of cash to get them off the ground, involved an element of risk and might take several months or years to yield a return. The answer was shared liability. A number of investors would come together to finance a venture and each would enjoy profit in proportion to the size of his investment. The queen and members of her court took up shares in the privateering ventures, exploratory voyages and colonizing enterprises of Hawkins, Drake, Cavendish and other bold mariners. Such activity was the origin of what became the joint stock company. Some such bodies were of recent origin when Elizabeth came to the throne. The Merchant Adventurers to New Lands and the Muscovy Company were set up during her predecessor's reign. But it was not only maritime activity that benefited from the principle of shared responsibility.

In 1568, Elizabeth granted charters to the Company of Mineral and Battery Works and the Mines Royal. There was an increasing demand for a variety of metal wares, from decorative ironwork for the mansions being built by the emerging gentleman-merchant class to pots and pans for humbler abodes; from agricultural tools to cannon. There were blast furnaces operating in the Weald of Kent and Sussex and in the Forest of Dean. There were specialist toolmakers working in towns such as Birmingham and Sheffield, but the finer and more intricate items were imported from Germany. The man who set himself the task of improving both the quality and quantity of native production was William Humfrey, goldsmith and assay master at the royal mint. He seems to have been someone with a good line in smooth patter and a desire for the quick buck. He had already been implicated in some shady operations at the mint. However, he won the confidence of William Cecil (later Lord Burghley) and travelled to Augsburg, home of Europe's finest armourers, in search of experts who could be persuaded to move to England and set up foundries and ateliers there. In 1565, he was able to report that he had made a deal with one Christopher Schütz:

That the said Christopher shall by his cunning erect mill or mills in such convenient place as shall be found meet for the plating of iron and steel, whereby may be made with it in this realm armour of such goodness and temperature as shall be thought most meet for the service of the Queen's majesty; also to make wire of iron and steel, which works are thought sufficient to set the people of some whole city on work, and for all manner [of] battery and wire works to be made of copper, and the mixed metal [brass] with the calamine stone [zinc], in such convenient place as shall be thought meet, which is also . . . like to set cities and towns to work . . .[7]

Humfrey's sales pitch was wildly optimistic, particularly if he envisaged English workmen being able to turn out armour comparable to the magnificent, elaborately decorated suits produced by the craftsmen of Augsburg and Nuremburg. However, the two companies were set up. The Mines Royal, financed by German money, began operation by extracting copper ore at Keswick. The Company of Mineral and Battery Works discovered zinc ore (calamine) in Somerset but failed to perfect the production of battery (i.e. beaten) utensils of brass. Nor did it have much more success in producing copper wire. Customers complained about the quality of the English wire and delivery delays. Iron wire, principally required to make the combs (cards) used in carding wool, proved more profitable.

It seems that workmen and investors soon began to see through William Humfrey. He dressed extravagantly and affected a luxurious lifestyle, doubtless to project a necessary 'image' of success. After only a year, he withdrew (or, perhaps, was forced to withdraw) from the companies. Now, still in association with Schütz, he turned his attention to lead production. The partners developed a new kind of smelting furnace using water power and installed it near Sheffield to work the ore coming from old Derbyshire mines. The furnace was Humfrey's only real success. It was more efficient and more economical with fuel than traditional smelting processes. Sadly for Humfrey, his success was his undoing. Midland landowners, such as the Earl of Shrewsbury, were so impressed that they set up mills on their own estates. Humfrey was still fighting in the courts to protect his patent rights when he died in 1579.

Humfrey was very far from being alone in pioneering new English industries and reinvigorating old ones. Government's desire to render the country as self-sufficient as possible, coupled with the ambition of landowners eager to exploit their estates in new ways created a climate in which men with new ideas could flourish. While the Earl of Shrewsbury was establishing ironworks at Chatsworth, his friend, Robert Dudley, Earl of Leicester, was doing exactly the same at Cleobury in Shropshire. The royal favourite was the largest landowner in the Midlands and Welsh border area and as ready to invest in blast furnaces as in privateering voyages. His iron master was a local man, John Weston, an adventurous young man, enthusiastic about the latest technology. Seeing that the Mines Royal was too preoccupied elsewhere to take up its copper mining rights in the South-west, Weston leased the Cornish mines and hired another German expert, Ulrich Fosse, to oversee the work. Unfortunately, the two men did not hit it off. There were frequent arguments between 'head office' and the 'workshop floor'. Fosse accused Weston of being a 'young scholar' who was only playing at being an industrialist. If there was any truth in this, Weston was not allowed the time to develop maturity as a businessman. He died suddenly in 1584.

It would be rash to label the expansion of industrial activity a 'revolution' but it certainly marked the beginning of an important diversification of business life. However, the manufacturing boom, which included a diverse range of activities beyond the production of metal goods (e.g. soap-boiling, sugar-refining, brewing and paper-making), was not without its cost. One was what, in today's jargon, we would call the threat to sustainable energy resources. Most of the manufacturing processes, at some point, involved burning wood. Other activities that made inroads into England's forests were shipbuilding, construction and domestic cooking and heating. This was beginning to become a matter for concern by the end of the reign. The answer – though it was but dimly realized at the time – was coal. In the last twenty years of Elizabeth's reign the import of coal into London trebled. It was known as 'sea coal' because it was brought to the capital, and other ports along the eastern seaboard, by coasters from Newcastle. The development of the coalfields of the North-east, the Midlands and South Wales was, according to one economist, 'little short of phenomenal'. Although most of the coal mined was sold within the region of production, this mineral fuel had become a major export overseas as well as to other parts of England. The production of Newcastle coal was in the hands of a consortium of some eighteen or twenty 'hostmen' or 'freehosts', who amassed considerable wealth from the trade. Indeed, they gained a reputation for profiteering. In 1590, the Lord Mayor of London complained to the Privy Council that the hostmen, 'Having coal pits of their own, and so engrossing the whole commodity, and reducing the trade into a few men's hands, have combined themselves to sell their sea coal at their own prices for their best advantage and the public detriment . . .'[8] The suppliers could claim that prices were fixed by the law of supply and demand. The market was king. Capitalism had come to stay. The age of Elizabeth was also the age of the entrepreneur.

10

DOCTORS AND DOCTORED

CASSIUS: *But soft, I pray you: what, did Caesar swound?*
CASCA: *He fell down in the market-place, and foamed at mouth, and was speechless.*
BRUTUS: *'Tis very like. He hath the falling sickness.*
CASSIUS: *No, Caesar hath it not; but you and I, And honest Casca, we have the falling sickness.*

Julius Caesar, I. ii. 250–5

What the Elizabethans called the 'falling sickness' we know as epilepsy. We understand that it is a neurological condition and one that, for most sufferers, can be managed. Managed, but not cured. The medical advances made over the last four hundred and fifty years have been prodigious, but we are still a long way from being complete masters of our mental and physical health (we cannot even cure the common cold) and that should make us wary of dismissing as 'primitive' the efforts of our sixteenth-century ancestors to deal with the ailments and diseases that afflicted them. In Shakespeare's day, one prescribed treatment for epilepsy was to prick the patient's little finger and with his/her blood to write on a piece of paper the mystic names Melchior, Jasper and Balthazar. This should be attached to the patient's clothing for a month while he/she recited daily three Paternosters and three Ave Marias. This, of course, did not rid the sufferer of the affliction but neither do our 'scientific' nostrums. The quest for perfect health is continuous and the doctors and physicians of the sixteenth century – for all that their therapies may seem quaint – were just as committed to it as our modern practitioners.

In an age when disease was a frequent visitor, when average life expectancy was thirty-five, and a quarter of all children born alive did not survive beyond the age of five, people turned – often in dire distress – to any who could offer hope of cure. The word 'doctor' might be translated as 'expert'. It indicated anyone who had mastered his subject to such a degree that he was qualified to teach others. There was a wide range of 'experts' available to Elizabeth and her subjects. At one end was the village wise woman who collected wild plants and concocted herbal remedies. Her ministrations were all that most Elizabethans could afford, though she was often viewed with suspicion because of her arcane knowledge and might be dubbed a witch by gullible folk who believed that her powers were of pagan or satanic origin. A more sophisticated operator was the apothecary who set up his shop in the high street, seeking to attract and impress passers-by with the paraphernalia of his profession.

> . . . in his needy shop a tortoise hung,
> An alligator stuff'd, and other skins
> Of ill-shaped fishes . . . and old cakes of roses,
> Were thinly scattered to make up a show . . .
>
> *Romeo and Juliet*, V. i. 42–8

Such tradesmen not only dealt in potions, unguents and perfumes, but might read horoscopes and even give medical diagnoses.

Those who considered themselves 'real' doctors regarded such practitioners with disdain. The 'qualified' men fell into two categories: physicians and barber surgeons. In crude terms, we might say that physicians worked from the inside out, while their rivals operated from the outside in. Physicians were the medical theorists of the day. They studied anatomy, sometimes working on the bodies of criminals to discover, for example, how muscles and tendons controlled movement and how the heart pumped blood. They based their studies on the principle that man is part and parcel of nature and this led them to experiment with the healing properties of plants and to consider how heavenly bodies influenced the health of their patients. The College of Physicians had been granted its charter by Elizabeth's father in 1518 and consisted of men who had obtained university degrees in medicine. Many of them had studied abroad, because the medical schools in centres such as Padua and Heidelberg were considered superior to those in the home universities. Professorships in physic or medicine had only been established as recently as 1546. There were other qualified physicians – men who, after examination, had been licensed by the Bishop of London, a practice which indicates the Church's long-standing relationship with the healing sciences.

The organization that vied with the College of Physicians for the lucrative trade of treating maimed or diseased bodies was the Company of Barber Surgeons, incorporated in 1540. Its members were much more 'hands on' in their approach to treating ailments. While the College, as its name suggests, was run on similar lines to academic institutions, issuing licences to applicants who had already studied for several years and obtained university degrees, the Company operated on more commercial lines. Young men wishing to become surgeons had to be apprenticed to a member of the Company and would only be licensed after proving their competence. The name 'barber surgeon' indicates the origins of this particular craft. Its exponents performed a wide variety of services for their clients. As well as trimming hair and beards, they extracted teeth, practised bloodletting (universally believed to be efficacious), lanced abscesses, branded criminals and set fractures.

It might appear from this that the various aspects of what we now consider to be the medical profession were well regulated but that is a long way from reality. For one thing, the two medical institutions, though operating a monopoly in London and its environs, had no authority in the provinces. What was happening throughout much of Elizabeth's reign was that the official bodies, as well as competing with each other, were striving to bring under control a profession that was being practised by hundreds of men who had no qualifications. The problem was that demand far exceeded supply. Illness and injury were so ubiquitous that there were innumerable potential patients willing to pay for treatment. The field was thus wide open to men who claimed to be competent in the curing of diseases or the setting of broken bones but who had no accreditation. Many were quacks who preyed on the vulnerable – those driven by pain or disability to hire anyone who offered to help them. But by no means all practitioners were con men or semi-skilled operators, as is demonstrated by the careers of two prominent Elizabethan doctors.

William Clowes, who rose eventually to the position of queen's surgeon, became a member of the Barber Surgeons' Company in 1569 but had not followed the route of apprenticeship ordained by the Company. In fact, we only know about his early training from his later acrimonious correspondence with the Company. He countered claims that he was ill-equipped to practise by asserting that he had established his career in 1563, at the age of nineteen, and that many grateful and influential patients would vouch for him. His principal patrons appear to have been the Dudley brothers, Earls of Leicester and Warwick. He served as surgeon in Warwick's naval expedition to Le Havre in 1563.

There was no better place to gain experience than aboard a ship of the queen's navy. Working one of these small vessels through the unpredictable waters of the Channel and the North Sea was hard and hazardous. On-board accidents were common enough without the added dangers of combat. But the use of gunpowder had greatly increased the hazards faced by sailors. Lead shot and wooden splinters might penetrate deep inside a man's body, not to mention the concussion or worse caused by falling spars. A shipowner was unlikely to send a crew to sea without a surgeon competent in resetting or amputating broken limbs or performing whatever emergency operations might become necessary. One of Clowes's more remarkable accomplishments was his operation on a sailor with broken ribs. Not only did he reset the ribcage on a ship ducking and weaving its way along the Channel, but he also successfully removed a fragment of bone from the patient's lung.

Such an outcome was, sadly, not common. A leading French surgeon of the day wrote a book for apprentices in which he laid down various rules of conduct. One read, 'It is always wise to hold out hope to the patient, even if the symptoms point to a fatal issue.' Descriptions of sixteenth-century operations and pictures of the surgical instruments employed suggest a very practical reason for such advice. Many a patient, if fully aware of the ordeal facing him and the likelihood of its failure, might well have opted for a quick death – thus depriving the surgeon of his fee. When a limb had to be amputated, a tight tourniquet was first applied above the site of the operation to prevent blood flow complicating the surgeon's work. The patient would then be restrained, usually by burly assistants strong enough to pin him to the chair or table. There

were, of course, no anaesthetics, though some practitioners placed faith in a well-known formula: 'Take of opium,
mandragora and henbane equal parts; pound and mix them
with water. Dip a rag in this and put it to the patient's nos-
trils. He will soon sleep so deep that you may do what
you wish.'[1] Such alleviation of pain was quite costly and
would not have been available to ordinary seamen and soldiers. All that could be done for them was the provision
of a stuffed pad to bite on, in order to stifle their screams.
After sharp knives had severed flesh and muscle, the bone
was cut with a saw. All that remained then was to cauter-
ize the wound. This was usually done with scalding hot
oil of elders, though some surgeons had come to realize
that this inflamed the wound as well as searing the veins,
arteries and nerve endings. They preferred some kind of
salve, such as might be concocted from eggs, oil of roses
and turpentine. If the patient survived the shock of this
treatment his problems were not necessarily over: there
was no understanding of septicaemia and post-operative
death from infection was common.

Ironically, the attendance of a surgeon at the birth of a
baby actually increased the threat to the mother. Puerperal
fever carried off a large number of women. In the majority
of cases, confinements were attended by the local midwives
who, if not professional, were, at least, experienced and gave
attention to cleanliness. Surgeons, on the other hand, were
less scrupulous (and, since there was no concept of clinical
hygiene, they had no reason to be). They and their tools
frequently conveyed germs from one patient to another. Of
course, that applied not only to maternity cases. The unwit-
ting transfer of infection must have carried off thousands
of men, women and children who entrusted themselves to
the surgeon's knife during the reign of Elizabeth. It certainly inhibited the development of operations that were
more invasive than the amputation or resetting of limbs.
This, in turn hampered the acquisition of knowledge about

the workings of the human body. The surgeon had little opportunity to explore the internal organs of living people and the examination of dead bodies was restricted by law.

Throughout his career Clowes was employed on more naval expeditions. When he was not at sea, between 1564 and 1570, he served as naval surgeon at Portsmouth. He made a point of spreading the knowledge gained in treating seamen and published treatises on gunshot wounds and syphilis (the latter the first in English). It was not until 1576 that he obtained a prestigious position in London, as surgeon at St Bartholomew's Hospital (already over four hundred years old and the most ancient such establishment in the capital). As well as this lucrative position, Clowes also acted as consultant surgeon and apothecary to Christ's Hospital at Newgate, the educational foundation established by Elizabeth's half-brother, Edward VI. Doubtless, it was as much Dudley patronage as his own reputation that won him these coveted positions. In 1585, we find him accompanying the Earl of Leicester as surgeon to the army he led to the Low Countries. Court friends further advanced his standing. In the following year, it was as a result of the queen's 'favour and good liking', that he became surgeon to the navy and, in 1588, he went to sea again, aboard the flagship, *Ark Royal*, when the fleet sailed to confront the Spanish Armada.

Clowes certainly needed influential backers because he was frequently at odds with the top brass of the Barber Surgeons' Company. He was accused of incompetence and even of corrupt practices. It takes little reading between the lines to conclude that Clowes was not the easiest of men to get on with. His intermittent war of words with his superiors sometimes escalated into physical violence. In 1577, he was in trouble for brawling with George Baker, another of the queen's surgeons. It was only in 1588 that he was admitted (we may suspect, with some reluctance) to the governing body of the Company.

What particularly galled Clowes were the restrictions imposed upon him by the lines of demarcation between surgeons and physicians. He was under obligation not to offer medicine to his patients or diagnose their complaints. To someone like Clowes, who had an enquiring mind and a compassionate heart, it was particularly frustrating not to be able to help when sailors or children in his care went down with fever or some other illness. In fact, he paid little heed to professional restrictions (which was one reason for his brushes with authority). For example, he carried out his own research into the causes of scurvy and, two centuries before Captain Cook made the same discovery, identified poor diet as the problem. To the end of what was, by the standards of the day, a long life, Clowes kept himself up to date with international advances. In the 1590s he readily followed the advice of French surgeon, Jacques Guillemeau, regarding cauterization by tying the ends of exposed arteries.

If Clowes was 'prickly' it was because he cared passionately about the wellbeing of his patients. It was his claim that he would never refuse to give the benefits of his skill and experience to anyone in need – 'even infidels'. He passed on his knowledge to the next generation and his *Approved Practice for all Young Surgeons* became a standard textbook for many years. Incompetence and quackery infuriated him. He was particularly scathing of naval surgeons who, once appointed to a ship, absconded with the money advanced to them for the purchase of instruments. Clowes himself became a wealthy man, owning properties in London and the country. It is not surprising that this dedicated surgeon died, in 1604, by contracting plague.

Among Clowes's few close friends was fellow surgeon John Banister. His career followed a similar pattern. Born in Huntingdon in 1532/3, he appears to have practised in Nottingham in the early stage of his career. He, too, was a protégé of the Dudleys. He, too, became a naval surgeon

and may have saved the Earl of Warwick's life by successfully and speedily extracting a poisoned bullet during the
campaign of 1563. What set him apart from most of his
colleagues was that soon afterwards he went to Oxford to
study medicine. By 1572, he was in London and admitted
to the Barber Surgeons' Company on the basis of having
served an apprenticeship in Nottingham. Like Clowes, he
saw no valid reason for the separation of the two medical
disciplines. In one of his many books he observed, 'Some
of late have fondly affirmed that the chirurgeon hath not to
deal in physic. Small courtesy is it to break faithful friendship . . . for the one cannot work without the other, nor
the other practise without the aid of both.'[2] But he was up
against the rigid traditionalism of the professional establishment and it was 1593 before he received a licence from
the College of Physicians to practise medicine as well as
surgery – and only then because the queen ordered the
College to grant it.

Banister's published works included notes on a wide
variety of clinical procedures, including treatments for
pleurisy and ulcers. However, his main claim to fame lies
in the realm of anatomy. The dissecting and examination of
cadavers was a science still in its infancy. Andreas Vesalius,
one of the greats in the history of medicine, taught at the
university of Padua and it was there that he published his
revolutionary treatise, *On the Fabric of the Human Body*,
in 1543. Hitherto, generations of students had been taught
the rudiments of anatomy based on the writings of the sec-
ond-century philosopher-surgeon, Galen. Not only was
their knowledge based on ancient texts and entirely second-
hand, but those texts were wrong. Galen had constructed
his descriptions of human anatomy from the dissection of
monkeys. As often happens with discoveries that challenge
traditional convictions, Vesalius's ideas were slow to find
acceptance. When Thomas Vicary wrote the first English
treatise on anatomy in 1547, he still projected the Galenic

model. This was despite the fact that, in 1540, the Barber Surgeons' Company had been given permission to dissect two bodies of executed criminals every year. Thirty years later it was still the case that very few students had the opportunity for hands-on examination of the human body.

Banister was one of the pioneers determined to change this. He was instrumental in having the number of anatomy lectures in the Barber Surgeons' Hall increased to four a year and it seems that he gave most of them. These demonstrations were open not only to apprentices of the Company, but to all freemen of the City and their guests. As far as one man could, Banister broke down the barriers and banished the taboos connected with dead bodies.

Among the most notable physicians of the day was the eccentric William Turner, the 'father of modern botany'. One moral we might draw from his life is that religious persecution can have positive results. This north countryman was entered at Pembroke College, Cambridge, where he took a master's degree and stayed as a fellow. He was caught up in the Protestant fever that spread through the university in the 1530s, eventually took deacon's orders and spent much of his time on unlicensed preaching tours. He was very much a law unto himself and defied the rules of the Church by taking a wife. Not wishing to be hauled before the ecclesiastical court, he prudently left England in 1541. Eventually he reached Bologna, enrolled in the university there and studied for an MD. He continued to travel, maintaining himself and his family by practising as a physician. But his contact with leading radical reformers made him into a religious extremist and a very forthright one. His first published work was a polemical tract, *The Hunting and Finding out of the Romish Fox*.

Turner possessed to a high degree that skill which is vital to physicians – observation. He made copious notes and sketches on the natural phenomena he encountered – birds, animals, but especially plants. On his return, during the Protestant regime of Edward VI, he prospered and was one of the physicians at court, though his extreme views, choleric temper and odd behaviour caused frequent embarrassment. One of his tricks was setting his pet dog to jump on the table and pull bishops' hats off. When Catholic Mary came to the throne Turner set off on his travels again. He was a restless pilgrim, ever driven onwards by curiosity. He had already written the book on which his fame chiefly rests but now he added fresh material and his *New Herbal* eventually consisted of three parts, lavishly illustrated with woodcuts. The work was both scholarly and accessible to non-specialists. Although he logged the Latin names of the hundreds of plants (300 species in England alone) he lovingly described, he also quoted the titles by which they were commonly known. He even made up names that would help people to identify them. Thus, for example, he dubbed antirrhinum 'Calf's Snout'. In the same way he paid equal heed to the properties of plants recorded by earlier scholars and the claims made for them in popular culture. Where he could prove, by experiment, that an old wives' tale was just that, he discarded it, but if he thought there might be some truth in an old legend he set it down in his book. Turner described the properties and uses to which leaves, flowers and roots might be put in cooking and the preparation of unguents but his main interest was in considering their medicinal applications. Here is a typical extract:

Wormwood hath astringent or binding together, bitter and biting qualities, heating and scouring away, strengthening and drying. Therefore it driveth forth by the stool and the urine also choleric and gallish humours out of the stomach. But it voideth most chiefly the gall of choler that is in the urine.[3]

Until very recent times wormwood was used in the western world and it is still employed extensively elsewhere as a purgative and an aid to digestion. Turner was also correct in his observation that this plant eases irritation of the gall bladder.

Turner devoted much of his time and energy in the 1560s to religious controversy and was among those Puritans who campaigned to rid the English Church of the last vestiges of 'popery'. However, this did not deflect him from his work as a naturalist, botanist and physician. He wrote treatises on the curative properties of wine and on the efficacy of drinking and bathing in spa waters. He described the composition and uses of ointments, pointing out that these should only be purchased from qualified medical practitioners and not from the kind of 'prating, runagate peddlers' who could be found in any market, selling their useless and even potentially harmful fake cures.

The year after Turner's death (1568), John Gerard (not to be confused with the Jesuit missionary – see above, pp. 123–4) was admitted to the Company of Barber Surgeons. This Cheshire-born practitioner not only followed the path blazed by Turner, he also helped to close the gap between the surgeons and the physicians which Clowes and Banister found so galling. In 1586, when the College of Physicians decided to establish a garden for the cultivation of medicinal herbs, it was Gerard they appointed to take charge of it. It was established on ground belonging to Lord Burghley in the region of Chancery Lane. Here Gerard grew over a thousand species of plants. Many of them were native to Britain but others were specimens collected by mariners on their travels or provided by European scholars with whom he corresponded. By this time plants such as the potato and tobacco were being introduced from the Americas. Objects that gave people a tangible connection with the New World, about which voyagers brought back strange tales, were regarded with fascination and even hope. Might not new discoveries produce the long-awaited answers to old maladies? In *The Merry Wives of Windsor* Falstaff seems convinced that the potato has aphrodisiac qualities. As his assignation with Mistress Page and Mistress Ford draws closer, he invokes heaven, 'Let the sky rain potatoes; let it thunder to the tune of "Greensleeves" ' (V. v. 11–13).

There is some disagreement about Gerard's own travels. He claimed to have visited many lands but may have made only one voyage, as a young man, to Russia and the Baltic. He certainly had no compunction in incorporating other men's discoveries with his own in his encyclopedic *Herbal or General History of Plants Gathered by John Gerard of London*, published in 1597. This work, with its 1,800 woodcuts, became, for many years, a standard reference book. Like its predecessors, Gerard's *Herbal* inevitably mixed entrenched legend with scientific observation. For example, it confidently asserted that a certain species of goose hatched from 'barnacles' on a foreign tree, branches of which were washed up on European coasts. The myth arose from the fact that the crustacean in question had a shape resembling the head of a goose. Since these migratory birds never bred in northern climes, it was assumed that their generation must follow a pattern different from that of other species. However, Gerard's life work was a valuable compendium for physicians who were called upon to treat a wide variety of human ailments. Thus, the author wrote of digitalis, concocted from foxgloves, which in more recent times has been used in the treatment of heart conditions, that it was valuable for the eradication of 'slimy phlegm and naughty humours'. He regarded basil as efficacious for dispelling melancholy and helping patients who could 'hardly make water'.

Medical practice, based on observation and experiment, was gradually emerging from the chrysalis of ancient knowledge, which had changed little since classical times. Basic to the understanding of individual physical and mental well-being was the philosophical proposition that human beings were meant to live in tune with nature. To achieve this it was necessary to maintain harmony between internal, external and cosmic forces. The internal forces were four 'humours', each located in a specific organ: black bile, centred in the gall bladder, yellow bile, lodged in the spleen, phlegm, positioned in the lungs, and blood, issuing from the liver. When one or other of these was dominant, the sufferer's health and personality would produce symptoms which the physician could deduce. The concept of the humours was taken as axiomatic by all. In *The Taming of the Shrew*, Petruchio acts the tyrant in order to bring the vile-tempered Katherina to heel. Depriving her of meat, he insists,

> I tell thee, Kate, 'twas burnt and dried away,
> And I expressly am forbid to touch it;
> For it engenders choler, planteth anger;
> And better 'twere that both of us did fast,
> Since, of ourselves, ourselves are choleric,
> Than feed it with such over-roasted flesh.

IV. i. 154–9

Audiences at the Globe would know that anger – a hot, dry humour – was produced by yellow bile and that physicians prescribed fasting from overcooked, dried-out food, which could only exacerbate the condition. Excess of blood made people hot-headed and lustful and part of the appropriate treatment was bleeding, by opening veins or applying leeches. Overmuch phlegm would push an otherwise calm, sensitive person into lazy, unemotional behaviour and nostrums might be prescribed which produced a sensation of heat. From a black bile imbalance sprang despondency and depression like that of Viola's listless, lovesick maiden, who,

> . . . with a green and yellow melancholy,
> She sat like patience on a monument,
> Smiling at grief . . .

Twelfth Night, II. iv. 111–13

Black hellebore, plenty of warmth and music were among the holistic cures prescribed for melancholic disorder.

When Queen Elizabeth was smitten with smallpox in October 1562, we might expect that the very best medical attention would have been summoned. It was – but all to no avail. There was no cure for this disease, which killed about fifty per cent of all who suffered from it and left most of the other fifty per cent badly scarred. The only way the worst could be averted was to encourage the fever to take its course and produce pustules, which eventually burst. When this did not happen, panic-stricken councillors, desperate to try anything that would avert the prospect of rival contenders for the vacant throne, summoned the extraordinary Burchard Kranach, a German engineer-cum-physician-cum-fortune-teller. Kranach, whose name was usually anglicized to 'Burcot', had arrived in England many years before to mine and smelt metals, which he had done with some success. But he also had a more questionable reputation as an apothecary and peddler of fake medicines. Kranach applied the 'red treatment', a remedy long customary throughout mainland Europe. Since small-pox, it was believed, resulted from a dominance of phlegm, the cold, moist humour, the way to counter it was to apply heat. The queen was wrapped in red (the colour of flame) flannel and laid before a blazing fire. Whether or not the heat helped, the disease did reach its climacteric, the pustules broke out and the fever passed.

Smallpox and syphilis were two common serious diseases and were considered similar because of their shared symptoms. Both produced pockmarks. Those of small-pox were smaller than those of syphilis – hence its name. Syphilis was known as the 'great pox' or, more often just 'the pox'. The Elizabethan world was wholly ignorant of the causes of epidemic disease. This was especially tragic because there was already in existence a book that laid the foundation for the science of epidemiology. In 1546,

Girolamo Fracastoro, a native of Verona, had published *De Contagione et Contagiosis Morbis*. In this he distinguished the three ways in which infection spreads: direct physical contact; contagion from infected objects, such as clothing and utensils; and infection carried through the air by 'seminaria, the seeds of disease which multiply rapidly and propagate their like'.[4] The Italian had, thus, deduced the existence of bacteria. Sadly, it would be three hundred years before the implications of this discovery led to effective preventative medicine. The root cause of syphilis was, of course, understood but could not be avoided because contraception, like abortion, was illegal and for the same reason: man should not interfere with the divine gift of procreation. This left the field wide open for the dissemination of 'remedies' based on old wives' tales and quackery, such as mildly acidic vaginal insertions. The commonest treatment of the disease was mercury, applied as an ointment or ingested in pills. This gave rise to the well-known saying, 'A night in the arms of Venus leads to a lifetime spent with Mercury'. This did produce results but the side effects were unpleasant – sweating and gum disease being among the least distressing. Moralists were not slow to point out that prevention (i.e. abstention) was better than cure.

Plague was a frequent visitor and occasionally reached epidemic proportions. Parish records for Bristol indicate that the worst years were 1565, 1575 and 1603. In the first of these years, there were 1,800 deaths out of a population of about 11,000. 'Plague', however, was a term that covered many conditions with similar symptoms, such as fever and skin sores, so we cannot base accurate assessments on these figures – not that precise diagnosis was of great concern to the sufferers and their families. A visiting diplomat commented that such disease was most prevalent among the lower orders and suggested that this was because of their 'dissolute mode of life'. The reality, as we now know, was that living conditions for everyone, but especially the poorer members of society, encouraged the animals, insects and microbes that spread infection. Flies settled on food on market stalls and in kitchens. Domestic waste was tipped into streets. Rotting animal carcases and vegetables lay piled in alleyways. Water came from pools and rivers near where sheep and cattle grazed. By 1558, most towns had water brought into the centre in conduits, many provided as bequests by charitable citizens, but these did not necessarily guarantee purity since the water was mostly brought in from nearby rivers. John Stowe in his *Survey of London* (1603) indicated the kind of problems that constantly beset the City authorities in their attempts to keep the capital provided with a fresh water supply. He described one major undertaking in 1589, aimed at cleaning the Fleet Brook, which ran close by the western wall. A special municipal tax having been raised,

> the money amounting to a thousand marks was collected, and it was undertaken, that by drawing diverse springs about Hampstead Heath into one head and course, both the city should be served of fresh water in all places of want, and also by such a follower [a kind of mill wheel] as men call it, the channel of this brook should be scoured [i.e. the mud of the riverbed should be diverted] into the river of Thames, but much money being therein spent, the effect failed, so that the brook by means of continual encroachments upon the banks getting over the water and casting of soilage into the stream, is now become worse cloyed [clogged] and choken than ever it was before.[5]

The water arrived at communal fountains and troughs where it was collected by servants in buckets (probably seldom cleaned) for domestic use. No one expected water to be potable. The common drinks taken regularly were ale and beer. The only sewage 'system' in place was that provided by the night soil men who collected waste from pails and latrines and dumped it in pits away from centres of habitation. People were not reticent about urinating or voiding their bowels.

Population rose steadily during the reign. Unemployed and ambitious men gravitated towards the towns. All this led to overcrowding. Cities and major towns had originally been enclosed by defensive walls. That meant that, for generations, as many citizens as possible had crammed their dwellings within the urban perimeter. Spaces between houses were filled with new buildings and extra storeys were added to existing ones. Sixteenth-century landlords, like their counterparts in all ages, regarded 'bricks and mortar' as an investment and, since urban demand exceeded supply, they were well placed to maximize profits. They built on what had been garden plots and they subdivided once-spacious town houses into what we would now call 'flats'. The Earl of Shrewsbury was typical when he had his London residence on Coldharbour with its pleasant view across the Thames demolished and, 'in place thereof builded a great number of small tenements now letten out for great rents'.[6] Though the comparatively peaceful Tudor era had made possible the development of suburbs, residence in salubrious areas beyond town walls tended to be the exclusive preserve of wealthy citizens. Most townsfolk lived in what were, by modern standards, crowded, unsanitary wens.

Unsurprisingly, high summer was the plague season. When food festered in kitchens and rats gorged themselves on scraps lying in the streets infections spread rapidly. The minority of town-dwellers who could afford to do so moved out to their country residences in the warmer months. Elizabeth went on progress every summer, touring with her entourage the country estates of her more prosperous subjects and visiting her own palaces away from Westminster. There was one very practical reason for this: after a few days in any one location the overfull latrines used by hundreds of courtiers and servants made it malodorous. Apothecaries did a roaring trade in perfumes and sweet-smelling herbs which customers applied to their kerchiefs or carried in pomanders (small fretted boxes), so that they could hold them to their noses. Nor were they above pointedly letting other people know that they stank: they used 'casting bottles' to sprinkle malodorous associates. It is easy to see why Elizabethans linked disease to 'foul airs' and noxious odours. They kept well away from anyone smitten with plague or fever.

Isolation was strictly enforced on sufferers. Beyond encouraging the disease to take its course as rapidly as possible little could be done. At crisis times opportunist quacks came forward with their 'cures', prepared to risk infection for a quick profit. In fact they were little worse than the 'professionals'. Physicians had no idea how to conquer plague and its related maladies. Medical knowledge had not advanced since the mid-fourteenth century, when French physician, Guy de Chauliac, had advocated applying a poultice of onions and figs cooked in butter to the buboes, before lancing them with a red-hot needle.

Just as every community was expected to solve its own unemployment problems and prevent vagrancy, so the care of the sick and infirm was a charge laid upon each neighbourhood. This was, indeed, accepted as a Christian duty and had originally been overseen by the Church. The closure of monasteries by Henry VIII threatened to put an end to several hospitals that had been run by monks and nuns. If these services were to continue, responsibility would need to be shouldered by municipal authorities or private charities. In many places the situation was put to the local people. The London historian, John Stowe describes one such public meeting:

> . . . they were by eloquent orations persuaded how great and
> how many commodities would ensue unto them and their
> city, if the poor of diverse sorts which they named were taken
> from out their streets, lanes and alleys and were bestowed

and provided for in hospitals . . . and therefore was every man moved, liberally to grant what they would impart towards the preparing and furnishing of such hospitals . . .[7]

We may doubt how enthusiastic all the citizens were about contributing to something their forefathers had enjoyed at no cost but, throughout the realm, by various combinations of public impost, private philanthropy, corporate charity (by bodies such as the London livery companies and provincial trade guilds) and royal grants of land, many ancient foundations were preserved. One such was St Bartholomew's Hospital in Smithfield. At the beginning of Elizabeth's reign the physician in charge was Thomas Vicary, another important figure in Tudor medical history. He was the author of *A Treasure for Englishmen, containing the Anatomy of Man's Body*, which remained, for generations, an indispensable textbook for students of surgery. In later years William Clowes occupied the position of surgeon to St Bartholomew's and, at the very end of the reign, one of the giants of English medicine had charge of the patients at 'Barts'. This was William Harvey, the discoverer of the circulatory system of the blood. These leading practitioners all had many lucrative clients but were contractually bound to attend poor patients, 'one day in the week throughout the year'.

A more specialist institution was the Hospital of St Mary of Bethlehem on Bishopsgate Street, just beyond the City wall. 'In this place people that be distraught in wits are by the suit of their friends received and kept . . . but not without charges to their bringers in.'[8] This was the notorious Bedlam, London's madhouse. There was no understanding of mental disease. People were admitted to St Mary's by concerned family members or friends who could not cope with their odd or violent behaviour. As well as these private inmates, the governors took in a few poor sufferers who had no other means of sustenance.

The Keeper had no medical qualifications. He was simply there to keep order – and to take his fees. As well as the money paid by the relatives of the inmates, his emoluments included admission charges to the general public, for 'going to Bedlam' was a popular recreation for citizens and visitors to the capital, who derived amusement from the antics of the unfortunate men and women confined there. During the latter part of Elizabeth's reign the hospital fell into a deplorable state of disrepair. When the authorities made a long-overdue inspection in 1598 they discovered 'that it is so loathsomely, filthily kept [as to be] not fit for any man to come into the said house'.

The best advice that could have been given to any of Queen Elizabeth's subjects was 'Don't get ill'.

II

SCHOOLS AND SCHOOLMASTERS

GREMIO: *I promised to enquire carefully*
About a schoolmaster for the fair Bianca;
And by good fortune I have lighted well
On this young man; for learning and behaviour
Fit for her turn, well read in poetry
And other books – good ones I warrant ye.
HORTENSIO: *'Tis well; and I have met a gentleman*
Hath promis'd me to help me to another,
A fine musician to instruct our mistress . . .

The Taming of the Shrew, I. ii. 162–70

When Bianca's rival suitors wish to gain access to the object of their affections they plan to do so by insinuating tutors into her household who will be able to act as intermediaries. By the time Elizabeth came to the throne it was quite accepted that young ladies of leisure should not only be accomplished in the pursuits suitable for their sex, such as needlework and playing the virginals (the very name may suggest performance upon it as most appropriate for modest maidens), but should be competent in Latin and well read in the classical authors. The extension of education to women was one of the more remarkable outcomes of that social revolution brought about by the Renaissance and the Reformation. Formal training in schools, universities and the inns of court was still only available for boys and adolescent males because nature had designated their sex to control all social units from the home to the nation. Or so it was believed. But such exclusivity was undermined in the sixteenth century by two unprecedented phenomena. The first was the dynastic imperative which placed women on European thrones. Elizabeth was queen because the Tudor male line had petered out, and she was not the only member of her sex who found herself at the helm, making policy, negotiating with foreign rulers and sending armies into battle. Mary Stuart ruled in Scotland (until she was driven into exile), Catherine de Medici held supreme power in France after the death of her husband, and a succession of remarkable Habsburg women acted as regents in the Spanish Netherlands. To be well fitted for high office any woman needed an understanding of politics, which could best be acquired by a study of classical history and philosophy. The second phenomenon was the open Bible. By the time Elizabeth came to the throne, reading of the Holy Scriptures in the vernacular had become part of the birthright of all English men – and women. Mary had tried to suppress this revolutionary text, but this had only made its champions more determined to place it at the centre of the nation's religious life. Protestant exiles returned from their continental havens with a new translation, which rapidly gained popularity – the Geneva Bible. Once it was established that all Christians ought to make God's word their primary study it followed logically that women were under as much obligation in this regard as their fathers, brothers and husbands. The Bible was the single most powerful stimulus to the spread of education in England and one corollary of this was the appearance of a number of well-read and erudite women.

The queen herself set the pace in the emancipation process. By the time of her accession Elizabeth was the best-educated monarch ever to have occupied the English throne to that point. Few of the Biancas in her realm could have matched her intellectual accomplishments. She had mastered classical Latin and Greek, was fluent in French and Italian and scarcely less accomplished in Spanish. She could discourse on theological questions with her bishops and explore complex political issues with councillors and ambassadors. Some of the credit for this must go to her teachers. In her early years, she shared with her brother, Prince Edward, the ministrations of a remarkable fellowship of humanist tutors, who represented the intellectual avant-garde of their day (see p. 3, pp. 202–3). Foremost among them was Roger Ascham. He had lectured in Greek at Cambridge and been closely involved in the arguments between traditionalists and radicals over changes in curricula and teaching methods before being promoted to royal service. Day by day Elizabeth read Greek and Latin texts with her tutor, including the New Testament in its original language. She found him stimulating, not only for his deep learning but also for his 'liberated' attitude to life. Ascham was no narrow-minded pedagogue, so steeped in his studies as to have little contact with everyday reality. He loved a joke and had a wide range of interests, including archery and cock-fighting. He was often broke, probably because he accumulated gambling debts. He was argumentative and this, too, often landed him in trouble. But, as far as education was concerned, he had one conviction that endeared him to the princess (and later to the queen): he believed that learning should be enjoyable. Ascham was separated from his royal pupil during the reign of Mary, whom he served as Latin secretary. Elizabeth retained him in this position and their old friendship resumed.

In 1563, he was dining with William Cecil and other courtiers when mention was made of a number of pupils who had run away from Eton because they were being beaten. This news made Ascham angry and his reaction was noted by his companions, who urged him to set down in a book his own ideas about teaching and learning. The result was *The Schoolmaster – a plain and perfect way of teaching children to understand, write and speak in the Latin tongue.* Ascham took very seriously the task of recommending a regimen for training the sons of gentlemen for the responsibilities they would later undertake as leaders of local and national society. 'God knoweth,' he warned, 'that nobility without virtue and wisdom is blood indeed, but blood truly without bones and sinews; and so of itself, without the other, very weak to bear the burden of weighty affairs.'[1] One wonders whether he had any current members of the queen's government in mind.

He spent five years on the book, pouring into it all the experience and wisdom he had accumulated throughout a lifetime spent in various educational environments. He wrote with passion, earnestly rejecting old methods and attitudes. He had still more to say, for *The Schoolmaster* was unfinished at his death (1568). Basic to his programme was a good relationship between teacher and pupil. 'In my opinion,' he declared, 'love is fitter than fear, gentleness better than beating, to bring up a child rightly in learning.' Ascham challenged current conventions in the way gentlemen's sons were reared. It was the custom for boys to stop formal school study at fourteen or fifteen (unless they were going straight on to university) and to spend some time having their minds 'broadened' by foreign travel. This, the writer deplored. It was wrong to take a boy away from his books just when his mind was learning to appropriate and apply the truths he had learned. Education should continue to the age of seventeen. As to foreign travel, that was the best way, Ascham insisted, to introduce him to unsavoury vices and expunge from his memory all the virtuous impulses and lofty thoughts imparted by his education. When it came to the actual mechanics of teaching, Ascham wanted, above all things, to see children develop a real love of books; to value the texts for themselves and not just as exercises in mastering the structure of dead languages. He saw little value in imparting the rules of grammar for their own sake. What he advocated was direct interaction with the chosen text. First it should be translated into English, then, after a few days, it should be rendered back into the original language. The pupil's version could then be compared with the original, and linguistic lessons learned. Of equal importance to the substance of *The Schoolmaster* is its language. Ascham chose to write his book in English at a time when Latin was still considered more appropriate for works of scholarship. He wanted his ideas to circulate as widely as possible and in this he was successful; his mould-breaking book, published in 1570, was reprinted at least seven times during the reign. How rapidly or otherwise his principles prevailed it is difficult to say. *The Schoolmaster* reveals to us not only the recommendations of the reformer, but the common practices against which he appealed – such as the use of corporal punishment. What certainly had an influence in literary circles was its style. At a time when there was no standardized written English and the vernacular was considered a debased and uncouth tongue in comparison with Latin, Ascham showed that his native language could be written with fluency and simplicity. *The Schoolmaster* is one of the literary stepping stones that lie between Tyndale's New Testament and the plays of Shakespeare.

The revolution in education did not only affect the upbringing of boys. The queen was not the only woman to have benefited from it. Let us consider the life and influence of the age's most formidable bluestocking. It used to be said that the ghost of Lady Anne Bacon could sometimes be observed wandering the inns of court, wringing her hands and bewailing the worldliness of the members, who enjoyed lewd plays and dances, behaviour she strongly and consistently denounced throughout her long lifetime. At the age of twenty-five, in 1553, Anne became the second wife of Sir Nicholas Bacon (see above, Chapter 1). After her husband's death in 1579, she remained unmarried until her own demise in 1610. Throughout her long widowhood, Anne devoted herself to forwarding the Puritan cause and, especially, to guiding her sons, Anthony and Francis (see below, Chapter 13) along the path of righteousness.

Anne was a by-product of the 'Cambridge School' to which Ascham belonged, a group of the finest scholars in mid-century England. These radical humanist thinkers had, in their turn, been instructed by the great Erasmus and were part of a Europe-wide network of idealistic reformers who wanted to change society and who believed that education freed from the shackles of medieval practice was the best tool to achieve this. Foremost among them were scholars appointed to Prince Edward's household, such as John Cheke and Roger Ascham. Another scholar also attached to Edward's court was Anthony Cooke. Although not, as far as records show, a member of the same university as the others, Cooke was certainly one of the group and shared their radical ideas. During Mary's reign he went into exile on the continent and further developed his theological position in discussion with the leading continental reformers. By the time he returned, he had taken up more extreme views on some of the religious issues of the day and this, coupled with his argumentative nature, probably explains why he failed to achieve a prominent position in Elizabeth's government. However, he stayed close to others who did gain preferment. One of his daughters was married to William Cecil and another, Anne, as we have seen, was the second wife of Nicholas Bacon.

One of the more remarkable innovations of the

Cambridge School was the conviction that the girls of prominent families should receive an education which, though different in some ways, was no less demanding than that of their brothers, for, although they were destined for different roles in life, boys and girls should aim for the same goal of education – the virtuous life. Cooke wholeheartedly espoused this principle. His five daughters were trained with the same intellectual rigidity as their four brothers. Anne was taught Latin, Greek and Italian and received some instruction in Hebrew. In 1548, when she was no more than twenty, she claimed a place in the literary firmament by translating from the Italian a book of sermons by Bernardino Ochino, an ex-Capuchin friar and one of the more maverick figures of the Reformation. But her major contribution to the religious life of England was her translation of Bishop Jewel's *Apologia Ecclesiae Anglicanae* (1564), which set out clearly the differences between the English Church and the Church of Rome. Her book became a primary text in the Elizabethan religious settlement.

In fact, Anne's Puritanism carried her well beyond the moderate Protestantism the queen wished to establish. She was patron and protector of outspoken radicals and was tireless in advocating further reform. She corresponded with bishops and councillors and never allowed her status as a 'mere woman' to stand in the way of making her opinions known. 'I think for my long attending in court and a chief councillor's wife,' she insisted in one of her letters, 'few women in my position are able to be alive to speak and judge of such proceedings and worldly doings of men.'[2] Much of Anne's energies were devoted to guiding her older sons through the snares and pitfalls of the wicked world. The boys attended Gray's Inn, like their father before them, and their mother was particularly concerned by the students' custom of putting on plays and other impious revels. Unsurprisingly, the young Bacons found their parent's well-meant advice irksome. In one letter Anthony accused his mother of having 'a sovereign desire to overrule your sons in all things, how little soever you understand either the grounds or the circumstances of [their] proceedings'.[3] Among the brothers and their friends the puritanical old lady became something of a joke. It may have been they who suggested that Anne Bacon's spirit would never find rest as long as high-spirited students indulged themselves in irreligious frivolities. If so the Gray's Inn legend of Anne's ghost long outlived them. It goes without saying that Anne and her husband paid the closest attention to the education their children received at all stages of their development. They employed chaplains of sound Puritan convictions as tutors to the boys and the girls. The Cambridge college selected for all four of their sons was Trinity, because the current master was Robert Beaumont, an old friend of Sir Nicholas, who had spent years of exile in Geneva and returned with a passion for removing from English public life the last vestiges of popery. But it was not sufficient to ensure that the Bacon boys were in a Puritan ambience; their parents also provided them with their own private tutor and, when the young men travelled in Europe to further their education, they were accompanied by approved companions to keep them on the straight and narrow.

The object of education (particularly that available to the upper classes) was the virtuous life. Virtuous citizens were the building blocks of a happy commonwealth. Thinkers of the Renaissance/Reformation were in no doubt that education was the key to the brave new world they wished – and expected – to see. They had turned their backs on medieval methods of learning, which relied, in large part, on studying the interpretations placed on Scripture and the early fathers of the Church by later scholars. They went back to the original texts – both sacred and secular – to rediscover and reapply the wisdom of the ancients. This wider approach to learning was made possible by the growing availability of books, which became cheaper because printing techniques improved and growing demand made possible longer print runs. Scholars pondering the nature of the perfect state now had at their disposal the works of all the philosophers and historians of antiquity who had written about those political and ethical problems common to societies of all ages. This was why educational theorists regarded familiarity with the classics as vital to young people who would be the future movers and shakers of Elizabethan society.

Yet, there was only one book that could, unfailingly, steer the young student in the right direction, as an act of Elizabeth's first Parliament plainly stated. It decreed that schoolmasters should 'accustom their scholars reverently to learn such sentences of Scripture as shall be most expedient to induce them to all godliness'. Reading the English Bible and hearing it read was the educational staple of the queen and all her subjects. Not only was it proclaimed and expounded in church, Sunday by Sunday, it was also the basis of formal education in the godly home, where the family worshipped together and where the children were instructed by a private tutor. Such a tutor might be the parish priest, a private chaplain or a young scholar fresh out of university.

But, of course, most children and young people did not live in such a privileged environment. If they were to enjoy the luxury of formal education they had to 'go to school'. This effectively excluded the majority. Most children were either born in poverty, with no prospect of acquiring those practical skills that would enable them to find gainful employment, or they were raised in busy households where, from an early age, they had to help their parents work the land, tend the animals, fetch and carry the raw materials of their craft, watch over younger siblings or cook food. Sporadic efforts were made to tackle the problem of unoccupied or under-occupied children. In 1570, the burghers of Norwich instituted a scheme of practical tutelage. They formed a corps of women who could teach such basic practical skills as spinning. This scheme was so successful that some nine hundred children between six and ten were soon earning sixpence a week by their labour. Parents who aspired to give their offspring a better start in life than they had enjoyed or who wanted them to be able to read the Bible could probably find someone locally to provide basic instruction in reading and writing. It might be the parish priest or the chaplain from the 'big house' or a widow with time on her hands. For a small fee or, in some cases, as a pure act of charity, such a person would take in boys (and sometimes girls) of four or five years. Such petty schools or dame schools taught pupils their 'letters' with the aid of a hornbook – a frame holding a printed alphabet or some other text covered by a transparent sheet of horn.

A royal injunction of 1559 decreed, 'No man shall take upon him to reach but such as shall be allowed by the ordinary [diocesan bishop] and found meet as well for his learning and dexterity in teaching as for sober and honest conversation and also for right understanding of God's true religion.'[4]

It was a wise regulation, designed to ensure that the structure of society was not threatened by people who might instil subversive ideas into the next generation of the queen's subjects. But the laws of supply and demand, stimulated by the age's new-found passion for general education, ensured that the reality was much more flexible – at least at the primary level. The government was well advised to keep tabs on teachers because education *was* potentially subversive. Queen and Council were faced with a dilemma. Social stability – and, therefore, the peace of the realm – depended on everyone keeping to his/her appointed place in society. Boys should follow their fathers' trades. Young men should receive the training appropriate to their station in life – and no more. But, at the same time, the strength of the Protestant state depended in large measure on Elizabeth's subjects being well versed in the Holy Scriptures. That implied the spread of literacy, and, once people could read, there was no way of controlling what they read and what ambitions they might nurse as a result of what they read. The queen's difficulties with Puritans in general and Puritan members of Parliament in particular (see Chapters 3 and 4) sprang from a clash of loyalties. Godly MPs owed allegiance both to their sovereign and to the will of God as they understood it from their study of the Bible. John Knox, the firebrand preacher of the Scottish Reformation, mightily offended Elizabeth when he denounced queenly rule as the 'monstrous regiment of women' but she could not disagree with him when he urged, 'It is most expedient that schools be universally erected in all cities and chief towns, the oversight whereof to be committed to the magistrates and godly learned men of the said cities and towns.'5 Many Elizabethans took this to heart by founding or re-founding places of learning. Religious radicals did not have a monopoly of concern for rearing young men in the pursuit of virtue. The educational revolution that had begun during the reign of Edward VI brought together a wide variety of thinkers, philanthrop-ists and men of affairs. Nothing demonstrates this more clearly than the founding of what was, by the end of the century, the largest school in England.

By the time of Elizabeth's accession, Sir Thomas White was already in his fifties and had behind him a distinguished career as a merchant and a public benefactor. He was a Hertfordshire clothier who had grown rich on the wool trade. He was a member of the Merchant Taylors' Company, a London alderman and (in 1553) Lord Mayor. Over the years he showed himself to be a generous, even a reckless, benefactor. His largest single work of charity was the founding of St John's College, Oxford, to which he made several endowments between 1555 and his death in 1567. All this generosity brought him close to bankruptcy as the declining traditional cloth trade reduced his income.

He also found himself out of favour at court because of his religious opinions. He had been a firm supporter of Catholic Mary and several of the fellows he had appointed at St John's were dismissed on religious grounds. It is interesting, therefore, that, in 1561, he should have joined in another philanthropic venture with Richard Hilles.

Hilles was another senior member of the Merchant Taylors' Company who had prospered mightily in trade (in 1582 he appeared on the 'London 100' list of wealthiest citizens). Of his religious propensities there can be no doubt. He had elected to stay in England during Mary's reign, outwardly conforming to the restored Catholicism of the regime, but had maintained a secret correspondence with reformers in exile and provided them with financial support. He continued to exchange letters with continental Protestant leaders in the new queen's reign. In 1566, reporting a rumour that Philip II was due to visit his Netherlands dominions, 'to restore and establish the popish superstition, idolatry and cruelty', he piously added,

> May God, in whose hands are the hearts of all princes, take away from this king and the rulers of this country their hearts of stone, and give them hearts of flesh, that being truly from the heart converted to Christ, they may be greatly grieved for their past sins and wickedness, and repent them of them; that they may obtain forgiveness and mercy from the Lord, and henceforth with all their might promote his glory.[6]

These two men joined forces to establish Merchant Taylors' School. Hilles gave £500 towards the purchase of roomy premises in Suffolk Lane, just to the north of Thames Street and the narrow alleys leading down to the river wharves. The new foundation was to provide free education for no fewer than a hundred poor boys. Another 150 were to be accepted on financial terms appropriate to their fathers' means. The brighter pupils were groomed for university places.

The scholar selected as the first headmaster was Richard Mulcaster, a forceful man in his early thirties, who had imbibed Cambridge humanism before graduating at Oxford. He represents the next stage in educational theory after Ascham. Though a master of classical languages, he departed from many of his fellows in the degree of importance he placed upon them. He was a passionate devotee of written English. Study of the classics, he insisted, was not the be-all and end-all of learning for all children. 'It is no proof,' he insisted in one of his educational treatises, 'because Plato praiseth it, because Aristotle alloweth it, because Cicero commends it, because Quintilian is acquainted with it, or any other else . . . that therefore it is for us to use.'[7] He believed that children should be well grounded in the vernacular and able to express their ideas and feelings clearly and stylishly in their own language before proceeding to explore their classical heritage. Mulcaster identified five essential ingredients for the instruction of children: reading, writing, singing, drawing and playing (exercise).

> By reading we receive what antiquity hath left us, by writing we deliver what posterity [requires] of us. By resembling with pencil, what aspectable [visible] thing is there, either brought forth by nature or set forth by art, whose knowledge and use we attain not unto? By the principle of music . . . we [have] such a glass wherein to behold the beauty of concord, and the blots of dissension, even in a politic body . . . And as so many principles appointed for the mind . . . thereto do make it most able to conceive with the soonest, and to deliver with the fairest, even so the one principle of exercise . . . maketh the body most active in all parts, to execute all functions both of necessity and praise . . .[8]

A healthy mind was one which had feasted on the rich intellectual fare offered by the world's greatest thinkers and, having ingested not only their wisdom, but also their ability to organize their thoughts, could develop a cogent and pleasing style of written English. But a well-trained child should also develop other skills for which he showed aptitude. Drawing, music and acting would help develop potential. His programme was completed with the inclusion of physical education in line with Juvenal's maxim, *mens sana in corpore sano*. One of the games he advocated was football and he claimed to have invented the team version of that sport. Mulcaster's experience at Merchant Taylors' School convinced him of the value of bringing together pupils of different backgrounds. Gentlemen's sons were not necessarily more brainy than boys from poor homes. The only educational disadvantage the latter suffered was that they might not be able to complete their school course because they were needed in their parents' business. But they could be given every chance and encouragement to advance as far as they could.

Mulcaster's ideas sound – and were – very advanced for their day. He worked them up into an educational programme that he believed should have universal application. That in itself was a revolutionary idea for there was no national curriculum; every teacher devised his own programme and his own methods of following it. Mulcaster's system was set forth in *Positions Wherein those Primitive Circumstances be Examined Which are Necessary for the Training-up of children* (1581). He did not embrace all the principles of other humanist pedagogues, such as Ascham. For example, he was not noted for sparing the rod. He believed that children, by nature, were inclined to disobedience and mischief and that this would gain the upper hand if they were not in 'awe' of their teacher.

> For if one need not to beat children to have them do ill, where-unto they are prone, we must needs then beat them for not doing well.

The queen's subjects would not respect authority if they were not forced to do so as children.

> And who can tell, what even he that under law is most obsequious and civil, would of himself prove, if law, which [is based on] awe, would leave him at liberty?[9]

The author was, by all accounts, a fierce disciplinarian who turned a deaf ear to the complaints of 'interfering' parents.

Where Mulcaster was in full agreement with Ascham was in his love of written English. Indeed, he went further, not only conceding that erudite books *could* be written in the vernacular, but that they *should be*. He was among the few men of his age who saw the potential of a standardized English which should, like Latin, be studied with the aid of a grammar book and a dictionary. It is no surprise that among Mulcaster's pupils were the young Edmund Spenser, author of *The Faerie Queene*, and Lancelot Andrewes, the mastermind behind the King James Bible. Equally it comes as no surprise that this stern but brilliant teacher fell foul of his paymasters of the Merchant Taylors' Company and went off in a huff in 1586. Time eventually healed the breach and when the liverymen needed a headmaster for St Paul's School, which they also ran, they turned to the venerable Mulcaster.

We must consider briefly the work of just one more educational pioneer. What Mulcaster did for English, William Kemp did for mathematics. He spent almost all of his fairly brief life (*c.*1560–1601) in Plymouth. He was a pupil of the grammar school there and, after his higher education in Cambridge, returned to take up the post of headmaster in the same school. He represented many dedicated men up and down the country who were turning school teaching into a respected profession. Respected and potentially lucrative. Kemp acquired several properties in the town and his wealth at death was assessed, after debts paid, at

£540. In 1588, when Plymouth was buzzing with preparations for the confrontation with the Spanish Armada, he published *The Education of Children in Learning*, dedicated to the mayor and corporation. The boys who came to his school were mostly of farming and mercantile families and it was with them in mind, rather than the sons of gentlemen, that he wrote. It may well have been the need to prepare young men in the skills of the counting house that prompted him to include arithmetic and geometry in his curriculum. He introduced the principles championed by continental scholars such as Petrus Ramus, a prodigiously gifted French philosopher whose career had been cut tragically short by the St Bartholomew's Day Massacre, the purge of French Protestants in 1572 and he wrote his own text, *The Art of Arithmetic*, to help other teachers.

By the end of the century schools like Kemp's were appearing in all parts of the country, either old foundations regenerated or new ones brought into being by private benefactors, municipal corporations or livery companies. Their creation indicates the rising demand for education at all levels of society and also the improving status of the teaching profession. Just how these factors interacted is illustrated by the history of one school that appeared in the Middlesex countryside not far from London. John Lyon was a well-to-do yeoman farmer who owned land in Middlesex and Hertfordshire, most of which is now covered by the urban and suburban sprawl of the metropolis. In 1572, he obtained a charter for a grammar school where thirty local boys would receive a free education. A condition set by the government stipulated that provision should be included in the benefaction for the upkeep of the road leading into the capital. For various reasons the school did not open until 1615 but when it did open it rapidly became popular – too popular. The charter granted the master the right to augment his stipend by taking in a few fee-paying pupils from outside the parish. The temptation was obvious. Not only did the early teachers accept more and more 'foreigners', gentlemen and even courtiers bought property in the locality in order to gain the necessary residency qualification for their sons to be taught gratis. Sadly, the families for whose benefit the school had been founded were being edged out. In this way Harrow School ceased to be a 'public school' in the original sense of the term and became what later ages would call a public school. It was not the only one.

Education had become a prized commodity and, as such, was bought up by those who could afford it. The same situation bedevilled further education. In 1587, Lord Burghley complained to the Vice Chancellor of Cambridge,

> I am credibly informed by the great complaints of divers both worshipful and wise parents . . . that through the great stipends of tutors, and the little pains they do take in the instructing and well governing of their pupils . . . the poorer sort are not able to maintain their children at the university; and the richer be . . . corrupt with liberty and remissness [because] the tutor is more afraid to displease his pupil through the desire of great gain, the which he hath by his tutorage, than the pupil is of his tutor.[10]

The increased demand for university places was stimulated by the growing numbers of young men – of all classes – who had received a grammar-school grounding and also by fashion. Residence for a year or two in one of the Oxford or Cambridge colleges was regarded as a suitable way of 'finishing' preparation for adult life. Inevitably, therefore, many youths in their later teens were attracted to university life not by the allure of further study, but by escaping from the restraints of home and enjoying themselves with others of their own age. On the other hand, as we have seen, the universities (and especially Cambridge) were the generators of exciting new ideas and there were students attracted there to hear the latest celebrity lecturers and preachers. It is scarcely surprising that, in such a turbulent age, the universities were places where paradoxes were the norm. They were backwaters at the cutting edge of radical intellectual development. They were wedded to their traditions but added new disciplines to their curricula. They banished arid scholasticism but the emphasis on Scripture inhibited scientific enquiry. By way of illustrating these trends let us consider the events and personalities responsible for the founding of new colleges during Elizabeth's reign.

This was the period when the two universities began to take on the appearance we know today. Colleges – the hostels where students lived and where most of their tutoring took place – had grown piecemeal over the previous three centuries. Now, benefactions and property dealing enabled impressive buildings to be erected and sites to be rationalized. The most obvious example is Trinity Great Court, the largest enclosed courtyard in Cambridge, which was under construction by the end of the reign. The fact that more and more sons of the nobility and gentry were spending time at the universities was reflected in the quality of accommodation provided. Halls were panelled and supplied with fireplaces. Hangings appeared on the walls. One sour historian of the seventeenth century remarked of St John's Cambridge, 'as the college began to rise in building, so it declined in learning'. If the importance of higher education were to be judged on the basis of the number of centres devoted to it, Elizabethan England would appear well down the league table. France, Italy, Spain and the German states each boasted more than twenty universities and the numbers were growing. There was no move to add to England's two universities. During the reign no new colleges were founded in Oxford and only three in Cambridge.

The first was Gonville and Caius, though, strictly

speaking, this was a re-foundation. John Caius was a student during the 1530s at what was then Gonville Hall. After graduation he went to study at the university of Padua, the leading centre in Europe for the study of medicine. On his return, he became a member (and eventually President) of the College of Physicians. He established a very lucrative practice in London and served as royal physician to Edward, Mary and Elizabeth. Meanwhile, his old college had fallen on hard times. Caius came to its rescue with lavish fresh endowment. He extended it to provide facilities for more teachers and students and modestly renamed it Gonville and Caius College. He was a staunch Catholic and eventually lost his position at court on the somewhat confused grounds that he was an atheist and a devotee of papist ritual. However, in Cambridge, his honoured position was never in doubt. One of his first acts of charity was to provide a home for Edmund Cosin. Cosin was the ex-Vice Chancellor and he had resigned because he could not accede to the Act of Supremacy. Dr Caius provided him with rooms in his college and here the dispossessed dignitary remained for at least four years. Little more is known about him. He seems to have died in straitened circumstances, forgotten and neglected for being on the wrong side in the religious conflict.

Caius became master of his college in 1559 and remained at the helm until shortly before his death. He continued to make improvements in the buildings. He also encouraged the study of medicine in Cambridge, obtaining permission to have the cadavers of two felons per year for dissection. But he was seldom at ease in a university that was leaning further and further towards Puritanism. His own loyalty to the regime was frequently questioned and opposition went well beyond polite disagreement. In 1572, the university authorities authorized the ransacking of his rooms. Vestments, pictures and anything that smacked of popery were smashed and burned. Shortly after this outrage, Caius resigned his position and retired to London, where, shortly afterwards, he died.

A more positive kind of Protestantism was shown by benefactors who saw the importance of the university in providing the Church with ministers and preachers well versed in the Bible and Calvinist doctrine. They financed scholarships and lectureships, supported tutors and gave support to radical teachers and preachers in the internal conflicts of the 1570s and 1580s, which often became very heated. It was specifically to provide the realm with a godly preaching ministry that the other two new colleges were founded – Emmanuel and Sidney Sussex. Another of the paradoxes we might discern in the life of the Elizabethan university is that, while it had become 'secularized' (i.e. no longer seen primarily as a training ground for the Church), the basic structure of courses remained much as it had done before the Reformation and was now seen by religious radicals as essential to the production of a godly preaching ministry. That meant encouraging 'sound' men to go through the long course leading to a theological degree. A student spent four years on the *trivium* – grammar, logic and rhetoric – in order to become a bachelor of arts, and then proceeded, for his master's degree, to study philosophy (which included arithmetic, geometry, music and astronomy). Only then might he proceed to one of the specialist studies – theology, medicine, canon law or civil law.

Sir Walter Mildmay was a financial bureaucrat who had the rare distinction of serving in the governments of all four Tudor sovereigns. By 1559, he was Chancellor of the Exchequer. He was also renowned for his oratory and on one occasion impressed the House of Commons with a speech of two hours. When he founded Emmanuel College in 1584 he was quite clear about his motive:

> The one object which I set before me in erecting this college was to render as many as possible fit for the administration

of the Divine Word and Sacraments; and that from this seed
ground the English Church might have those she can summon
to instruct the people and undertake the office of pastors,
which is a thing necessary above all others.[11]

The new buildings for the college clearly proclaimed its
theology. The chapel faced north, instead of the customary
east, and the communion table was so placed that recipients
could receive the elements seated around it. Ministers wore
no vestments and the official Prayer Book was not used.
Emmanuel's first master was one of the truly remarkable
pedagogues of his generation. Laurence Chaderton ruled
over his college for thirty-eight years. He was a brilliant
scholar and a demanding teacher. He was by all accounts
an electrifying preacher. On one occasion, having occupied the pulpit for two hours, he suggested that it was
time to draw his discourse to a close. But the cry went up
from the congregation, 'No, no, no, sir! In God's name,
go on!' Under his leadership Emmanuel became the biggest college in Cambridge. Strangely, it did not produce a
large number of clergymen. What it did produce was actually more important. The young men who passed through
Chaderton's hands were the future leaders of county society: the gentlemen, JPs and lawyers who would be the
backbone of resistance when the showdown with the monarchy came about.

Twelve years after the founding of Emmanuel, Sidney
Sussex College came into existence. The foundress was
Frances Radcliffe, widow of Thomas Earl of Sussex. The
noble couple were part of the court establishment. Sussex
was Lord Chamberlain of the Household and his wife was
one of the queen's ladies of the bedchamber. As well as the
benefits of royal favour that Frances enjoyed, she also had
to endure the bitter rivalries with which the court was riddled. Her husband was a long-standing enemy of the Earl
of Leicester and one reason for their enmity was Leicester's

support of Puritans. Sussex, it seems, was a pragmatist in matters of religion, with no emotional commitment to any confessional group. Frances, however, did favour the radicals and was recognized as a patroness by Puritans, some of whom dedicated their works to her. In 1581, Thomas Rogers, a Suffolk minister and troublesome controversialist, made her the dedicatee of a volume entitled with breathtaking universality, *The Faith of the Church Militant most effectually described in this exposition of the 84th Psalm . . . a treatise written as to the instruction of the ignorant in the ground of religion so to the confutation of the Jews, the Turks, atheists, Papists, heretics and all other adversaries of the truth whatsoever.* In it Rogers stressed the importance of education in spreading true religion. Doubtless this and similar entreaties influenced the countess's thinking when she pondered what contribution she could make to the Protestant cause. She could do little while her husband lived but, as she revealed in her will, for some years she set aside 'such money as she conveniently could' for a future great project. Sussex died in 1583, inveighing to the last against Leicester, 'the Gipsy'. His widow fell out of favour with the queen, perhaps as a result of certain scandals which were none of her doing or, perhaps, because of a too-outspoken Puritanism. Whatever caused the seclusion of her later years, it gave her the opportunity to make plans for her major benefaction. When she died in 1589, she left £5,000, the bulk of her estate, to the founding of a college as a 'good and godly monument for the maintenance of good learning'. The will was contested unsuccessfully by Frances's relatives and it was not until 1596 that Sidney Sussex College opened its doors. Its statutes were modelled closely on those of Emmanuel. Twenty years later it received its most famous student – Oliver Cromwell.

12

FUN AND GAMES

CASSIUS: *Will you go see the order of the course?*
BRUTUS: *Not I.*
CASSIUS: *I pray you, do.*
BRUTUS: *I am not gamesome: I do lack some part*
Of that quick spirit that is in Antony.

Julius Caesar, I. ii. 25–9

Anyone not 'gamesome' (a word sadly phased out of our common speech) in Elizabeth's England might have stood in need of a dose of the popular comedian Richard Tarlton. Whenever the queen was in a bad mood Tarlton could make her laugh and it was said that courtiers seeking some favour from Her Majesty sometimes employed the famous comedian as their spokesman. He represented a new phenomenon in English public life – the commercial theatre (see below, pp. 225–6).

Acting is an essential part of social life and all communities in sixteenth-century England had some experience of it, but it was during Elizabeth's reign that the foundations were laid of the acting profession as we know it today. Groups of skilled performers appeared who made their living by their craft. 'Stars' emerged, whose names were household words. Permanent theatres were built which attracted large audiences. Dramatic conventions were established. And gifted playwrights raised English drama to new heights. The blossoming of this new entertainment industry began in London. There were two reasons for this. The capital and its environs housed the largest concentration of the queen's subjects and, therefore, the largest potential audience. Also, the proximity of the court provided sophisticated, wealthy patrons on whose support bands of actors relied in the early decades of the professional theatre. But the story of Elizabethan drama is not wholly bound up in the lives of Shakespeare, Marlowe, Tarlton and their colleagues. Four streams fed into the broad stream of Elizabethan and Jacobean drama. They flowed from the Church, from the noble household, from the schoolroom and from the marketplace.

The pre-Reformation Church had used religious drama as a teaching aid. Major festivals were marked by mystery plays, so called because each scene was traditionally performed by a local craft or mystery guild. Like stained-glass windows, these performances provided a mix of biblical stories, legends of the saints and apocryphal material. Over the generations the Bible narrative had tended to become increasingly overlaid with extraneous stories and it was largely for this reason that they had been banned by the reformers.

The Protestant Church did not veto all religious drama. It was too popular and it could be made to serve the new theology. What the reformers did was build on another medieval tradition – the morality plays. These were allegorical in tone: various vices and virtues were shown competing for man's soul. After the mid-century such plays were given a new twist to reflect Protestant doctrine and, particularly, to point out the shortcomings of the

Catholic Church. Morality plays were essentially didactic but, because their subject matter was not limited by being tied to one or other festival of the liturgical year, the authors could be freer in their choice of characters and storylines. Particularly, they could use humour to drive home their message. A more common name for these pieces was 'interludes', which suggests that their origins lay within the context of a larger event. Whether in a guildhall or in the mansion of the local squire, the interlude was the 'cabaret spot' at a banquet or other celebration.

Entertainment was part of the function of noble and gentry households. A wealthy host wishing to delight and impress his guests employed the services of musicians, acrobats and actors to add variety to an evening feasting and dancing. Dramatic interludes might be provided by local amateurs, as portrayed in *A Midsummer Night's Dream*. As we have seen (see above, p. 24) when Elizabeth went on progress she was often offered rustic entertainment by villagers and estate workers who must have been overawed as well as excited to be performing before such an exalted audience. Shakespeare made fun of such amateurs when he presented his group of 'hempen homespuns' carefully preparing their interlude of *Pyramus and Thisbe*. Bottom warns that their 'lion' must not appear too fierce: '. . . if you should fright the ladies out of their wits, they would have no more discretion but to hang us; but I will aggravate my voice so, that I will roar you as gently as any sucking dove . . .' (I. ii. 70–3).

By the middle years of the reign, groups of strolling players had become a common feature of the emerging entertainment industry. While some set their sights on the top end of the market and hoped for employment by the nobility and gentry (as portrayed by the 'Players' in *Hamlet*), others travelled the marketplaces of the realm, putting on impromptu performances of folk plays, such as the adventures of Robin Hood. There was little of moral or religious

instruction to be found in the repertoire of these street performers. This was one reason for the persistent hostility of
many in authority – especially church leaders – to *all* actors.
The conviction continued to be held that they were a part of
that morally unstable underclass which included vagabonds
and criminals. There were good reasons for this assumption (see above, pp. 91–3). The dubious character of strolling
players was well known. Early in the next century Thomas
Middleton wrote a tragedy called *Hengist King of Kent*, but
the most popular part of it was a comic interlude about a
local dignitary conned out of his money and valuables by
a gang of thieves masquerading as a troupe of actors. This
sub-plot was so popular that the whole play was commonly
known as *The Mayor of Quinborough*.

Throughout the reign actors were unpopular with the
authorities. They were regarded as rootless undesirables
whose activities could not be properly policed because they
did not belong to any trade guild or professional body. The
Poor Act of 1572 attempted to bring such undesirables
within the purlieus of the law:

> . . . for the full expressing what person or persons shall be
> intended within this [category] to be rogues, vagabonds and
> sturdy beggars, to have and receive the punishment afore-
> said for [their] said lewd manner of life; it is now published,
> declared and set forth by the authority of this present parlia-
> ment that . . . all fencers, bearwardens, common players in
> interludes, and minstrels not belonging to any baron of this
> realm or to any other honourable personage of great degree
> [who] . . . shall wander abroad and have not licence of two
> justices of the peace at least . . . shall be taken, adjudged and
> deemed rogues, vagabonds and sturdy beggars, intended of by
> this present Act . . .[1]

The government was also aware of the propaganda
value of drama. The establishment made use of it to stir up
patriotic fervour or support for official policy. In January

1559, when Elizabeth made her progress from the Tower to Westminster for her coronation, she encountered a series of tableaux and orations featuring mythical personages both praising her and exhorting her. To take just one example, at Temple Bar a boy, robed and garlanded as a poet, recited verses of which this is typical:

> For all men hope in thee, that all virtues shall reign,
> For all men hope that thou, none error will support,
> For all men hope that thou wilt truth restore again,
> And mend that is amiss, to all good men's comfort.[2]

Public spectacle was an important element of government policy. So were the more private performances, which were presented to Her Majesty as part of the coronation celebrations. The message certainly went home to one foreign Catholic observer:

> As I suppose your Lordship will have heard of the farce performed in the present of her Majesty on the day of the Epiphany, and I not having sufficient intellect to interpret it, nor yet the mummery performed after supper on the same day, of crows in the habits of Cardinals, of asses habited as Bishops, and of wolves representing Abbots, I will consign it to silence, . . . Nor will I record the levities and unusual licentiousness practised at the Court in dances and banquets, nor the masquerade of friars in the streets of London nor the statue of St. Thomas stoned and beheaded, which is now thrown down entirely, and the stucco statue of a little girl placed in its stead;[3]

But what was sauce for the Protestant goose was also sauce for the Catholic gander. The Council was soon being made aware of ribald, anti-establishment interludes being performed in recusant homes in parts of northern England. There was a more refined tributary feeding the mainstream of Elizabethan drama. We have already seen that acting played a part in the life of many educational establishments. It was encouraged as a means of helping students to grasp classical literature. As a result many young men had developed a taste for theatrical performance by the time they reached their mid-teens. Publius Terentius Afer, better known as Terence, was standard fare in Elizabethan grammar schools. This second century BC Roman playwright was held by many to be the perfect exemplar for young students, both for the style and content of his writings. They were considered as essential for a rounded education in the sixteenth century as Shakespeare is for schoolboys and schoolgirls today. In order for young people to absorb the moral values behind these Latin comedies, scholars were encouraged to act them as well as read them. In several Oxford and Cambridge colleges, regular performances of classical drama were obligatory. We have already seen that student drama was a popular feature of life at the inns of court (see above, pp. 106–7). It was in this academic soil that what are now known as the first English comedies grew. They were the work of scholarly clerics. Nicholas Udall, one time headmaster of Eton College, wrote *Ralph Roister Doister* during the reign of Mary Tudor. John Still, who rose to be Bishop of Bath and Wells, penned *Gammer Gurton's Needle* (first printed in 1575) for performance at Christ's College, Cambridge. These pieces and others long lost are the most obvious antecedents of the plays written for the playhouses that sprang into being in the last decades of the reign. The rich and varied traditions of vernacular drama created a growing demand. This was met by the formation of yet more groups of travelling players and this, in turn, led to the proscriptive Act of 1572. Specifically exempted from this legislation were companies of actors who enjoyed the patronage of courtiers and other prominent subjects. Thus came into being professional troupes such as the Lord Chamberlain's Men and the Earl of Leicester's Men, with which Shakespeare and other dramatists were connected.

Richard Tarlton's career illuminates for us this tran-
sitional phase in the history of the emergent theatre. He
grew up in Shropshire but, some time in his youth, moved
to Essex. He tried his hand at various occupations, including those of swineherd, water-carrier and fencing-master.
By these means he obtained sufficient capital to set himself
up as an innkeeper. He maintained a hostelry in Colchester
before being drawn, like so many others, to the honeypot
of the capital, where he eventually kept an eating-house in
Paternoster Row, a street just north of St Paul's, frequented
by booksellers, statesmen and their clientele. It may well
have been customers of a literary frame of mind who were
drawn to Tarlton's establishment for the host offered them
more than just food and drink. He recited verse to them as
they ate and drank. Tarlton was an ugly man with a squint
but he turned these facial characteristics to his advantage
and illustrated his witticisms with grotesque grimaces. He
became particularly famous for his 'themes'. These were
poems or aphorisms made up on the spot on topics suggested by his guests. His ready – and usually bawdy – wit
brought him rapid acclaim. When the first acting companies
came into being in the 1570s Tarlton did not find it difficult to secure a place in the Lord Chamberlain's Company,
under the patronage of Thomas Radcliff, Earl of Sussex.

He rapidly became a celebrity. We know this, even
though we have no list of the roles he played. References to
him indicate that he excelled in at least two areas. One was
his skill at spontaneous repartee. This was something audiences loved. Almost every play presented at the capital's
growing number of theatres – even the most harrowing
tragedies – had a part for the fool or clown. He engaged
with the audience in off-the-cuff gags and ad-libbed around
the text. He also won fame as a dancer. It was the custom,
at the end of the play, for the company to perform one or
more jigs. These were enormously popular. They sent the
audience home with a spring in their steps.

Like modern celebrities, Tarlton paid for his fame by forfeiting his privacy. His fans wanted to know all about his personal, off-stage life and, as with today's 'stars', the paparazzi were ready to feed the public's curiosity. The sort of tales circulating about him were collected in books which began to appear in the 1590s and ran to several editions. It is impossible to know now how much the outrageous popular stories exceeded the reality or, indeed, whether the actor's true identity was swallowed up by the PR image. If we are to believe *Tarlton's Jests*, as one of the biographical compilations was entitled, the comedian was a fast-living, hard-drinking, short-tempered, argumentative, vulgar caricature of a man whose all-embracing satire was as cruel as his face was ugly.

Yet, he must have had a refined side to his nature, for he was a welcome figure at the royal court. In 1583, he became a member of the Queen's Company and was entitled to style himself one of the Grooms of Her Majesty's Chamber. Tarlton became a myth immediately after his death in 1588. It was widely believed that he died in poverty, having wasted all his money in a dissolute lifestyle. This was less than the truth, since, after his demise, relatives were squabbling in the courts over his estate, which amounted to several hundred pounds. His fame was kept alive for several decades, not only in printed anecdotes, but also in city streets, for Tarlton's grotesque visage was painted on numerous inn signs throughout London. The comedian's career in what was a new medium had been fairly brief but his image lodged itself in the minds of all who had seen him, and many more who had not, for two or three generations.

One reason why Tarlton became a hero with the hoi polloi was the continuing hostility of many in authority – especially church leaders – to the new playhouse culture. The theatres that were rapidly (we might almost say 'frenziedly') constructed between 1576 and 1600 had to be built

outside London because the City authorities set their faces
firmly against popular drama. It is not surprising, therefore, that the players were regarded as the people's heroes,
challenging pretentious bureaucracy.

Preachers – and not just Puritans – inveighed against
the moral dangers of the playhouse. According to the title
of one of Stephen Gosson's treatises, performers were the
Caterpillars of the Commonwealth. In another diatribe,
Plays confuted in five Actions (1582), he left the reader in
no doubt whatsoever about his opinions:

> Plays are the invention of the devil, the offerings of idolatry,
> the pomp of worldlings, the blossoms of vanity, the root of
> apostasy, the food of iniquity, riot and adultery . . . Players
> are masters of vice, teachers of wantonness, spurs to impurity,
> the sons of idleness. So long as they live in this order, loathe
> them.[4]

Gosson was no Puritan. Indeed, he had at one time been
a playwright (though an unsuccessful one). He followed a
conventional ecclesiastic career and ended his life as rector
of St Botolph without Bishopgate, a wealthy London living.
Nor did he dismiss all drama as corrupt. In an earlier work,
The School of Abuse (1579), he distinguished between
poetry, music and plays that extolled virtue and those that
pandered to man's baser instincts. Around the turn of the
century we find him in partnership with Edward Alleyn,
actor, impresario, theatre owner and philanthropist, setting up a charity for poor people in St Botolph's parish
(see below, pp. 232–6). Other writers took up the cudgels
in support of popular theatre and debate raged fiercely for
several years.

It was not just churchmen who objected to the actors –
and particularly their 'lewd' off-stage lifestyle. Ordinary
citizens, who enjoyed an occasional outing to the theatre,
did not want the theatre to be brought close to them. When

permission was granted for the construction of the Rose Theatre at Cripplegate in 1600, the locals were up in arms. They did not want the crowds attracted by performances. Particularly, they did not want the 'undesirables' who always appeared wherever large numbers gathered: prostitutes, beggars and petty criminals. The protestors fought tooth and nail to prevent the new building being constructed. The backers had to turn to their friends at court to overcome the opposition of local residents and JPs.

But not even prominent courtiers and Council members could overcome the opposition of London's governing body. Although the 1572 act had permitted public performances by companies licensed to prominent noblemen, the mayor and corporation of London stubbornly maintained their own right of censorship. When, in 1574, the Earl of Leicester's Men were refused permission to perform within the City, opposition continued. If the new drama was going to survive, it would have to do so in the suburbs. It did, of course, survive, simply because it could not resist the law of supply and demand. The popularity of drama held out to businessmen the prospects of huge potential profit. Enter the impresario.

England's first theatre family was the Burbages. James Burbage was a carpenter by trade before he joined the Earl of Leicester's Men. In 1574, he pooled his resources with those of his brother-in-law, John Brayne, to provide a permanent home that was outside the jurisdiction of the City fathers but close enough to be easily accessible to Londoners. It was called the Theatre and was built north of Bishopsgate in the area known as Shoreditch, a popular recreational space. By all accounts, the realm's first custom-built playhouse was an impressive building – and so it should have been; the couple had lavished £700 on its construction and decoration.

The entrepreneurs must have known they were on to a winner and the fact is proved by the frequent pulpit denunciations of their initiative and also by the other play-houses that were soon being built. A positive spate of new auditoriums appeared around London's perimeter. Within twenty years at least six purpose-built playhouses had been established, competing for custom. They did not all prosper. Fashions changed, audiences were fickle, opposition was relentless and partners fell out. All these plagued the Theatre. The land on which the playhouse had been built was owned by Giles Allen, who either was or had become an opponent of the drama. When the lease expired (1596), he refused to allow the premises to be used for the performance of plays. James Burbage's company – now the Lord Chamberlain's Men – had to move to the nearby establishment known as the Curtain. The following year, James died, and his sons, Richard (one of the stars of the Elizabethan stage) and Cuthbert, tried to salvage their business. They were further hampered by a series of legal wrangles with the heirs of John Brayne, their father's part-ner. Things turned very nasty and, in December 1598, the brothers took drastic action. While the landlord was out of town they gathered a posse together and did,

> riotously assemble themselves together, and then and there armed themselves with divers and many unlawful and offen-sive weapons, as namely swords, daggers, bills, axes and suchlike, and so armed did then and there repair to the said Theatre . . . and attempted to pull down the said Theatre . . . and having so done, did then also in most forceful and riot-ous manner take and carry away from thence all the wood and timber thereof unto the Bankside in the parish of St Mary Overys, and there erected a new playhouse with the said timber and wood.[5]

Thus was born the Globe, Shakespeare's 'wooden O', where he and the Lord Chamberlain's Men performed most or all of the Bard's repertoire.

The Bankside, extending eastwards from the southern end of London Bridge to Paris Gardens, was emerging as the principal entertainment area for the capital. Here were to be found the cockpits, bear- and bull-baiting arenas, gambling dens and bordellos to which citizens frequently resorted. The new playhouses evolved from the existing structures dedicated to public entertainment. Like the inn-yards, they consisted of three or four levels of public galleries facing a performance area. Like the cockpits and baiting arenas they were circular or polygonal in shape. They were, of necessity, open to the elements. During the winter months the acting companies toured the palaces and mansions of the queen and her leading subjects, performing on makeshift stages set up in the great halls. Theatre 'in the round' made possible – and, indeed, obligatory – interaction between actors and audience.

The performer who most excelled at spontaneous badinage and who took over from Tarlton as the comedic darling of the audiences was Will Kempe. So much was Kempe in demand that scenes quite dissociated from the plot had to be written into plays so that he could perform his antics. In some plays gaps were left in the script so that Kempe could fill them with his own buffoonery. The clown or the fool served as a dramatic bridge between stage and auditorium. Dressed in simple clothes or tatters and spouting homespun wisdom, he connected directly with the 'groundlings', the poorer members of the audience who occupied the standing space on the ground floor of the theatre. They loved his jigs and capers. They applauded his outwitting of socially superior and, supposedly, cleverer characters. Kings and councillors, bishops and generals might dominate the action of a play but the clown linked the action to the real world.

There was room here for conflict between serious playwrights and 'matinee idols'. Shakespeare and other talented writers could incorporate comic incidents into their plots to relieve tension or anchor high drama in the mundane. After the murder of the king in *Macbeth* a doorkeeper appears and engages in bawdy repartee with Macduff. But suppose the popular comedian tried to steal the show by adding his own gags. It may be that something of this sort caused bad blood between Shakespeare and Kempe. By the mid-1590s, the comedian, as well as being a star attraction, was a major partner in the Lord Chamberlain's Men. But, in 1599, he quit, concentrated on his solo career, travelled in England and abroad and then joined another company. In the meantime Shakespeare had written *Hamlet* and given the following lines to the prince, who was instructing a troupe of actors, come to perform at Elsinore:

> . . . let those that play your clowns speak no more than is set down for them; for there be of them that will themselves laugh, to set on some quantity of barren spectators to laugh too, though in the meantime some necessary questions of the play be then to be considered. That's villainous, and shows a most pitiful ambition in the fool that uses it.
>
> *Hamlet*, III. ii. 36–41

It is hard to believe that the audience would not have seen this as a reference to their recently departed hero.

By this time the entertainment industry was big business. The Burbages had acquired part of the site of the old Dominican monastery at Blackfriars, in the south-west corner of the City, and had turned it into an indoor theatre. This brought inevitable protest: the new venture was within the jurisdiction of the mayor and corporation. But there was a loophole in the law. Prohibition of acting in London only applied to *public* theatres. Owners of private property might adapt their buildings to accommodate performances for the benefit of elite audiences. Several owners had already done so. Such legal niceties did not impress local residents. Opposition was vociferous and relentless. It was not until 1608 that Richard Burbage, Shakespeare and their colleagues were able to begin performing at the Blackfriars Playhouse. Their audience was smaller and, because seat prices were more expensive, more select. But thanks to artificial lighting and more complex stage machinery the Lord Chamberlain's Men (by now the King's Men) were able to present comparatively elaborate plays and bring to a wider audience the kind of sophisticated entertainment hitherto associated only with court masques.

By the end of the century, the kings of the entertainment industry were Edward Alleyn and Philip Henslowe. Henslowe was a born entrepreneur, with a nose for anything that would make money. By 1587, when he was still in his early thirties, he had turned his hand to pawnbroking, selling timber and hides, and property speculation. The theatre was obviously by now a growth industry and Henslowe wasted no time in investing in it. He built the Rose playhouse, close to the south end of London Bridge. Henslowe made sure that his theatre outshone those of his rivals and in this he was so successful that, after five years, he was able to increase the size and facilities.

One of the actors at the Rose, currently performing with the Admiral's Men, was the twenty-six-year-old Edward Alleyn, who was enjoying celebrity status for his interpretation of demanding roles, such as Christopher Marlowe's Doctor Faustus and Tamburlaine the Great. In 1592, he married Henslowe's stepdaughter, Joan Woodward. It was both a love match and a business arrangement. Henslowe saw in the young man a level-headed and astute potential partner. In 1597, Alleyn retired from the stage to devote more of his time to management. Three years later, the partners built another playhouse on the far side of town, just beyond Cripplegate. With the Fortune they aimed to cater for a local clientele which did not find it easy to travel right across London for their entertainment. What Henslowe and Alleyn provided for them was a building that outclassed all the capital's other playhouses. Once again the champions of the theatre had to cope with fierce, organized opposition from local residents, but the new playhouse opened on schedule with Alleyn making a brief return to the boards in order to launch it.

Documents that have survived about the Henslowe–Alleyn business operation reveal a great deal about how they built up and maintained their commercial empire. Their carefully kept account books reveal that they leased their playhouses to other companies when they were not using them. They bought up properties adjacent to their premises. They made loans to their actors and, occasionally, had to bail them out of the debtors' prison. They also devoted much energy to trying to get into the bear- and bull-baiting business.

> When I'se come there, I was in a rage,
> I railed on him that kept the bears,
> Instead of a stake was suffered a stage
> And in hunks' house [the bears' cage] a crew of players.[6]

So grumbled a visitor to London who arrived at a dual-purpose venue, hoping to witness an afternoon's bear-baiting, only to discover that he had come on the wrong day – a play day. He had probably gone to the Hope playhouse, yet another of Henslowe's Bankside projects, erected early in James I's reign. It was more substantial than the earlier theatres, being built partly of brick and it had a movable wooden stage. This was taken down once a week (or, perhaps, once a fortnight) to accommodate the animal shows. Bear- and bull-baiting were serious rivals for the drama and Messrs Henslowe and Alleyn were far too astute to compete with the opposition when they could join it and claim a slice of the action.

What folly is this to keep with danger,
A great mastiff dog and a foul, ugly bear;
And to this only end, to see them two fight,
With terrible tearing, a full ugly sight.
And yet methink those men be most fools of all,
Whose store of money is but very small,
And yet every Sunday they will surely spend
One penny or two, the bearwarden's living to mend.
At Paris Garden each Sunday a man shall not fail
To find two or three hundreds, for the bearwarden's vaile
    [profit].[7]

When those words were written by the cleric-poet Robert
Crowley in 1550, the baiting of animals by dogs was a
long-established pastime, popular at all levels of society.
Queen Elizabeth loved it. Control of the sport – if such
it can be called – was consigned to a court official, the
Master of the Royal Game. He it was who issued performance licences to the owners of various venues. This was a
lucrative office and Henslowe and Alleyn made strenuous
efforts to acquire it. They succeeded early in the reign of
James I. According to the chronicler John Stow,

> ... there be two bear gardens, the old and new places, wherein
> be kept bears, bulls and other beasts to be baited. As also mas-
> tiffs in several kennels, nourished to bait them. These bears
> and other beasts are there baited in plots of ground, scaffolded
> about for the beholders to stand safe.[8]

These dedicated buildings were situated on the Southwark
side of the river and are marked on the earliest maps of the
area. Here crowds flocked to see a great beast tethered to a
stake and set upon by powerful hounds. They wagered on
the outcome of contests. They bought food and drink from
vendors and they screamed their excitement at the bloody
spectacle. Attendance at these shows could be hazardous.

On an afternoon in 1583 'the old and underpropped scaf-
folds round about the bear garden . . . overcharged with
people fell suddenly down, whereby to the number of eight
persons, men and women, were slain, and many other sore
hurt and bruised'.[9] About twenty bears were kept for performance in the Bankside arenas. They were seldom killed
in the fray – they were too valuable to their owners. The
excitement consisted in seeing how many dogs were badly
or fatally wounded in the contest. The owners of the arenas
were always on the lookout for fresh diversions to pull in
the crowds. One such was setting hounds to chase a horse
with an ape tied to its back. A more dangerous pastime
favoured by young men eager to display their bravery
was to allow a bear to run free in the arena for the macho
youths to try to catch his chain. In *The Merry Wives of
Windsor* Anne Page's suitor boasts, 'I have seen Sackerson
[a famous bear] loose twenty times and have taken him by
the chain' (I. i. 269–70). The noise made by enthusiastic
crowds carried a considerable distance and their feverish
behaviour had added the word 'beargarden' to our vocabu-
lary to describe a disorderly scene. But it was not just the
common people who enjoyed the baitings – such entertainments were laid on by the queen for the delight of visiting
foreign dignitaries. When the Earl of Leicester played host
to Elizabeth at Kenilworth in 1575, as well as arranging
sophisticated masques, plays, dances and banquets, he
staged a bear-baiting.

Henslowe and Alleyn were prime examples of
Elizabethan capitalism. Both of them died as wealthy men.
Their fortunes were built on ploughing the income from
their theatres into property dealing. Henslowe owned
a sizeable portion of Southwark where he lived most of
his life 'over the shop'. He never felt the urge to move out
into the country and set himself up as a landed gentleman.
Despite the opposition of moralists who objected to his
business proceedings, Henslowe was an influential and

respected member of the local community, a pillar of the church, a welcome visitor to the royal court and a generous philanthropist.

However, when it came to charity, Alleyn outdid his friend. In his will he left money for the foundation of ten almshouses. But the bulk of his estate, after provision for his widow, went to finance the College of God's Gift at Dulwich. Alleyn had invested in an estate at Dulwich, in the Surrey countryside, some ten kilometres south of Southwark, and here he established a foundation for the care of a dozen poor elderly people and the education of poor scholars. From these beginnings one of England's largest public schools was to develop. We have no reason to doubt Alleyn's philanthropic motives but it may be that he was always aware of criticism about the ways he had come by his fortune. In a letter to one of his critics he wrote: 'That I was a player I cannot deny; and I am sure I will not. My means of living were honest, and with the poor abilities wherewith God blessed me I was able to do something for myself, my relatives, and my friends.'[10]

The public playhouse took the place of the tiltyard as a venue for exciting spectacle. To what extent this was cause and effect is debatable; what is clear is that the rise of one occurred at the same time as the decline of the other. The waning of the feat of arms in England may be said to have begun in 1536. That was the year in which Henry VIII suffered a bad fall in the tiltyard. He was concussed for two or three hours and attendants genuinely feared for his life. The king, who had for years prided himself on his skill in the lists, never competed again. In 1559, Henry II of France *did* die as the result of a jousting accident. Such disasters tended to support the arguments of those who condemned martial arts as dangerous and vainglorious. But there were deeper reasons for the decline of knightly combat as participant and spectator sports in England (where the waning of interest was more rapid than in most European countries). Henry VIII's successors were a young boy and two women, none of whom could personally grace the tiltyard. The nature of warfare changed dramatically with the invention of small arms. The mounted knight was no longer the decisive participant (nor the romantic hero) on the battlefield. Royal tournaments continued to be held during Elizabeth's reign but they were gradually fusing with the court masque and the spectacle lay more in the elaborate costumes and theatrical paraphernalia than in the actual fighting. Francis Bacon regarded this display as the only reason for keeping the tradition alive:

> For jousts, and tourneys, and barriers, the glories of them are chiefly in the chariots, wherein the challengers make their entry; especially if they be drawn with strange beasts: as lions, bears, camels, and the like; or in the devices of their entrance, or in the bravery of their liveries, or in the goodly furniture of their horses and armour. But enough of these toys.[11]

The queen, it seems, preferred to see her courtiers competing in less hazardous exercises.

> Ten of my Lord of Hertford's servants, in a square green court, before her Majesty's window, did hang up lines, squaring out the form of a tennis-court, and making a cross line in the middle. In this square they (being stripped out of their doublets) played five to five, with the hand-ball, at bord and cord (as they term it), to the so great liking of her Highness.[12]

Whether this refers to a form of tennis or fives is not clear. Several forms of ball games involving special indoor courts or marked-out areas were popular at this time.

Such contests demanding special equipment or arenas were the preserve of the wealthy, but natural competitiveness was common at all levels of society. The most popular form of rustic contest was football. The actual form of the game varied considerably from one place to another.

Indeed, it did not always involve a ball, and the means of propelling it was not, in all traditions, confined to the feet. The common features were that it involved two sides of unspecified number, trying to get an object to a pre-ordained base while attempting to prevent the opposition doing the same. The one feature that all observers were agreed on was that football was a violent pastime. In 1583, Philip Stubbs, a Puritan Jeremiah, published *The Anatomy of Abuses: containing a . . . Brief Summary of such Noble Vices and Imperfections as now reign in many Countries of the World; but especially in . . . Ailgna* (i.e. England). Writing of football, Stubbs described it as

> . . . a bloody murdering practice [rather] than a fellowly sport or pastime. For doth not everyone lie in wait for his adversary, seeking to overthrow him and pitch him on his nose . . . By this means sometimes their necks are broken, sometimes their backs, sometimes their legs, sometimes their arms . . . Is this murdering play now an exercise for the Sabbath day?[13]

Such local 'wars' had been fought from time immemorial, usually between rival neighbouring villages. Stubbs may have been a killjoy of the kind satirized in Shakespeare's Malvolio (*Twelfth Night*), but he was far from being alone in regarding football as a reprehensible pastime. Interestingly, there existed a female version of the game. The courtier poet, Philip Sydney, in his *Dialogue of Two Shepherds* (1580) wrote,

> A time there is for all, my mother often says
> When she, with skirts tucked very high, with girls at football plays.

Most of what we can discover about the recreational habits of the Elizabethans comes from the pens of those who lamented changing customs. John Stow, in his *Survey of London* pointed out that Grub Street, 'of late years inhabited for the most part by bowyers, fletchers, bow-string makers, and such like, [is] now little occupied, archery giving place to a number of bowling alleys and dicing houses, which in all places are increased, and too much frequented.'[14]

Gambling was ubiquitous and, according to numerous contemporary reports, rife. Strict social divisions might govern peoples' leisure pursuits – hunting, falconry, coursing, fencing and tennis for the upper classes; football, skittles, rustic dance and wrestling for the lesser sort – but what united all sorts and conditions was the love of a wager. The queen played a variety of card games with her ladies. The young bloods of the court staked money on the result of a tennis match. But wherever men or beasts pitted their strength and skill against each other bystanders, high and low, eagerly wagered on the outcome. The results were often as dire in the sixteenth century as they are in the twenty-first.

> Common bowling alleys are privy moths [i.e. parasitic organisms], that eat up the credit of many idle citizens, whose gains at home are not able to weigh down their losses abroad, whose shops are so far from maintaining their play, that their wives and children cry out for bread, and go to bed supperless often in the year.[15]

13

PHILOSOPHERS

HORATIO: *O day and night, but this is wondrous strange!*
HAMLET: *And, therefore, as a stranger give it welcome.*
There are more things in heaven and earth, Horatio,
Than are dreamt of in your philosophy.

Hamlet, I. v. 164–6

In the play, Hamlet and his friends have just had an encounter with the ghost of Hamlet's father. This is a frightening experience and one that challenges Horatio's thinking about life and death. Hamlet's advice is, 'Since we do not understand everything, we should keep our minds open to new experiences. It would be quite wrong to dismiss the unfamiliar simply because it is unfamiliar or because it is rejected by traditional attitudes.' But such open-mindedness only unleashed further questions: 'Where is wisdom to be found? To what uses should it be put?' If ever there was an age when men challenged old, accepted truths and opened their minds to fresh ideas, that age was the sixteenth century. New concepts disturbed religion, politics,

art and science. Fifteen years before Elizabeth's accession, Copernicus proposed the hypothesis that the earth
circled the sun and not vice versa. Seven years after she
died, Galileo proved that it was so. Her first government
was exercised by the disturbing prophecies of the French
astrologer, Nostradamus, and prosecuted booksellers
offering his books to an eager public. 'Where was truth to
be found and how could evil falsehood be discerned when
politicians, scholars and theologians disagreed?' Such were
the questions that goaded scholars into probing several
branches of knowledge which corporately were known as
'natural philosophy'.

Practitioners became objects of awe and wonder to
other mortals, but they could also inspire suspicion
and fear. England's most famous magus, John Dee, discovered this to his cost in September 1583 when a mob broke
into his home, overturned his furniture, tore up his books
and smashed his chemical apparatus. This was a man who
was frequently consulted by Queen Elizabeth, had cast
her horoscope in 1558 to discern the most propitious day
for her coronation and who, in 1589, received a royal warrant that he might pursue his experiments in philosophy
and alchemy 'and none should check, control, or molest
me'.

As we shall see, Dee was, in part, responsible for his own
misfortunes, but the suspicions that inflamed his riotous
neighbours were ultimately a result of the gap between
scholars at the cutting edge of 'science' (a word coming
into popular parlance at this time to indicate knowledge
derived from observation, rather than belief based on
traditional teaching or revelation) and people of lesser education. Clever men might be held in awe or they might be
dismissed as cranks, heretics or Satanists. Sir Francis Bacon
observed 'Crafty men condemn studies, simple men admire
them, and wise men use them; for they teach . . . a wisdom
without them and beyond them, won by observation.'[1] Dee

was obliged to defend himself against charges of atheism in a published letter. He insisted that it was God who had implanted in him a

> desire to know his truth: And in him, and by him, incessantly to seek and listen after the same; by the true philosophical method and harmony; proceeding and ascending . . . from things visible, to consider of things invisible; from things bodily, to conceive of things spiritual: from things transitory and momentary, to meditate on things permanent: by things mortal . . . to have some [perception] of immortality. And to conclude . . . by the most marvellous frame of the whole world, philosophically viewed, and circumspectly weighed, numbered and measured . . . most faithfully to love, honour, and glorify always, the Framer and Creator thereof . . .'[2]

Not everyone was prepared to accept this assurance that the philosopher's speculations were kept within religious bounds. It seemed to them that the intellectual freedom claimed by scholars could, and often did, lead them into rejection of Christian truth.

It is not difficult to understand the bewilderment and apprehension many must have felt at the ideas being propounded by natural philosophers. Anyone who was middle-aged when Elizabeth ascended the throne had had his/her basic attitudes to life formulated by the Catholic Church and imposed by the Catholic Church, which claimed to exercise powerful sanctions in this world and the next. The Reformation had removed those restraints. He/she was now expected to rely on the open Bible and Protestant expounders of the open Bible. But there were clever men who, having rejected old orthodoxy, felt themselves free to question new orthodoxy. Worse than that, the unrestrained scholar might be lured into the study of the dangerous arts, with which mortals are forbidden to meddle. This is the theme of Christopher Marlowe's play

Doctor Faustus, first performed *c*.1592. The eponymous hero is damned for abandoning holy learning in favour of pernicious, esoteric subjects:

> . . . Divinity, adieu!
> These metaphysics of magicians
> And necromantic books are heavenly.
> Lines, circles, scenes, letters and characters –
> Ay, these are those that Faustus most desires.
> O, what a world of profit and delight,
> Of power, of honour, of omnipotence
> Is promised to the studious artisan?
> All things that move between the quiet poles
> Shall be at my command . . .
>
> I. i. 149–58

But all this was only part of the problem. Elizabethan truth-seekers also had to contend with both old superstitions and new discoveries.

Traditional beliefs, which we would now class as superstition, embraced ancient folklore, magic, natural remedies and astrology. Folk religion (which is simply a term for the survival of pagan beliefs predating Christianity) maintained a stubborn hold on the popular imagination. Patrons of the Globe did not find it odd that the fairy courts of Oberon and Titania should be presented as realistically as that of Duke Theseus in *A Midsummer Night's Dream*, or that Falstaff could believe that he was being set upon by sprites and goblins in Windsor Forest (*The Merry Wives of Windsor*). The fierce and erudite theological arguments that raged through much of the century can deceive us into thinking that these issues engaged the attention of large numbers of people. Nothing could be further from the truth. Ministers frequently complained about the level of ignorance displayed by their parishioners. The old religion had made few intellectual demands on churchgoers; they had simply been required to perform certain ritual duties. Many found it difficult to make the transition to a faith that expected them to reflect on the Bible and listen to frequent sermons. On the other hand, Elizabeth's subjects, from their earliest years, were familiar with the folklore that told of good and evil spirits who inhabited woods and wild places and entered men's homes to perform mischief or convey good luck.

Natural magic was not the monopoly of the 'little folk'. In a sermon of 1552, Bishop Latimer referred to common custom: 'A great many of us, when we be in trouble, or sickness, or lose anything, we run hither and thither to witches or sorcerers, whom we call wise men; when there is none so foolish and blind as they be . . . seeking aid and comfort at their hands.'[3] It was only natural that most people – who could not afford the ministrations of a physician – should turn to those members of their own communities who had a knowledge of herbal remedies and simples. It was but a short step from that to seeking the aid of 'experts' (whether charlatans or individuals who genuinely believed in their own arcane powers) when they were confronted by other problems: 'How can I cure my cows from a murrain?' 'How can I make the object of my desire return my affection?' 'What does the future hold in store for me?' Such experts – 'wise men' and 'wise women' – claimed access to the spirit world and used a bewildering array of spells, incantations, nostrums and rituals in treating their clients. Often they employed a mixture of Christian prayers, astrological invocations and mere gobbledegook.

Write these words: 'Arataly, Rataly, Ataly, taly, aly, ly', and bind these words about the sick man's arm nine days, and every day say three *Pater Nosters* in worship of St Peter and St Paul, and then take off that and burn it and the sick shall be made whole.[4]

This was just one of thousands of formulae which Elizabeth's subjects believed in or to which they clung desperately in times of trouble.

John Dee was a man intoxicated by learning. When he was a student at Cambridge in the 1540s he spent eighteen hours a day at his books and subsisted on four hours sleep. He was, in very truth, a scholar born, convinced that the spiritual and physical realms would yield their secrets to the seeker who diligently and tirelessly plied his craft. Dee was not content to remain an academic, confined by the walls and the traditional methods of a university. At the age of twenty, he made the first of a series of visits to famed foreign scholars. In Louvain he studied law and made the acquaintance of the great geographer, Gerard Mercator. Months later we find him in Paris lecturing on Euclidian and Pythagorean mathematics. He was, or so he later asserted, acclaimed as such a prodigy that audiences crammed the lecture halls to hear him speak. On his return to England, he was offered inducements to lecture at Oxford, but he was determined to retain his independence and, to that end, sought patrons at the royal court. In Mary's reign, Dee's Catholic orthodoxy was called into doubt. This was scarcely surprising since, in his ceaseless self-promotion, he did not hesitate to seek support among Princess Elizabeth's group of intimates.

The 1560s saw this restless maverick constantly on the move again – Louvain, Venice, Hungary, even the Island of St Helena. He favoured hoped-for patrons with treatises and observations on a range of subjects – mathematics, astronomy, alchemy, ciphers. He made himself an object of curiosity by showing visitors to his house in Mortlake, west of London, the collection of alchemical and mathematical instruments he had brought from abroad. But none of his efforts brought the financial rewards he considered his due. He was not reticent about pointing this out to Cecil:

> My intent and studious doings is well known unto your
> honour, and the most part of all Universities in Christendom
> (and farther), that for this twenty years last past, and longer
> ... I have had a marvellous zeal, taken very great care, endured
> great travail and toil, both of mind and body, and spent very
> many hundred pounds, only for the attaining some good
> and certain knowledge in the best and rarest matters Math-
> ematical and Philosophical.[5]

Dee did not allow the Elizabethan establishment to ignore him, but most of Elizabeth's courtiers regarded him as a curiosity. For his part, Dee was only prepared to accept patronage on his own terms. When he was offered ecclesiastical preferment he declined because he was not prepared to tie himself into a system entailing pastoral responsibilities.

He was helped in maintaining a high profile by the public's fascination with astronomical phenomena. When a supernova appeared in the constellation of Cassiopeia in 1572 or a spectacular comet blazed across the sky in the winter of 1577, many people turned to Dee to enquire what these heavenly manifestations portended. Few people doubted that such dramatic stellar events must 'mean' something. The connection between cosmic phenomena and the affairs of men had been believed for centuries. Shakespeare knew of it from his reading of ancient history: 'When beggars die there are no comets seen;/The heavens themselves blaze forth the death of princes' (*Julius Caesar*, II. ii. 30–1).

The study of heavenly bodies and their influence had entered the world of European scholarship via both the classical world and the Islamic world. Men and women adrift on the uncertain seas of this life looked to the stars just as mariners took astronomical readings to set their courses. To the sixteenth-century mind it seemed evident that the clockwork motions of the spheres were superior to the vagaries of human experience and that, therefore, individuals would order their own lives more satisfactorily by aligning themselves with what was going on in the heavens. Astrologers made their money by casting horoscopes for their clients, based on the alignments of the planets at the time of their birth, and advising them on when to embark on important undertakings. Businessmen and mariners sought favourable portents before embarking on their enterprises. Physicians and surgeons calculated the most propitious dates for performing operations and prescribing medicines. Esoteric knowledge hitherto only available to the well-educated was increasingly attainable at all levels of society, thanks to the ubiquity of the printing press. Many people fell into the habit of buying an almanac every year. These manuals, as well as providing a calendar, gave notice of major astronomical events and made forecasts based upon them of what was likely to happen in the world of men. Astrological prophecy assumed an important place in the lives of ordinary people. The specialist astrologer divided his subject into three branches. Horary astrology related to major political and business affairs. Natural astrology, which was concerned with the calculation of horoscopes, covered the destiny of individuals. Judicial astrology foretold future events.

When Dee wrote his begging letter to Cecil, he included what can only be referred to as a bribe. He promised that, in return for generous patronage, he would, by means of astral revelation, locate mines of silver and gold. Elizabeth was always interested in moneymaking schemes that might help her to balance the books without reliance on Parliament. Mining and metallurgy were currently developing as techniques for adding to personal and national wealth (see above, p. 29). Dee, himself, seems to have had an interest in prospecting for silver in Devon. The government was certainly on the lookout for pioneering voyages and new technologies that might lead to valuable discoveries or inventions that would enable England to compete with Spain and Portugal. However, on this occasion Cecil resisted Dee's get-rich-quick scheme. He may well have called to mind the occasion early in the reign when the queen had been conned by a foreign alchemist into believing that he could 'create' gold.

Alchemy, to which Dee devoted much attention, was another branch of esoteric knowledge with an impressive ancestry. While the astrologer looked to the stars to reveal their secrets, the alchemist explored the properties of the earth's mineral and vegetable resources. He burned, he dissolved, he mixed, he distilled, ever searching for new efficacious – and profitable – discoveries. The theoretical basis of alchemy was the hypothesis of the unity of matter. According to this understanding of reality, everything in the physical universe was composed of four elements – earth, air, fire and water. By the application of the appropriate processes, substances could be changed but preserve their common essence. This seemed obvious to the most casual observer. Did not water turn into ice or steam? Did not wood become ash or smoke? Why then should not, for example, base metals be transmuted into gold? It was only necessary to discover the philosopher's stone that could effect this transformation. Such theoretical possibilities could be exploited by charlatans who, by employing strange-looking apparatus and spouting impressive gobbledegook, could gull the unwary into parting with money for the elixir of life or a love potion or some other concoction which would magically fulfil their desires. Magic? Or science? To the uninitiated there was no discernible difference. However, to the serious scholar, like John Dee, impelled by the pursuit of pure knowledge, alchemy provided as valid a pathway as astronomy, physic, mathematics or any other of those branches of intellectual endeavour that made up natural philosophy.

It was in the 1580s that Dee began devoting an increasing

amount of time and energy to what we would today call clairvoyance, the summoning of beings from the spirit world to make revelations. Among his scientific/magical paraphernalia he had a crystal globe in which, he believed, spirits would appear – if approached in the right way. The 'right way' involved the employment of an intermediary, a seer, or what we would now call a psychic medium. From 1582 to 1589, Dee's seer was Edward Kelly, a young man from Worcestershire who had had run-ins with the law for fraud or coining and, as a result, both of his ears had been cropped. To cover this loss he wore a black skullcap, which gave him an impressive appearance that enhanced his other-worldly appearance.

The most convincing rogue is the rogue who has convinced himself. Dee and Kelly were engaged in a career of mutual self-persuasion. It is important to realize that this famous pair was far from being a unique mystical double act. Elizabethan court records contain many references to offenders who 'claimed to obtain treasure by invocation of spirits'. Unique Dee and Kelly may not have been, but they were international celebrities of unrivalled fame. They moved in the highest circles and their antics fascinated leading members of the royal court as well as foreign dignitaries. This led to an extended European tour, during which the couple demonstrated their skills to the Holy Roman Emperor and several rulers of German principalities. A series of bizarre adventures led to Kelly making ever more extreme demands of his companion (backed, of course, by endorsements from the spirit world). Eventually Dee was persuaded to agree that all their possessions, including their wives, should be held in common. They parted company in 1589 when Dee decided to return to England. Kelly believed his prospects were rosier in Bohemia, where a wealthy court lavished money and lands on him. For a few years, the necromancer enjoyed a life of great luxury, but eventually, having failed to supply his patron with large quantities of gold, he was imprisoned and died (1597–8) as the result of a fall while trying to escape.

Dee's fortunes went into a steady decline after his return. Though warmly welcomed by Elizabeth, who continued to believe in him when others did not, the scholar failed to gain the rewards necessary to sustain himself and his household in comfort. In his last years, he was reduced to selling off some of his treasured books and apparatus to obtain the necessities of life.

Had Elizabeth's subjects only had the novel ideas of natural philosophers to contend with there would have been more than enough to challenge old convictions and excite with new wonders, but there were others who presented them with news of discoveries just as novel and intriguing. While scholars pored over their books or their alembics, mariners were probing the secrets of newly discovered lands and coming back with eye-widening tales. Some were fictions designed to amaze 'the folks back home', or to win them another brimming tankard in the alehouse. They told of ship-swallowing sea monsters, of headless men whose faces were in the middle of their chests; of the terrible Amazons who captured men in order to create the next generation of female warriors and, after conception, murdered their mates; of the 'golden one', El Dorado, who ruled a secluded kingdom of unimaginable wealth. But they also revealed to their enthralled listeners new marvels that really did exist, such as the asphalt lake in Trinidad, the men in small canoes who hunted mighty whales, the wives who were burned on their husbands' funeral pyres, the exotic fruits and medicinal herbs (some of which they brought home in the hope of growing them in England). Elizabeth's subjects were discovering that the world was bigger and contained more wonders than their forefathers could ever have imagined. Moreover, the hope was beginning to emerge that they might play a major role in it.

John Dee wrote more than eighty books, pamphlets

and fragmentary studies on a wide range of subjects. In one of them, *General and Rare Memorials Pertaining to the Perfect Art of Navigation* (1577), an interesting term appears for the first time in history: the 'British Empire'. Ever since Henry VIII's paid academics had scoured libraries for ancient documents to prove 'this realm of England is an empire' free from papal interference in its affairs, the myth of imperial destiny had been tied up with the Tudor dynasty. Several factors combined to produce this hubristic self-identification. England still laid claim to France and many of Elizabeth's subjects could remember her father's military exploits in trying to make good that claim. When Mary Tudor lost Calais, England's last continental toehold, the humiliation was widely felt. The voyages of Hawkins, Drake, Chaloner and their compeers (see above, Chapter 8) were profit-driven, but national pride was also involved. With their country excluded from continental Europe, England's sea captains were determined to make their mark in other parts of a world that was getting 'bigger' with every new maritime adventure. It was John Dee and other natural philosophers who provided both a philosophical raison d'être for expansionism and practical information for effecting it.

Dee added to his encyclopedic other pursuits an interest in antiquarian matters. He made several trips to Wales, looking at ancient monuments and gathering books and documents about the Celtic rulers of the pre-Conquest centuries. From these sources he deduced that Elizabeth had a long and unbroken ancestral line reaching all the way back to the Trojan Brut. Not content with that, he asserted from legendary accounts of early voyages, such as that of Madog ab Owain Gwynedd, that the Tudor dynasty had a claim to lands in North America. All this was grist to the mill of councillors such as Dudley and Walsingham who were urging an unwilling Elizabeth to assume the role of leader of Protestant Europe.

Dee's knowledge of mathematics and astronomy was greatly valued by captains and their commercial backers who were planning voyages into little-charted or unknown regions. Martin Frobisher consulted the magus about his attempts to reach China via a north-west passage in the 1570s. When Sir Humphrey Gilbert received a charter from the queen to seek out and colonize lands not hitherto claimed by another prince, he took advice from John Dee. This gained him a stake in Newfoundland, Elizabeth's first overseas possession. And in the same year (1583) Dee was again consulted by Adrian Gilbert, eager to take up the north-west challenge which his brother, Sir Humphrey, had been forced to abandon. Months later, he found an influential new patron in Sir Walter Raleigh who founded England's first – but short-lived – North American colony at Roanoke (1585–6).

In the pre-Armada years when maritime rivalry with Spain and Portugal was at its height and patriotic feeling ran high, exploration was in the air and catching the imagination of both adventurous captains and patriotic scholars. While Raleigh's unfortunate colonists were desperately trying to survive at Roanoke, a thirty-two-year-old clergyman was serving the English ambassador in Paris in the office of chaplain. But Richard Hakluyt's time was devoted less to pastoral duties than to eagerly reading books and gathering information on the voyages of foreign mariners. He had already indicated what was to become his lifelong passion in a treatise written at the behest of his patron, Sir Walter Raleigh: *Particular Discourse Concerning the Great Necessity and Manifold Commodities That Are Like to Grow to This Realm of England by the Western Discoveries Lately Attempted* (1584).

The principles which lay at the root of Hakluyt's lifelong passion were those enunciated by the Dutch scholar, Hugo Grotius, whose *Mare Librum* (*The Free Sea*) he translated in 1609. No European power had a prior claim on unsettled territory. The Treaty of Tordesilas (1493), which had divided the globe into Spanish and Portuguese spheres of interest, had no validity. The world's oceans were open to all and only by establishing settlements could any nation lay claim to possessions. However, the major fruit of Hakluyt's monumental endeavours was *The Principal Navigations, Voyages and Discoveries of the English Nation*. This first appeared in 1589 and was followed by enlarged versions until 1600, when the final, three-volume edition was published. This 'colonialists' Bible' brought together details and accounts accumulated from books, letters and interviews with men who had sailed the seven seas. It was a remarkable compendium of geographical information – most of it first-hand – about the world which lay beyond the shores of Elizabeth's island nation.

Among the pioneer thinkers of this period two more are worthy of note. In 1592, Thomas Harriot, a thirty-two-year-old Oxfordshire mathematician, was facing charges of being a member of an atheists' coven run by his patron, Walter Raleigh. He was just one of the coterie of advanced thinkers that the royal favourite gathered around himself, primarily to further the work of American colonization. Harriot was basically a mathematician but, as with other natural philosophers, his studies took him into a variety of related fields – astronomy, cartography, mechanics, optics and physics. He was valuable to Raleigh because he sought practical applications for his discoveries. Thus he developed improved navigational tables and instruments, and studied ballistics with a view to improving the effectiveness of cannon. Quite how he came under fire for supposed irreligion is not clear and, fortunately, the charges were dropped, but Harriot's experience underlies once again the suspicion and hostility often directed at the breed of scholars at the cutting edge of new technology.

In 1584, Harriot had been a member of the disastrous Roanoke expedition and was fortunate to be one of the settlers who returned safely the following year. Raleigh was anxious to ensure that what was essentially a failed expedition should appear in the most favourable light and it was Harriot who produced a report on the venture stressing the potential of the American colony (including the introduction of tobacco).

Harriot's career was threatened by the fall from favour of his patron. The person who came to his rescue was another nobleman, Henry Percy, Earl of Northumberland. He was provided with a house on an estate at Isleworth, Middlesex, a handsome pension and servants to cater for his needs. For the scholar this peace and security was a privilege enjoyed by few contemporaries outside academic circles. Here he continued his reading and experiments. He also maintained a correspondence with foreign scholars like the German astronomer Johannes Kepler, who regarded him as the leading mathematician in England, and, perhaps, in Europe.

Thomas Digges was fortunate among scholars in two ways. He was born into a substantial gentry family and had the resources to pursue his interests. He also became an assistant to John Dee. This occurred after the death of his father, early in Elizabeth's reign. He was, thus, virtually adopted by the great magus when he was at the height of his celebrity. He proved himself a gifted pupil and Dee described him as 'my most worthy mathematical heir'. When he was only in his mid-twenties the young mathematician came to the attention of the international academic fraternity in 1572 with a treatise on the supernova. He had no hesitation in boldly condemning traditional astronomy and declaring his support for the new Copernican understanding of the cosmos. He became the first author to explain the new heliocentric theory *in English*. It is difficult for us now to realize what an impact that had. When the new ideas 'escaped' from their scholarly, Latin prison into the ordinary everyday world it challenged, worried and bewildered people. It threw into question, not just people's knowledge of astronomy, but their understanding of God and their own role in the great scheme of things.

Digges was no ivory tower scholar. He took seriously his role in national affairs. He became an MP, attended every session of the 1572 and 1584 Parliaments and served on various committees. He was also a vigorous member of the group centred round Robert Dudley and John Dee that called for active intervention in the Netherlands in support of the international Protestant cause. He made a tour of the Low Countries in 1578, making copious notes on Spanish fortifications in the hope that an English military expedition was imminent. He was determined that his studies should bear practical fruit. His most important work, *Stratioticos* (which was first published in 1579 and went through further editions between then and 1590) was written with the aim of 'reducing the sciences mathematical from demonstrative contemplations to experimental actions for the service of my prince and country'.

The government made use of his services and his enthusiasm. In 1582, they gave him overall charge of the rebuilding of Dover Harbour. When Elizabeth was finally persuaded to come to the aid of beleaguered Netherlands Calvinists in 1585, Digges was appointed muster-master and trench master in the force sent over under Dudley's leadership. In *Stratioticos* he had covered a wide range of military matters. As well as providing instruction on the use of arithmetic and algebra in a military context, Digges set out his ideas on how an army should be efficiently and effectively employed. Unfortunately, when faced with the reality of mismanagement, corruption and party strife (see above, pp. 125–33), Digges was forced to acknowledge the need for fundamental reform. He fell foul personally of the faction opposed to Dudley and was made to take much of the blame for the failure of the Netherlands' expedition. When, in 1594, he was discharged from his post, he was still personally out of pocket to the tune of more than a thousand pounds.

It would be a mistake to think that the enemies of the new sciences were drawn entirely from the ranks of the undereducated, like the protestors who vented their spleen on John Dee's library and workshop. In the freethinking atmosphere of Elizabeth's England there was a great deal of scepticism around.

> This is the excellent foppery of the world, that, when we are sick in fortune, – often the surfeit of our own behaviour, – we make guilty of our disasters the sun, the moon, and the stars; as if we were villains by necessity, fools by heavenly compulsion, knaves, thieves, and treachers by spherical predominance, drunkards, liars, and adulterers by an enforced obedience of planetary influence; and all that we are evil in, by a divine thrusting on.
>
> *King Lear*, I. ii. 132–41

So says Edmund in *King Lear* and many playgoers would have agreed with the sentiment. The intellectual freedom, which had permitted Dee and other advanced scholars to challenge traditional religious and philosophical dogma, could be, and was, turned against them. Scepticism was fuelled by extravagant claims and prophecies that went very wrong. In 1583, the conjunction of Jupiter and Saturn was hailed as a sign of the end of the world. Holinshed describes the expectation and trepidation with which the fatal date was anticipated: '. . . the common sort of people, yea and no small multitude of such as think scorn to be called fools . . . whilst they were in expectation of this conjunction, were in no small imaginations, supposing that no less would have been effectuated than . . . was prophesied.'[6]

By the end of the century, battle was fiercely engaged between several defenders of ancient certainties and a new, bolder school of thinkers prepared to confront the old ideas head-on. One English contributor to the increasingly heated debate was John Chamber, a Calvinist cleric who taught at Oxford and, later, Eton College. We know little about him apart from his fierce denunciation of astrology. He dismissed Dee and his ilk as 'number flingers' in his *Treatise Against Judicial Astrology*. From his own astronomical observations and particularly from the appearance of the 1572 supernova he deduced the heresies that 'there be more planets than seven, whose courses are unknown to us' and that stars, supposedly fixed in their relation to the earth, in fact, kept 'their several circuits and motion'.[7] This evoked a heated response from a certain Christopher Heydon – *A Defence of Judicial Astrology*. Chamber riposted with *A Confutation of Astrological Demonology or The Devil's School*. Another controversialist weighed in with *The Madness of Astrologers*. The argument rumbled on and the sixteenth century went out in a blaze of controversy. These debates were not merely esoteric slanging matches between academics. Heydon, for example, was a parliamentarian and a political partisan who was involved in and destroyed by Essex's rebellion. In the closing years of the century, professional and amateur scholars were eagerly – one might almost say, desperately – seeking what one Italian philosopher called 'an intellectual instrument bringing about out of the known a knowledge of the unknown'.[8] Thinkers in all areas of human endeavour were like men stumbling about in a forest. They had forsaken the old paths leading to truth – Catholic dogma, popular mythology, classical learning – and could only debate among themselves the merits of their own partial understandings. Would no one come to their aid, point them in the direction of sunlit glades and meadows flooded with divine light? Yes, there was such a one. His name was Francis Bacon.

We began our rubbing of shoulders with the high and low of Elizabeth Tudor's England with some reflections on the career of Nicholas Bacon, adviser to the girl queen who ascended the throne in 1558. We have caught occasional glimpses of his wife and widow, the redoubtable Lady Anne Bacon and we have observed something of the career of Francis Bacon as lawyer, politician and supporter of the ill-fated Earl of Essex. But, as the life of the Virgin Queen drew towards its close, Francis Bacon and his remarkably original way of thinking pointed towards a new age.

Bacon was, perhaps, the victim of his own intelligence. He possessed a brilliant analytical mind. This meant that what seemed obvious to him was often far from obvious to others. He also had an unfortunate, arrogant manner that led him to express his opinions with little regard for the sensitivities of others or, indeed, for his own reputation. This was demonstrated in 1593 when his behaviour in the House of Commons angered the queen. Bacon owed his seat as knight of the shire for Middlesex to his uncle, Lord Burghley, but instead of showing due deference to the government or, at least, maintaining a discreet silence on major policy issues, he expressed strongly his opposition to details of the latest taxation demand. He complained that what was proposed would place too heavy a burden on the queen's subjects and breed discontent. 'We are here to search the wounds of the nation,' he insisted, 'not to skin them over.' This did not go down well and certainly blighted Bacon's hope of gaining the Attorney-Generalship in 1594 (see above, pp. 110–11).

As a man with extravagant tastes, Bacon felt particularly acutely his failure to achieve the preferment (and the financial concomitants) that he considered to be his due. He had to endure at least one brief stay in a debtors' prison. On such occasions he was wont to declare his intention of abandoning law and politics in order to devote himself entirely to natural philosophy. In actual fact, he never did give up his quest for public office and, after various vicissitudes, he would become Lord Chancellor and Viscount

St Albans. His later career belongs to the reign of James I, but by 1603 he had already given evidence of an amazing breadth of vision. His printed works would eventually embrace law, history, education, astronomy, mathematics, physical sciences, politics and medicine. So wide and deep was his interest in man and the cosmos that some nineteenth-century literary experts propounded the theory that Bacon was the *real* author of the works of Shakespeare. Particularly, it is clear that before the old queen died he had developed the main philosophical principles that constituted what became known as the 'Baconian method'.

Bacon was irritated by the arguments and counter-arguments of Elizabethan philosophers, which, in his view, generated more heat than light. He set out his own creed in a letter of 1592 to Lord Burghley:

> ... I have taken all knowledge for my province; and if I could purge it of two sorts of rovers, whereof the one with frivolous disputations, confutations and verbosities, the other with blind experiments and curricular traditions and impostures, hath committed so many spoils, I hope I should bring in industrious observations, grounded conclusions, and profitable inventions and discoveries.[9]

Bacon detected in both scholastic theologians and alchemists the same intellectual flaw – they began with hypothesis and proceeded to test it by logical argument and/or experiment. Thus, for example, alchemists worked from the basic assumption of the unity of matter and accepted that transmutation was possible. Catholic theologians, working from the same understanding of the physical universe, proposed that the bread and wine of the mass were *really* changed into the body and blood of Christ (even though their outward appearance – their 'accidents' – did not alter). The ground rules for all natural philosophy had been laid in the twelfth and thirteenth centuries when scholars, exploring their ancient Greek progenitors, had evolved a synthesis of Aristotelian logic and Christian orthodoxy. Aristotle's intellectual schema had been set out in his *Organon*. Bacon's detailed response, the *Novum Organum*, was not published until 1620 but had by then matured over several years. In brief, what he asserted was that the old philosophy put the cart before the horse. Instead of making a hypothesis the basis of intellectual enquiry, one should observe reality and, by subjecting it to close scrutiny ('induction'), discern the principles that governed it. He also insisted that all natural philosophy should be 'useful', i.e. it should lead to inventions, such as the compass and the telescope, or to systems of thought, such as mathematics, which can be applied in various technologies.

Francis Bacon has been called the father of experimental science, the daystar of empiricism. With him we look forward into a new age, the age of Isaac Newton, the Royal Society and the Enlightenment. In the ideas that teemed in his brain (many emerging but half formed) we may discern the seeds, not only of great advances in medical science, but also principles we now regard as basic, such as the separation of Church and state and the rejection of slavery.

But Bacon was nurtured in the Elizabethan world. It was the personal, political and philosophical conflicts of that age that tutored him and trained his remarkable mind. Out of all the profound and intricately argued books that he wrote it was his little collection of *Essays* that became the most popular. First offered to the world in 1597, the book grew larger through two editions in 1612 and 1625 and has scarcely been out of print ever since. In this amalgam of reflections on some sixty topics, we touch the mind of the Elizabethan age, just as we do when we read Shakespeare, Spenser or Marlowe. So let the last word be with Nicholas Bacon's greater son. As he analyses what makes kingdoms great, there is more than an element of prophecy in his words:

The kingdom of heaven is compared, not to any great kernel, or nut, but to a grain of mustard-seed; which is one of the least grains, but hath in it a property and spirit hastily to get up and spread. So are there states great in territory, and yet not apt to enlarge or command; and some that have but a small dimension of stem, and yet apt to be the foundations of great monarchies.[10]

NOTES

Chapter 1   The Statesman

1. R. H. Tawney and E. Power, *Tudor Economic Documents* (1951), i. 326–7.
2. Ibid., 325.
3. T. E. Hartley, (ed.), *Proceedings in the Parliaments of Elizabeth I* (Leicester, 1981), 34–5.
4. Cf. R. Tittler, *Nicholas Bacon: The Making of a Tudor Statesman* (1976), 90.
5. Cf. D. MacCulloch, *Suffolk and the Tudors* (Oxford, 1986), 91.
6. H. Robinson, (ed.), *The Zurich Letters*, 2nd series (Cambridge 1842), 287.
7. H. Ellis, *Original Letters, Illustrative of English History* (1824–46), ii. 264.
8. E. Lodge, *Illustrations of British History* (1838), ii. 119.
9. Cf. Tittler, *Nicholas Bacon*, 183.
10. Cf. J. E. Neale, *Elizabeth I and her Parliaments, 1559–1581* (1953), 363.

Chapter 2   King Land

1. Shakespeare, *Titus Andronicus*, IV. i. 59.
2. Cf C. Read, *Mr. Secretary Cecil and Queen Elizabeth* (1955), 312.
3. D. Wilson, *Sweet Robin* (1981), 221.

4. Cf. J. Lees-Milne, *Tudor Renaissance* (1951), 109.
5. William Harrison, *Historicall Description of the Island of Britain* (1577), II, ch. I. ii. 9–10.
6. Ibid.
7. *Records of Building at Longleat*, 3.213, Thynne Archives, Longleat.
8. Lees-Milne, *Tudor Renaissance*, 102–3.
9. Ibid.
10. Tawney and Power, *Tudor Economic Documents* (1951) I. 85.
11. Ibid.
12. Ibid., I. 87–8.
13. Harrison, *Historical Description*, ch. II. iv. 1.

Chapter 3   The Parliamentarian

1. Cf. P. W. Hasler, *The House of Commons 1558–1603* (1981), i. 37.
2. Ibid., i. 279–80.
3. Ibid., i. 49–50.
4. Ibid., iii. 395.
5. Ibid., iii. 596.
6. Ibid.
7. Cf. J. E. Neale, *Elizabeth I and her Parliaments 1559–1581* (1953), 185–6.
8. Ibid., 205.
9. The History of Parliament, 'Wentworth, Peter (1524–97), of Lillingstone Lovell, Oxon.' <http://www.historyofparliamentonline.org/volume/1558-1603/member/wentworth-peter-1524-97>
10. Acts of the Privy Council, (ed.) J. P. Dassent (1900), xxiv. 269.

Chapter 4   Three Men of Religion

1. Shakespeare, *Macbeth*, V. v. 24–8.
2. W. Nicholson, (ed.), *The Remains of Edmund Grindal* (Cambridge, 1843), 211.
3. J. G. Nichols, (ed.), *The Diary of Henry Machyn, Citizen and Merchant Taylor of London from A.D. 1550 to A.D. 1563* (Cambridge, 1848), 265.
4. H. Robinson, (ed.), *The Zurich Letters, 1558–1579*, 1st series (Cambridge, 1842), 214–15.

5. Cf. P. Collinson, *Archbishop Grindal 1519–1583* (1979), 203.

6. Ibid., 242–6.

7. P. Caraman, trs., *William Weston, The Autobiography of an Elizabethan* (1955), 25.

8. Ibid., 24.

9. Ibid., 99.

10. Ibid., 101.

11. Cf. A. J. Loomie, 'Guy Fawkes in Spain: the "Spanish Treason" in Spanish Documents' in *Bulletin of the Institute of Historical Research* (November 1971), 25.

12. G. Townsend and S. R. Cattley, (eds.), *Acts and Monuments of John Foxe* (1839), VIII. 281.

13 Cf. P. Collinson, *Archbishop Grindal*, 117.

14. J. L. Black, *The Marprelate Tracts* (Cambridge, 2008), 10.

Chapter 5   A Clutch of Villains

1. G. B. Harrison, *Elizabethan Journals, 1591–1603* (1938), 22.

2. J. Chandos, (ed.), *In God's Name: Examples of Preaching in England, 1534–1662* (1971), 88.

3. J. Strype, *Annals of the Reformation* (Oxford, 1824), i. 392.

4. J. Schofield, (ed.), *Works of James Pilkington* (Cambridge, 1842), 540–1.

5. J. Earle, *The Autograph Manuscript of Microcosmographie* (Leeds, 1966), 146.

6. British Library, Lansdowne MS, 20.

7. J. B. Black, *The Reign of Elizabeth* (Oxford, 1959), 276.

8. G. Ungerer, 'Mary Frith alias Moll Cutpurse in life and literature', *Shakespeare Studies*, 18 (2000), 69.

9. R. H. Tawney and E. Power, (eds.), *Tudor Economic Documents* (1924), iii. 346.

10. *A Collection of Seventy-nine Black-Letter Ballads and Broadsides, printed in the Reign of Queen Elizabeth . . .* (1867), 16–17.

11. G. B. Harrison, *Elizabethan Journals*, 221–3.

Chapter 6   The Lawyer

1. I. Alston, (ed.), *Sir Thomas Smith, De Republicca Anglorum* (Cambridge, 1906), 89.

2. Ibid., 86.
3. Cf. A. Underhill, *Shakespeare's England* (1917), i. 398.
4. A. D. Boyer, *Sir Edward Coke and the Elizabethan Age* (Stanford, 2003), 270.
5. P. W. Hasler, *The House of Commons 1558–1603 (1981)*, i. 623.
6. T. Birch, (ed.), *Memoirs of the Reign of Queen Elizabeth* (1754), i. 152–3.
7. Boyer, *Sir Edward Coke*, 270.
8. Ibid.
9. E. Coke, *The Fourth Part of the Institutes of the Laws of England* (1644), 65.
10. Boyer, *Sir Edward Coke*, 213.

Chapter 7   The Soldier

1. J. S. Nolan, *Sir John Norreys and the Elizabethan Military World* (Exeter, 1997), 247–8.
2. C. Hughes (ed.), *The Defence of the Realm* (Oxford, 1906), 13.
3. S. Turnbull, *The Art of Renaissance Warfare* (2006), 210.
4. *Calendar of State Papers Domestic, 1595–1597* (1869), 365–6.
5. Hughes, *Defence of the Realm*, 56–7.
6. C. Edelman, *Shakespeare's Military Language: A Dictionary* (2005), 350.
7. C. G. Cruickshank, *Elizabeth's Army* (Oxford, 1966), 291.
8. L. S. Marcus, J. Mueller, and M. B. Rose (eds.), *Collected Works of Elizabeth I* (Chicago, 2000), 326.
9. E. G. Atkinson (ed.), *Calendar of State Papers Irish, 1596–7* (1893), 242.

Chapter 8   Ships and Shipmen

1. R. Hitchcock, *A politique platte for the honour of the prince, the great profit of the public states, the relief of the poor, the preservation of the rich. The reformation of rogues and idle persons and the wealth of thousands that know not how to live . . .* in R. H. Tawney and E. Power, *Tudor Economic Documents* (1924), iii. 250.
2. Cf. D. Childs, *Tudor Sea Power* (2009), 60.
3. Cf. S. Usherwood (ed.), *The Great Enterprise: The History of the Spanish Armada* (1978), 33.
4. Ibid., 45.

5. Ibid., 51.
6. J. S. Cummins (trs.), *Succeros de las Islas Filipinas* (Hakluyt Society, 1970) 2nd series, no. 140.
7. Cf. D. B. Quinn (ed.), *The Last Voyage of Thomas Cavendish 1591–1592* (1975), 56.
8. Ibid., 110.
9. Ibid., 128.

Chapter 9   Merchants and Merchandise

1. W. Herbert, *The History of the Twelve Great Livery Companies of London* (1834), 120–4.
2. G. Unwin, *The Gilds and Companies of London* (1963), 246.
3. R. H. Tawney and E. Power (eds.), *Tudor Economic Documents* (1924), i. 214–15.
4. A. Pettegree, *Foreign Protestant Communities in Sixteenth-Century London* (Oxford, 1986), 292.
5. Tawney and Power, *Tudor Economic Documents*, i. 327.
6. C. L. Kingsford, (ed.), *A Survey of London by John Stowe* (Oxford 1908), i. 193.
7. Tawney and Power, *Tudor Economic Documents*, i. 244.
8. Ibid., i. 267.

Chapter 10   Doctors and Doctored

1. Cf. D. Guthrie, *A History of Medicine* (1945), 107–8.
2. Ibid., 151.
3. G. T. L. Chapman and M. N. Twiddle (eds.), *William Turner, a New Herbal* (Cambridge, 1995), i. 32.
4. Guthrie, *History of Medicine*, 166.
5. C. L. Kingsford (ed.), *A Survey of London by John Stowe* (Oxford, 1908), i. 13.
6. Ibid., i. 237.
7. Ibid., *op. cit.*, ii. 24–5.
8. Ibid., i. 165.

Chapter 11   Schools and Schoolmasters

1. J. Simon, *Education and Society in Tudor England* (Cambridge, 1966), 340–1.
2. Lambeth Palace Library, MS 651, fol.156.
3. Ibid., MS 650, fol. 228.

4. W. H. Frere and W. M. Kennedy (eds.), *Visitation Articles and Injunctions of the Period of the Reformation* (1910), iii. 21.
5. Cf. Simon, *Education and Society*, 287.
6. H. Robinson (ed.), *The Zurich Letters 1558–1579, 1st series* (Cambridge, 1842), 174.
7. Cf. Simon, *Education and Society*, 353.
8. R. Mulcaster, *The Elementary* (1582), Scholar Press facsimile (1970), 19f.
9. R. Mulcaster, *Positions* (1581), 67.
10. Simon, *Education and Society*, 360.
11. Cf. H. C. Porter, *Reformation and Reaction in Tudor Cambridge* (Cambridge, 1958), 239.

Chapter 12   Fun and Games

1. R. H. Tawney and E. Power, *Tudor Economic Documents* (1924), ii. 328–9.
2. S. Anglo, *Spectacle, Pageantry and Early Tudor Policy* (Oxford, 1969), 352.
3. Ibid., 344.
4. Cf. P. Simpson, 'Actors and Acting' in *Shakespeare's England* (Oxford, 1917), ii. 241.
5. Cf. W. Archer and W. J. Lawrence in *Shakespeare's England* (Oxford, 1917), ii. 291–2.
6. A. Nicoll, *Shakespeare Survey* (Cambridge, 1955), viii. 106.
7. R. Crowley, *Select Works* (Early English Text Society, 1872), extra ser. xv. 16.
8. C. L. Kingsford (ed.), *A Survey of London by John Stowe*, ii. 54.
9. *Holinshed's Chronicle* (1587), iii. 1353.
10. *Oxford Dictionary of National Biography*.
11. F. Bacon, 'Of Masques and Triumphs' in *Essays* (ed.) H. Milford (Oxford University Press, 1902), 108.
12. J. Nichols (ed.), *The progresses and public processions of Queen Elizabeth* (1823) cited by A. F. Sieveking, in *Shakespeare's England*, ii. 459.
13. P. Stubbs, *Anatomy of Abuses* (1595), 138–9.
14. Kingsford, *Survey of London*, ii. 79.
15. Nichols, *Queen Elizabeth*, 465.

Chapter 13 Philosophers

1. F. Bacon, 'Of Studies' in *Essays* (ed.) H. Milford (Oxford University Press, 1902), 139.
2. J. Dee, 'A Letter Containing a Discourse Apologetical', in J. Crossley (ed.), *Autobiographical Tracts* (Manchester, 1851), 72.
3. G. E. Corrie (ed.), *Sermons of Hugh Latimer* (Cambridge, 1844), 53.
4. Cf. K. Thomas, *Religion and the Decline of Magic* (1978), 213.
5. H. Ellis, *Original Letters of Eminent Literary Men of the 16th, 17th and 18th Centuries* (Camden Society, 1843), 34.
6. T. Buckmaster, *An Almanack and Prognostication for the Year 1583*, v.
7. J. Chamber, *A Treatise Against Judicial Astrology* (1601), 18.
8. Cf. W. J. Bowsma, *The Waning of the Renaissance 1550–1640* (New Haven, 2000), 187.
9. J. Spedding, R. L. Ellis and D. D. Heath, *The Works of Francis Bacon* (1857–74), viii. 109.
10. F. Bacon, 'Of the True Greatness of Kingdoms and Estates', *Essays*, 81.

BIBLIOGRAPHY

Place of publication is London unless otherwise specified.

A Collection of Seventy-nine Black-Letter Ballads and Broadsides, printed in the Reign of Queen Elizabeth . . . (1867).

Acts of the Privy Council (ed.) J. P. Dassent (1900), XXIV.

Alford, S., *Burghley* (New Haven, 2005).

Alston, I. (ed.), Sir Thomas Smith, *De Republicca Anglorum* (Cambridge, 1906).

Anglo, S., *Spectacle, Pageantry and Early Tudor Policy* (Oxford, 1969).

Archer, W. and W. J. Lawrence in *Shakespeare's England* (Oxford, 1917).

Armada 1588–1988 (1988).

Atkinson, G. E. (ed.), *Calendar of State Papers Domestic 1595–1597*, ed. R. Lemon and M. E. A. Green (1869).

Bacon, F., *Essays* ed. H. Milford (Oxford, 1902).

Birch, T. (ed.), *Memoirs of the Reign of Queen Elizabeth* (1754).

Black, J. L., *The Marprelate Tracts* (Cambridge, 2008).

Bowsma, W. J., *The Waning of the Renaissance 1550–1640* (New Haven, 2000).

Boyer, A. D., *Sir Edward Coke and the Elizabethan Age* (Stanford, 2003). -

Buckmaster, T., *An Almanack and Prognostication for the Year 1583*.

Calendar of State Papers Irish, 1596–7 ed. R. Leman and M. E. A. Green (1893).

Caraman, P. (trs.), *William Weston, The Autobiography of an Elizabethan* (1955).

Chamber, J., *A Treatise Against Judicial Astrology* (1601).

Chandos, J. (ed.), *In God's Name – Examples of Preaching in England, 1534–1662* (1971).

Chapman, G. T. L., and Twiddle, M. N. (eds.), *William Turner, a New Herbal* (Cambridge, 1995).

Childs, D., *Tudor Sea Power* (2009).

Coke, E., *The Fourth Part of the Institutes of the Laws of England* (1644).

Collinson, P., *Archbishop Grindal 1519–1583* (1979).

— —, *Elizabethans* (London and New York, 2003).

— —, *Godly People* (1983).

— —, *The Elizabethan Puritan Movement* (1969).

Corrie, G. E. (ed.), *Sermons of Hugh Latimer* (Cambridge, 1844).

Coward, B., *Social Change and Continuity in Early Modern England 1550–1750* (1988).

Crowley, R., *Select Works*, Early English Text Society, extra ser. xv (1872).

Cruickshank, C. G., *Elizabeth's Army* (Oxford, 1966).

Cummins, J. S. (trs.), *Succeros de las Islas Filipinas*, Hakluyt Society, 2nd series (1970).

Dee, J., 'A Letter Containing a Discourse Apologetical', in J. Crossley (ed.), *Autobiographical Tracts* (Manchester, 1851).

Earle, J., *The Autograph Manuscript of Microcosmographie* (Leeds, 1966).

Edelman, C., *Shakespeare's Military Language: A Dictionary* (2005).

Edwards, F., *The Elizabethan Jesuits* (Phillimore, 1981).

Ellis H., *Original Letters, Illustrative of English History* (1824–46).

— —, *Original Letters of Eminent Literary Men of the 16th, 17th and 18th Centuries* (Camden Society, 1843).

Frere, W. H., and W. M. Kennedy (eds.), *Visitation Articles and Injunctions of the Period of the Reformation* (1910).

Guthrie, D., *A History of Medicine* (1945).

Haller, W., *The Rise of Puritanism* (New York, 1957).

Harrison, G. B., *Elizabethan Journals, 1591–1603* (1938).

Harrison, W., *Historicall Description of the Island of Britain* (1577).

Hasler, P. W., *The House of Commons 1558–1603* (1981).

Hassell Smith, A., *County and Court: Government and Politics in Norfolk, 1558–1603* (Oxford, 1974).

Herbert, W., *The History of the Twelve Great Livery Companies of London* (1834).

Holinshed's Chronicle (1587).

Hughes, C. (ed.), *The Defence of the Realm* (Oxford, 1906).

Kingsford, C. L. (ed.), *A Survey of London by John Stowe* (Oxford, 1908).

Knyvett, Sir Henry, *The Defence of the Realme 1596*, (ed.) C. Hughes (Oxford, 1906).

Lees-Milne, J., *Tudor Renaissance* (1951).

Lodge, E., *Illustrations of British History* (1838).

Loomie, A. J., 'Guy Fawkes in Spain – the "Spanish Treason" in Spanish Documents' in *Bulletin of the Institute of Historical Research* (November, 1971).

MacCaffrey, W., *The Shaping of the Elizabethan Regime* (1969).

MacCulloch, D., *Suffolk and the Tudors* (Oxford, 1986).

Marcus, L. S., J. Mueller and M. B. Rose (eds.), *Collected Works of Elizabeth I* (Chicago, 2000).

Mulcaster, R., *Positions* (1581).

Mulcaster, R., *The Elementary* (1582) Scholar Press facsimile, 1970.

Neale, J. E., *Elizabeth I and her Parliaments, 1559–1581* (1953).

Nichols, J. (ed.), *The progresses and public processions of Queen Elizabeth*, 1823 cited by A. F. Sieveking, in *Shakespeare's England*.

Nichols, J. G. (ed.), *The Diary of Henry Machyn, Citizen and Merchant Taylor of London from A.D. 1550 to A.D. 1563* (Cambridge, 1848).

Nicholson, W. (ed.), *The Remains of Edmund Grindal* (Cambridge, 1843).

Nicoll, A., *Shakespeare Survey* (Cambridge, 1955).

Nolan, J. S., *Sir John Norreys and the Elizabethan Military World* (Exeter, 1997).

Oxford Dictionary of National Biography

Pettegree, A., *Foreign Protestant Communities in Sixteenth-Century London* (Oxford, 1986).

Porter, H. C., *Reformation and Reaction in Tudor Cambridge* (Cambridge, 1958).

Quinn, D. B. (ed.), *The Last Voyage of Thomas Cavendish 1591–1592* (1975).

Read, C., *Lord Burghley and Queen Elizabeth* (1965).

——, *Mr Secretary Cecil and Queen Elizabeth* (1955).

Records of Building at Longleat, 3.213, Thynne Archives, Longleat.

Robinson, H. (ed.), *The Zurich Letters containing the correspondence of several English bishops and others . . . during the early part of the reign of Queen Elizabeth*, 2nd series (Cambridge, 1842).

Rowse, A. L., *Sir Richard Grenville* (1977).

Schofield, J. (ed.), *Works of James Pilkington* (Cambridge, 1842).

Sharpe, K., *Selling the Tudor Monarchy* (New Haven, 2009).

Simon, J., *Education and Society in Tudor England* (Cambridge, 1966).

Simpson, P., 'Actors and Acting' in *Shakespeare's England* (Oxford, 1917).

Spedding, J., R. L. Ellis and D. D. Heath, *The Works of Francis Bacon* (1857–74).

Strype, J., *Annals of the Reformation* (Oxford, 1824).

Stubbs, P., *Anatomy of Abuses* (1595).

Tawney, R. H. and E. Power (eds.), *Tudor Economic Documents* (1951).

The Hakluyt Society, *Documents concerning English Voyages to the Spanish Main 1560–1580* (1932).

Thomas, K., *Religion and the Decline of Magic* (1978).

Tittler, R., *Nicholas Bacon, The Making of a Tudor Statesman* (1976).

Townsend, G. and S. R. Cattley (eds.), *Acts and Monuments of John Foxe* **(1839).**

Turnbull, S., *The Art of Renaissance Warfare* (2006).

Underhill, A., in *Shakespeare's England* (1917).

Ungerer, G., 'Mary Frith alias Moll Cutpurse in life and literature' in *Shakespeare Studies*, 18 (2000).

Unwin, G., *The Gilds and Companies of London* (1963).

Usherwood, S. (ed.), *The Great Enterprise: The History of the Spanish Armada* (1978).

Wagner, J., *The Devon Gentleman* (Hull, 1998).

Wernham, R. B., *Before the Armada* (1971).

Wilson, D., *Sweet Robin* (1981).

Woolley, B., *The Herbalist* (2004).

Yates, F. A., *The Occult Philosophy in the Elizabethan Age* (1979).

INDEX